Analyzing Social Science Data

Analyzing Social Science Data

David de Vaus

SAGE Publications
London • Thousand Oaks • New Delhi

© 2002 David de Vaus

First published 2002

 SAGE Publications Ltd
6 Bonhill Street
London EC2A 4PU

SAGE Publications Inc
2455 Teller Road
Thousand Oaks, California 91320

SAGE Publications India Pvt Ltd
32, M-Block Market
Greater Kailash - I
New Delhi 110 048

British Library Cataloguing in Publication data

A catalogue record for this book is available
from the British Library

ISBN 0 7619 5937 8
ISBN 0 7619 5938 6

Library of Congress control number available

£24.79

Typeset by SIVA Math Setters, Chennai, India
Printed and bound in Great Britain by Athenaeum Press, Gateshead

Contents

List of Figures

List of Tables

Preface

This book is designed primarily for social science students and researchers. It deals with some of the common issues that confront students, postgraduates and practising researchers alike by selecting 50 key problems in data analysis.

The selection of 50 key problems (Chapters) is somewhat subjective. No doubt the problems could have been divided up differently, and other writers with different experience and expertise would have selected different issues and proposed different solutions. My selection of 50 problems is a distillation of the difficulties frequently faced by students and practising researchers, often marring their work.

The 'problem approach' in this book is somewhat different from the normal strategy in texts and courses on data analysis where the focus is primarily statistical. My experience has been that, even with excellent books and teachers, students often complete these courses without a 'feel' for data analysis and are not well equipped to face the real world of research, with its messy and uncompliant data. The students learn about statistics but not about data analysis.

I have adopted a 'problem' approach in this book because identifying and solving problems is what characterizes research for students and more experienced researchers alike. The problem approach should help readers become more critical consumers of research by enhancing their awareness of the issues surrounding the satisfactory analysis of data.

By providing an accessible treatment of many of the day-to-day problems that researchers confront when analyzing data, the book aims to provide information unavailable in any other single book. Some of the practices are conventions that have simply evolved and have not even been systematically treated in print.

Throughout the book instructions have been provided to execute the data analysis strategies using the SPSS computer package. This package was selected because of its wide use. In most cases the menu based instructions rather than syntax commands are provided. These instructions are correct for version 10.0.5 of SPSS for Windows. Instructions for earlier versions may vary slightly.

The overall aims of the book are:

- to assist researchers in mastering the *art of data analysis* and to help students recognize that quantitative analysis is far more than the routine application of statistical tests;
- to identify some of the most common problems that are encountered in the analysis of quantitative social science data;
- to outline ways of detecting whether these problems exist in a given data set;
- to provide a range of ways of dealing with these problems and assistance with deciding which solution is best suited to the situation.

1

How to Code Data

What is the Problem?

Coding is a method of representing categories and values of a variable so that:

- responses are converted to a form suited to statistical analysis;
- data become more manageable by grouping similar responses.

Since coding produces the raw material for data analysis it can fundamentally affect the quality of the analysis. The two central problems of coding are:

- deciding on coding schemes;
- minimizing coding errors.

How to Structure and Store Codes

Since coding is designed to facilitate computer-based statistical analysis, the codes have to be stored in such a way that computer programs can access and interpret them. Most statistical analysis programs require coded data to be stored in a particular form which I call a *variable-by-case data grid*. The main characteristics of such a grid are:

- Each column represents a variable.
- Each row represents a case.
- Each cell contains the response (or value) of a particular case to a specific variable.
- Responses are represented as a code: an abbreviated representation of the response for that case on that variable.

	marital	divorce	age	sex	race	region	srcbelt	vote92	pres92	cappun
283	NEVER MARRIE	NAP	18-33	FEMALE	WHITE	Midwest	Suburbs	DID NOT VOTE	NAP	FAVOR
284	MARRIED	NO	18-33	FEMALE	WHITE	Midwest	Suburbs	VOTED	PEROT	FAVOR
285	DIVORCED	NAP	34-49	MALE	WHITE	Midwest	Smaller town	VOTED	CLINTON	FAVOR
286	MARRIED	NO	50 and older	MALE	WHITE	Midwest	Smaller town	VOTED	BUSH	FAVOR
287	MARRIED	NO	34-49	FEMALE	WHITE	Midwest	Smaller town	VOTED	BUSH	FAVOR
288	NEVER MARRIE	NAP	18-33	FEMALE	WHITE	South	Suburbs		NAP	FAVOR
289	MARRIED	YES	34-49	MALE	BLACK	South	Suburbs	VOTED	CLINTON	FAVOR
290	DIVORCED	NAP	50 and older	FEMALE	WHITE	South	Larger city	VOTED	CLINTON	FAVOR

Figure 1.1   *Variable-by-case data grid with labels*

	marital	divorce	age	sex	race	region	srcbelt	vote92	pres92	cappun
283	5	0	1	2	1	2	2	2	0	1
284	1	2	1	2	1	2	2	1	3	1
285	3	0	2	1	1	2	3	1	1	1
286	1	2	3	1	1	2	3	1	2	1
287	1	2	2	2	1	2	3	1	2	1
288	5	0	1	2	1	3	2	.	0	1
289	1	1	2	1	2	3	2	1	1	1
290	3	0	3	2	1	3	1	1	1	1

Figure 1.2   *Variable-by-case data grid with codes*

- Each case must have a 'response' or value for each variable.
- Each case has one and only one value (code) per variable.
- The order of the variables in the file containing coded responses will be the same for every case.
- The same set of codes will be used for all cases on a given variable.

Figure 1.1 provides an example of a variable-by-case data grid in which the actual responses are entered in each cell. The data grid is a small part of the data grid for the US General Social Survey. It indicates actual responses for eight cases (rows) for ten variables. Each cell contains the actual responses for each case. Notice that for case 288 there is a dot rather than an actual value for the variable VOTE92 – this is the 'code' given to a non-response to this question. Figure 1.2 presents the same grid but numeric codes replace the actual answers.

Decisions to Make

Translating answers into numeric codes requires a series of decisions including:

- the type of codes to use – *numeric* or *alphanumeric* (words and letters);
- when to produce a coding system – *before* or *after* collecting data;
- how to code *non-responses*;
- methods of coding *multiple answers* to the one question;

- the method of coding *open-ended* questions – whether to use a pre-established coding scheme or to create one from the responses;
- *how many* codes for the variable – the level of detail to which responses will be coded.

Should Numeric or Alphanumeric Coding be Used?

Numeric coding involves allocating numbers to responses, as illustrated in Figure 1.2. Alphanumeric coding may use letters such as A, B, C, D, E rather than numbers 1, 2, 3, 4, 5. More often, however, alphanumeric coding involves the use of words (e.g. Yes, No; Male, Female; or I voted for X because …). In nearly all cases where variables are to be used for statistical analysis responses are coded numerically.

Should Codes be Produced Before or After Collecting Data?

When data are collected using a predetermined set of categories, codes can be allocated to these answers before collecting the data. This *precoding* can eliminate the need to manually code later and can improve the accuracy of data entry (see p. 9). Figure 1.3 provides examples of precoded questions.

How Should 'Non-Responses' be Coded?

Since every case must have a code for each variable, a system must be developed for coding non-responses to questions. Non-responses may occur because people:

- were not required to answer (question did not apply);
- refused;
- provided an illegible answer;
- responded 'don't know'.

You may wish to distinguish between different types of non-response by allocating separate codes to each type. This provides maximum flexibility during later data analysis.

To avoid confusion, distinctive codes are allocated to non-responses. For variables where only single-digit codes are required, non-responses are often coded 8, 9 or −1. For variables that require two-digit codes (e.g. age), non-responses are given codes such as 98, 99, −1. The important thing with allocating codes for missing or invalid responses is to:

- make them distinctive;
- make them as consistent as possible across questions (e.g. always −1 or always 9 for single-digit variables, always 99 for two-digit variables).

Here are some statements about general social concerns. Please say whether you strongly agree, agree, disagree or strongly disagree with each of these statements.

	Strongly agree	Agree	Neither agree nor disagree	Disagree	Strongly disagree
The death penalty should be reintroduced for murder.	☐₁	☑₂	☐₃	☐₄	☐₅
The smoking of marijuana should NOT be a criminal offence.	☐₁	☐₂	☐₃	☐₄	☑₅

Figure 1.3   *Examples of precoded questions*

How to Code Multiple Answers to the One Question

Respondents might give several responses to the same question. For example, in response to a question about the anticipated major problem facing the world in 10 years' time a person may identify several possibilities. Problem 2 (see p. 10) discusses methods of coding this type of question.

Approaches to Coding Open-ended Questions

Open-ended questions are not so readily precoded. Open questions fall into four categories:

- closed questions with an open-ended category (e.g. Other, please specify);
- open-ended questions to which there is a defined range of possible responses (e.g. religious group, country of birth, occupation);
- self-coding open questions (e.g. age, number of children);
- open-ended questions to which there is a wide and undefined range of possible responses (e.g. What, in your opinion, is the most important problem facing the world today?).

For open questions of the first two types a set of codes can be developed before collecting data. Self-coding variables are numeric variables, such as income in dollars and age, where the answer is already in numeric form. Answers to these questions are suitable for statistical analysis and do not require further coding. To code the fourth type of open question it is best to look at answers before developing a coding system (see pp. 15–16).

Table 1.1   *Three-level coding scheme for religion*

Level 1: Broad (single-digit codes)	Level 2 Narrow groups (three-digit codes)	Level 3 Detailed classification (four-digit codes)
1 Buddhism	**2 Christianity**	***223 Orthodox***
2 Christianity	201 Anglican	2231 Albanian Orthodox
3 Hinduism	203 Baptist	2232 Antiochian Orthodox
4 Islam	205 Brethren	2233 Greek Orthodox
5 Judaism	207 Catholic	Autocephalic Greek
6 Other religions	211 Churches of Christ	Orthodox Church of Australia
7 No religion	213 Jehovah's Witnesses	Greek Orthodox (Australian
	215 Latter Day Saints	Archdiocese)
	217 Lutheran	Greek Orthodox
	221 Oriental Christian	(Old Calendar)
	223 Orthodox	2234 Macedonian Orthodox
	225 Presbyterian	2235 Romanian Orthodox
	and Reformed	The Lord's Army
	227 Salvation Army	2236 Russian Orthodox
	231 Seventh-day Adventist	Orthodox Church in America
	233 Uniting Church	(Australian Mission)
	240 Pentecostal	Russian Orthodox
	280 Other Protestant	(Ecumenical Patriarchate)
	290 Other Christian	Russian Orthodox
		(Moscow Patriarchate)
		2237 Serbian Orthodox
		2238 Ukrainian Orthodox
		Ukrainian Autocephalic
		Orthodox Church
		2239 Orthodox, not elsewhere
		classified
		Byelorussian Autocephalic
		Orthodox Church
		Old Believers (Russian)
		Old Orthodox Church of
		the Holy Nativity
		Polish Orthodox

Whether to Use Other People's Codes or Develop Your Own

Some excellent coding schemes have been developed for common demographic variables. Where these exist it normally makes sense to use them, since they have been carefully developed and enable comparisons between your results and those from other studies.

Many established classification schemes (e.g. Table 1.1) employ a *multilevel coding scheme* which allows the variable to be coded to different levels of detail. Table 1.1 gives a scheme for classifying religions. At the first, most

Table 1.2   *Examples of coding and classification schemes for core demographic variables*

Variable	URL
Standard Occupational Classification (SOC)(USA)	http://stats.bls.gov/soc/soc_home.htm
Employment status (UN)	http://www.ilo.org/public/english/bureau/stat/class/icse.htm
Industry (UK)	http://www.statistics.gov.uk/nsbase/themes/compendia_reference/Articles/downloads/structur.pdf
Diseases and Related Health Problems (UN)	http://www.who.int/msa/mnh/ems/icd10/icd10.htm
Education (UN)	http://unescostat.unesco.org/en/pub/pub0.htm
Race and Ethnicity (USA)	http://198.137.240.91/textonly/OMB/fedreg/directive_15.html
Countries (Australia)	http://www.abs.gov.au/ausstats/abs@.nsf/StatsLibrary? Open View then select link to ABS classifications and select catalogue 1269.0
Languages (Australia)	http://www.abs.gov.au/ausstats/abs@.nsf/Stats Library? Open View then select link to ABS classifications and select catalogue 1267.0
Religion (Australia)	http://www.abs.gov.au/ausstats/abs@.nsf/StatsLibrary? OpenView then select link to ABS classifications and select catalogue 1266.0
Crime/Offences (Australia)	http://www.abs.gov.au/ausstats/abs@.nsf/StatsLibrary? Open View then select link to ABS classifications and select catalogue 1224.0
Causes of Death (Australia)	http://www.prometheus.com.au/healthwiz/142death.htm

general, level we have the major world religions, along with a general code for other religions and for no religion. The second level distinguishes between the main groupings within a specific religion (e.g. within Christianity we can code different Christian groups). The third level of coding provides most detail. The extract in Table 1.1 makes some very fine-grained distinctions between different types of Orthodox Christianity. Notice the structure of the numerical codes that accompany this classification: the first digit in all the codes indicates the first-level classification (2 = Christian), the second and third digits indicate the second-level classification (223 = Orthodox), while the fourth digit indicates the third-level classification (2237 = Serbian Orthodox).

The decision about the level of detail at which to code depends on various factors, including the likely make-up of the sample, the sample size and the way in which the data will be used. If the sample is likely to consist mainly of Christians we would want to code beyond the first level to enable the distinction to be made between religious affiliations. If everyone belonged to the one group the variable would be of little value in later data analysis (see pp. 48–53). If the sample is fairly small it is unlikely to be worth coding at the third level since these fine distinctions are unlikely to be of much use.

Table 1.3   *First- and second-level codes in an open coding scheme*

First-level codes		Second-level codes	
Codes	Broad type of problem	Codes	**Specific environmental problem**
1	Social	501	Overcrowding
2	Economic	502	Air quality
3	Moral	503	Water quality
4	Military	504	Scarcity of resources
5	**Environmental**	505	Extinction of species
6	Political	506	Greenhouse problems
7	Religious	507	Ozone problems
8	etc.	508	Salinity
		509	Deforestation
		510	etc.

However, this would depend on the nature of the sample. If the sample consisted of migrants from eastern Europe these finer distinctions might be important for the analysis.

There are many excellent coding schemes available. Some of these can be found on the websites listed in Table 1.2.

Fixed coding schemes are inappropriate for some open questions. Suppose that you have asked people what they think will be the major problem facing their country in 10 years' time. Since you do not want to impose your range of possibilities on respondents, you have asked an open-ended question.

To code the responses you should examine the first 50–100 responses (or more if you keep finding new responses). Try classifying these responses into broad groupings. This will require some trial and error. Once these broad headings are developed, you should assign a code to each broad grouping. Then, examining the specific responses, see if there are some distinctions that you should make within each broad grouping. Assign specific codes to these subcategories, but make sure that you retain the broad-level code as the first digit of the code. You might possibly then develop a third-level classification and codes.

Table 1.3 illustrates a set of first-level codes that might emerge from an examination of responses to the major problems question. One type of problem might be broadly classified as 'environmental'. The table illustrates some of the possible subcategories within the environmental grouping. The end product of developing a coding scheme from responses to open-ended questions should have a similar structure to the pre-existing coding schemes.

When developing codes, try to make the categories and codes flexible so that additional codes can be added later as more questionnaires are examined. Use multiple-digit codes so that there are plenty of spare codes if they are needed. For example, allow two digits for specific environmental problems so that you can have up to 99 different codes.

How Detailed Should the Coding be?

There is no simple answer to this question. The fineness of the coding scheme will depend on the:

- size of the sample;
- importance of making particular distinctions;
- way in which the data will be analysed;
- likely distribution of cases within the sample.

However, the general guideline is to code for more rather than less detail. This is particularly true if you are not quite sure how you will analyse the data or how many cases will belong to any one category. The main rationale for detailed coding is that you can always collapse categories at a later stage (see pp. 34–38) but you cannot expand broad categories to reveal finer detail if you have only coded at the broad level.

How to Minimize Coding Error

The best way of reducing coding error is to reduce the number of steps involved in coding and data entry. The fewer the steps, the smaller the chance of error.

How to Reduce Coding Mistakes

A number of procedures can help increase the accuracy of coding:

- Include codes *next to* responses to fixed-choice questions. Data entry operators can then enter data directly from questionnaires (see Figure 1.3).
- Use automated coding programs. For complex coding, such as occupational coding, computer programs are available to allocate codes based on descriptive information.
- Develop written coding schemes and continually update these with guidelines and decisions that are made while coding.
- Use several coders and introduce consistency checks.
- Where electronic data collection methods are used (e.g. Computer Assisted Telephone Interviewing – CATI, web-based surveys, e-mail surveys), they can be programmed to disallow responses outside a

specified range of codes and to disallow the wrong type of response code (e.g. alphanumeric rather than numeric). While these safeguards cannot eliminate incorrect 'within-range' responses they can eliminate 'out-of-range' errors.

- Electronic data collection methods automatically code responses and build a database, thus eliminating the need to code at all.

How to Reduce Data Entry Errors

A number of procedures can help improve the accuracy of data entry:

- Automate the data entry by using electronic data collection methods.
- Use a data entry template. Some electronic questionnaires that do not automatically code and create a data file will still automatically generate a data entry form that simplifies manual data entry. (e.g. SPSS Data Entry).
- Use professional data entry personnel. If manual data entry is required, use trained people who are much more likely to enter data accurately than inexperienced people.
- Use double data entry methods. This involves entering data from the same questionnaire twice. Where the second attempt differs in any way from the first attempt, the data entry operator is alerted to the discrepancy.
- Choose data entry software correctly. If a special data entry program such as SPSS Data Entry is unavailable, then more common software can assist with data entry. Avoid entering codes into a text file or word-processing file. A spreadsheet can be useful since the layout of a spreadsheet is the same as the variable-by-case data grid. Even better are database programs. These can be programmed easily to create a data entry form for each person. These forms provide an intuitive method for entering codes and can be programmed to build in data integrity checks.

2

How to Code Questions with Multiple Answers

What is the Problem?

When coding any variable a case must belong to *one and only one category* of the variable. However, some questions allow respondents to provide more than one answer. The problem then is how we code multiple answers to a single question.

What are Multiple-Response Questions?

To identify a solution it is helpful to examine first how the problem arises. There are four main types of question that are widely used in questionnaires and produce multiple responses:

- *Closed question – select as many answers as apply*. This question provides respondents with a single question, but instead of asking them to select only one response allows them to select all that apply (Table 2.1).
- *Closed question – ranking responses*. A different type of multiresponse closed question asks respondents to rank the set of responses (Table 2.2). Rather than selecting some responses, this method requires that each possible answer receives a response.
- *Open questions – limited number of responses*. Open-ended questions that allow a set number of responses (Table 2.3) can produce a large number of possible answers which require particular strategies for coding and analysis.
- *Open questions – unlimited number of responses*. This type of question is similar to the previous type except that there is no limit on the number of responses that can be given (Table 2.4).

The solution to the problem of coding multiple responses to a single question lies in distinguishing between a *question* and a *variable*. While an answer to a single question often only requires a single variable to contain the response code, a single question can produce a number of variables.

Table 2.1 *Closed multiresponse question*

From the list below select the main pressures on your life at the moment (select all that apply).

☐ Financial   ☐ Relationship with my children
☐ Job insecurity   ☐ Relationships with people at work
☐ Uncertainty about the future   ☐ Housing problems
☐ Health   ☐ What the future holds for my children
☐ Relationship with my partner   ☐ Education

Table 2.2 *Closed multiresponse question requiring ranking*

The list below describes various features of jobs. When looking for a job, what are the things you look for most and least? Please rank each of the job features below from most important to least important. Place a 1 in the square next to the most important; a 2 in the square for the second most important; a 3 in the third most important; and a 4 in the square for the job feature that is least important to you. Please place a number in each square and do not use the same number more than once.

☐ A good income so that you do not have any worries about money

☐ A safe job with no risk of closing down or unemployment

☐ Working with people you like

☐ Doing an important job which gives you a feeling of accomplishment

Table 2.3 *Open question with a limited number of responses*

Thinking about the future, what do you think will be the three most important problems facing this country in ten years' time?

1. _____

2. _____

3. _____

Where respondents provide several responses to a question, the solution is to create a *set* of variables to 'hold' those responses to the question. There are two approaches to developing these sets of variables:

- multiple-dichotomy method;
- multiple-response method.

The application of these two approaches can be explained in relation to each of the four question types outlined above.

Table 2.4   *Open question with the option of unlimited responses per person*

Thinking about the future, what do you think will be the main problems facing this country in ten years' time. (You can mention more than one problem.)

_____

_____

_____

How to Code Multiple Responses to a Closed Question

When respondents can 'select as many answers as apply' the multiple answers can be coded using the multiple-dichotomy and multiple-response methods.

Using the Multiple-Dichotomy Method

Using this method, each of the possible responses is treated as a separate variable to which respondents provide either a yes answer (by selecting it) or an implied no answer (by not selecting it). For the life pressures question in Table 2.1, this method results in 10 separate variables (Table 2.5). Respondents are then coded for each of the 10 variables. If they selected all 10 variables they would receive a yes code for each variable. If they selected just two options they would receive a yes code for those two variables and a no code for the remaining eight.

Using the Multiple-Response Method

Instead of creating a separate variable for each response category, this approach involves creating a separate variable to contain each of the responses provided by an individual. Since most people will only select two or three responses to the pressures question and no one will probably select all ten pressures, we do not need to create ten variables. The multiple-response method involves the following steps:

1. Determine the maximum number of responses given by any person (for this example assume that no one selected more than four pressures).
2. Create four variables. Let us call them PRES1, PRES2, PRES3, PRES4.
3. Create 10 categories for each variable. Each category will represent the ten different pressures. Use the same set of categories for each of the four variables. Because each variable will contain all ten pressures this is called the multiple-response method (as opposed to a simple dichotomous yes/no coding).

Table 2.5 *Multiple-dichotomy method for multiple-response questions*

Variable number	Is this a pressure?	No (code = 0)	Yes (code = 1)	Total N
1	Financial	380	620	1000
2	Job insecurity	630	370	1000
3	Uncertainty about the future	680	320	1000
4	Health	640	360	1000
5	Relationship with my partner	710	290	1000
6	Relationship with my children	650	350	1000
7	Relationships with people at work	850	150	1000
8	Housing problems	880	120	1000
9	What the future holds for my children	550	450	1000
10	Education	780	220	1000

Table 2.6 *Coding multiple responses for three cases*

CASE	PRES1	PRES2	PRES3	PRES4
A	2	8	−1	−1
B	5	−1	−1	−1
C	2	5	6	10

4. For each case code the responses into the four pressure variables. This can be illustrated with the examples of three cases in Table 2.6. Case A nominated two pressures (job insecurity and housing problems). This person's two responses would be coded into the first two pressure variables (PRES1, PRES2). The remaining two pressure variables (PRES3, PRES4) would be coded −1 to indicate that no information was coded to those variables for this case. Case B nominated only one pressure. This response would be coded into PRES1, with the remaining pressure variables being coded −1. Case C listed four pressures (job insecurity, relationship with partner, relationship with children, and education). These four responses would require the use of all four PRES variables.

Table 2.7 illustrates the coding and distributions of the same 1000 cases as were coded using the multiple-dichotomy method (Table 2.5). In this table these same cases are coded into the four PRES variables using the multiple-response method. Notice that the number of people who indicated a particular pressure is the same as with the multiple-dichotomy method. The selections of a particular pressure are simply represented in a different way using the two methods.

Table 2.7   *Multiple-response method for multiple-response questions*

Code	Is this a pressure?	PRES1	PRES2	PRES3	PRES4
1	Financial	270	160	110	80
2	Job insecurity	120	140	65	45
3	Uncertainty about the future	90	100	85	45
4	Health	90	200	50	20
5	Relationship with my partner	70	70	130	20
6	Relationship with my children	90	80	125	55
7	Relationships with people at work	30	50	35	35
8	Housing problems	20	60	30	10
9	What the future holds for my children	120	65	195	70
10	Education	100	40	45	35
−1	No response	0	35	130	585
	Total N	1000	1000	1000	1000

Table 2.8   *Multiple 'dichotomy' coding for ranking questions*

	Variables			
Codes	INCOME	SECURITY	PEOPLE	ACCOMP
Ranked 1st	400	250	200	150
Ranked 2nd	300	250	300	150
Ranked 3rd	200	200	400	200
Ranked 4th	100	300	100	500
N	1000	1000	1000	1000

How to Code Ranking Questions

Rank-ordered responses can be coded using the same general logic as outlined above.

Using the Multiple 'Dichotomy' Method

In Table 2.2 there are four responses to rank, so the multiple 'dichotomy' method will result in four variables – one for each of the responses. The only difference is that instead of a simple yes/no set of responses (i.e. a dichotomous response) the possible ranks become the categories of each variable. Where there are more than two items to be ranked there will be more than two categories used for these variables. Since any job characteristic could receive one of four possible ranks the variable used for that job characteristic will have four categories – one for each possible rank. The resulting variables will indicate, for each job characteristic (e.g. INCOME), how often

Table 2.9 *Multiple-response coding for ranking questions*

	Variables			
Codes	FIRST ranked characteristic	SECOND ranked characteristic	THIRD ranked characteristic	FOURTH ranked characteristic
Income	400	300	200	100
Job security	250	250	200	300
Nice people at work	200	300	400	100
Feeling of accomplishment	150	150	200	500
N	1000	1000	1000	1000

it was ranked first, how often it was ranked second and so forth. Table 2.8 illustrates the distribution of 1000 cases using this approach. Four variables (INCOME, SECURITY, PEOPLE and ACCOMP) are created. Each has the categories to indicate the number of people who ranked a given variable first, second, third and fourth.

Using the Response Method

The logic of the multiple-response method can be used for ranking questions. Using this approach, the ranks become the variables and job characteristics become the categories. The resulting variable (e.g. FIRST rank) will indicate the number of times income was ranked first, security was ranked first and so on (see Table 2.9).

How to Code Open Questions with Multiple Answers

Multiple responses to open-ended questions can be handled with the multiple-dichotomy and multiple-response methods.

Using the Multiple-Response Method

This method can be applied to the open question in Table 2.3 using the following steps:

1. Create three variables (PROB1, PROB2 and PROB3).
2. Examine the responses provided by respondents.
3. Create categories for PROB1 for each of the problems listed.

4. Use the same categories for PROB2 and PROB3.
5. For each respondent, code the problems listed into the variables PROB1, PROB2 and PROB3.

Using the Multiple-Dichotomy Method

The multiple dichotomy method can be applied to open questions with a maximum number of responses in the following way:

1. Examine the responses provided to the question.
2. Compile a list of the problems (e.g. environment, overpopulation, no jobs, poverty, crime, low birth rate, moral decline, ...).
3. Where appropriate, combine very similar problems.
4. For each problem in your list create a separate variable with the values 0 and 1 (e.g. ENVIR, POP, NOJOBS, POV, CRIME, BIRTH, MORALS, ...). If a total of 20 different problems were listed across the sample, create 20 different variables.
5. Code each respondent on each of the variables. Where the respondent listed the specific problem, code them as 1. Otherwise code them as 0.

When there is no maximum number of responses to open questions the same basic coding strategies can be used. The only difference is in the way the multiple-response method is implemented. Where respondents are restricted to three responses, only three variables are required to contain these responses. Where there is no limit on the number of responses, you will first need to examine each case and determine the largest number of responses any case has provided. Then create that number of multiple-response variables to contain each response.

Using SPSS

The variables that are used with either the multiple-dichotomy method or the multiple-response method should be created when setting up the initial database. Decisions about the method of dealing with multiple responses should be made at this stage and the variables should be coded accordingly. There is nothing to prevent you using both methods in the same database – it simply requires more coding and data entry.

3

Can the Respondent's Answers be Relied on?

What is the Problem?

Data analysis relies on measurements being both reliable and valid. A *reliable* measure is one for which we can depend on obtaining *consistent* responses. A set of scales is reliable if it gives the same reading each time the same person steps on it (assuming the person does not change weight). A questionnaire item is reliable if it elicits dependable and consistent answers from people. Remember, however, these answers may not be accurate answers. A set of scales that consistently underweighs is still reliable. A question that consistently overestimates happiness is nevertheless reliable (see pp. 25–27).

If we cannot rely on the responses that a questionnaire item elicits then any analysis based on such data will be suspect. If the results we obtain from a sample could just as easily be different if we administered the questionnaire again, how much confidence can we have in any of the findings?

We must, therefore, use reliable items, but this requires a way of evaluating how reliable our measurement instruments are. Would we obtain similar data if the same questions were given to the same people again?

We cannot just use measures because others have found that they are reliable. A measure's reliability can change over time, can vary in different contexts, with different samples and on the method of administering the questions. It is therefore important to assess the reliability of our questions and data.

How to Assess Reliability

A range of methods of evaluating the reliability of measures have been developed. Unfortunately there is no single method that is suitable for all situations.

The Test–Retest Method

This is intuitively the most straightforward way of assessing reliability. Since reliability is the consistency with which a response is obtained, simply administering a question to the same sample on two occasions and correlating their answers on the two tests should indicate the question's reliability. If the correlation between the test and retest responses is high enough the question is considered reliable. The particular correlation used would depend on the level of measurement of the variables (Problem 36).

The advantage of this approach is that it is easy to understand and can be used for single questions or a set of questions.

However, the test–retest method faces substantial problems in social science research. These problems include the following:

- It is often impractical to administer the questions to a sample on two occasions.
- It can be difficult to distinguish between real change and lack of reliability. Since there has to be some gap between the test and the retest, it is possible that the sample will change between the two tests. There is no simple way of knowing whether different responses between the test and retest reflect instrument unreliability or real change.
- The administration of the first test can produce changes in the sample (this is called *reactivity*) and this, rather than lack of reliability, could be responsible for difference between test and retest answers.
- If the gap between the test and retest is relatively short then *memory* effects may come into play. Respondents may remember the way they answered the question previously and this may cause them to answer in a consistent way at the retest, thus inflating the apparent reliability.

The Panel-of-Judges Method

A different approach, especially with observational data, is to test the reliability of the way data are *coded*. Suppose we have a video of a group of people in a particular situation and wish to code the nature of the interactions. A single observer may code the interactions in a particular way (e.g. conflict events, level of tension, degree of co-operation, degree of hierarchy in group, differences in male/female behaviour in group). To the extent that such coding requires subjective judgement the codes may be unreliable. To test the reliability of such codes a second judge will be asked to independently code the video along the same dimensions. The level of agreement between the two judges is used to indicate the reliability of the coding. The statistic used to measure the level of agreement between two judges is called *Cohen's kappa*.

While this method can be appropriate for observational coding or for coding open-ended questions, it is not of much use for the type of data collected from questionnaires with fixed sets of responses, where judgement coding is not an issue.

The Parallel-Forms Method

This method is designed to avoid the problems of the test–retest method. Rather than giving people the *same* measures on two *different* occasions, this method gives the same respondents two different but equivalent measures on the one occasion. The correlation between these two equivalent tests is used as a measure of the reliability of the tests. Thus, if we had two equivalent tests of self-esteem, they would be given to respondents at the same time. This approach is designed to imitate the test–retest method. It eliminates the difficulties of not being able to retest, of actual change occurring between test and retest, of memory problems and reactivity effects.

The difficulty with this approach is that it can be difficult to obtain truly equivalent tests. Even where they are available, the method can result in long and apparently repetitive questionnaires.

Internal Consistency Methods

There are a variety of internal consistency methods, but they have a key feature in common. They all administer one multi-item measure at a single point of time to a single sample. They evaluate the reliability of the set of measures by examining the consistency with which people answer each item in the set. Where items that are meant to measure the same underlying concept are answered in a consistent way the set of items is regarded as being reliable. In other words, reliability is estimated by examining the consistency with which *different items* express the *same concept,* rather than by looking at the consistency with which the same item is answered over time. All the measures of internal consistency indicate reliability using a coefficient ranging from 0 to 1. The higher the value the more reliable the set of questions.

AVERAGE INTER-ITEM CORRELATION   This approach simply obtains the correlations between each of the items used to measure the concept and calculates the average of these correlations (see Table 3.1).

AVERAGE ITEM–TOTAL CORRELATION   Rather than correlating each item with each other item, this approach correlates each item with the total of the other items and then obtains an average of these item–total correlations. The bottom row of Table 3.2 indicates the correlation of each item with the set of the other items.

Table 3.1   *Inter-item correlations*

	Item 1	Item 2	Item 3	Item 4
Item 1	1.00			
Item 2	0.55	1.00		
Item 3	0.33	0.38	1.00	
Item 4	0.44	0.48	0.40	1.00

Average = 0.43

Table 3.2   *Item-total correlations*

	Item 1	Item 2	Item 3	Item 4	Total
Item 1	1.00				
Item 2	0.55	1.00			
Item 3	0.33	0.38	1.00		
Item 4	0.44	0.48	0.40	1.00	
Total	0.56	0.60	0.45	0.58	1.00

Average of item–total correlations = 0.55

SPLIT-HALF CORRELATIONS   This method is similar to the parallel-forms method, except that it randomly divides the items into two groups. The hope is that all the items will form part of the final measure.

Having split the items into two groups, the responses *within* each of the two groups are combined and then the two halves of the scale are correlated. In the above example of Tables 3.1 and 3.2 one half might consist of Item 1 and Item 3 while the other half consists of Item 2 and Item 4. The split-half method tends to underestimate the reliability of a set of items so a correction, called the *Spearman–Brown prophecy coefficient*, is normally applied. In this case this would lead to a corrected reliability coefficient of 0.71.

CRONBACH'S ALPHA   This test of reliability builds on the logic of the split-half method. Instead of relying on one split-half test, it looks at all the possible split-half correlations. If there are four items there are three possible sets of split-half correlations that could be computed:

1.   Item **1**, Item **2** with Item **3**, Item **4**;
2.   Item **1**, Item **3** with Item **2**, Item **4**;
3.   Item **1**, Item **4** with Item **2**, Item **3**.

In effect, Cronbach's alpha coefficient of reliability is equivalent to calculating each possible split-half coefficient and obtaining the average of these split-half coefficients. For the variables in the example in Tables 3.1 and 3.2, Cronbach's alpha is 0.75. An alpha of 0.7 is normally considered to indicate a reliable set of items.

KUDER–RICHARDSON COEFFICIENT The Kuder–Richardson reliability coefficient is conceptually similar to Cronbach's alpha, except that it is based on dichotomous items that have simple yes/no categories. Alpha, on the other hand, is based on items with multiple response categories.

Which of the Reliability Tests Should be Used?

For single-item measures there is little choice. The test–retest method is the only available method since all the other methods rely on multiple items. With multi-item measures the internal consistency measure is the best method. It does not encounter the problems of the test–retest method and does not require the development of an 'equivalent' parallel form.

Of the internal consistency measures Cronbach's alpha is the most widely used and is the most suitable. The strength of alpha is that it provides the most thorough analysis of patterns of internal consistency. Rather than relying on the way in which an individual variable is related to others (average inter-item correlation or average item-total correlation), it examines how groups of variables are related to groups of other variables and is therefore less affected by the idiosyncrasies of an individual variable. Alpha is preferable to the split-half method because it does not rely on just one split-half coefficient (a different split would result in a different coefficient) but on all the possible combinations of splits.

Using SPSS

Cohen's Kappa

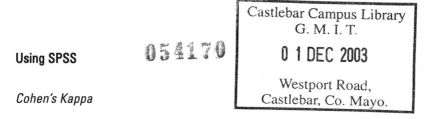

Analyze ▾
   Descriptive Statistics ▶
      Crosstabs…
         Row(s): Input Y variable
         Column(s): Input X variable
         ☑ Suppress tables
         Statistics…
           ☑ Kappa
         Continue
     OK

Inter-Item Correlations

Analyze ▾

    Correlate ▶

        Bivariate…

            Variables: Select variables to correlate

            Correlation Coefficients

                ☑ Pearson

            Test of Significance

                ☑ Two-tailed

            ☐ Flag significant correlations (untick)

            Options…

                Missing Values

                      ⊙ Exclude cases pairwise

                Continue

            OK

or

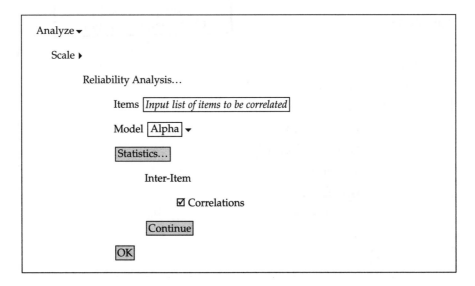

Analyze ▾

    Scale ▶

        Reliability Analysis…

            Items Input list of items to be correlated

            Model Alpha ▾

            Statistics…

                Inter-Item

                    ☑ Correlations

                Continue

            OK

Item–Total Correlations

Analyze ▾

    Scale ▶

        Reliability Analysis…

            Items: | Input list of items to be correlated |

            Model: | Alpha | ▾

            | Statistics… |

                Inter-Item

                    ☑ Correlations

                Descriptives for

                    ☑ Scale if item deleted

                | Continue |

        | OK |

Split-Halves Method

Analyze ▾

Scale ▶

    Reliability Analysis…

        Items | Input list of items to be correlated |

        Model | Split-half | ▾

        | OK |

Cronbach's Alpha

Analyze ▾

    Scale ▶

        Reliability Analysis…

            Items: | Input list of items to be correlated |

            Model: | Alpha | ▾

            | Statistics… |

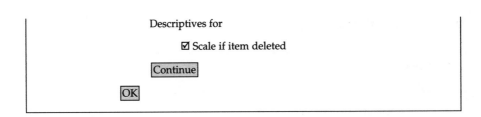

Kuder–Richardson Coefficient

Obtain Cronbach's alpha. This is the same as the Kuder–Richardson coefficient if the variables being tested are all dichotomous.

4

How to Check that the Right Thing is being Measured

What is the Problem?

Any data analysis is only as good as the measures it uses. Since most social science analysis relies on using relatively concrete measures of more abstract concepts we face the problem of knowing whether our measures actually measure what we say they do. This is the problem of *validity*. We must somehow be confident that our relatively concrete questions actually tap the concepts we are interested in. The real problem, however, is that there is no conclusive way of establishing validity.

To understand the nature of the problem of validity, it is important to understand the nature of validity itself.

What is the Difference Between Validity and Reliability?

The concepts of reliability (Problem 3) and validity are often confused. *Validity* flows from the use to which we put a set of measures. We must match the measure and the concept properly. A set of scales may be a valid measure of weight, but is an invalid measure of health. *Reliability* is the extent to which measures elicit consistent responses. Scales that indicate that a person is 75 kg one minute and 65 kg the next minute provide an unreliable measure of weight.

Trochim (2000a) provides a useful way of thinking about the relationship between validity and reliability (Figure 4.1):

- A valid measure is 'on target'. A reliable measure consistently hits the same place on the target. A reliable and valid measure will consistently hit the bull's eye (Figure 4.1a).
- A reliable but invalid measure will be consistent but consistently off target, i.e. consistently wrong (Figure 4.1b).
- An unreliable but valid measure is scattered unpredictably around the target in a random fashion (Figure 4.1c). Because the error is unsystematic the measure is valid.

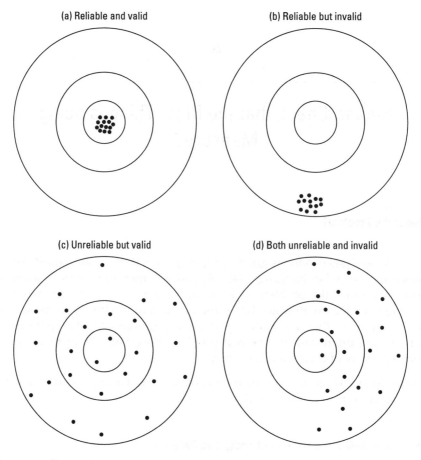

Figure 4.1 *The relationship between reliability and validity*

- An unreliable and invalid measure would not hit the same place consistently and would be biased in terms of the part of the target it hits (Figure 4.1d).

Another way of understanding reliability and validity is in terms of two types of measurement error – random error and non-random error (Carmines and Zeller, 1979):

- Non-random (systematic) error (Figures 4.1b and 4.1d) results in invalid measures.
- Random error affects the degree of reliability. The greater the random error (Figure 4.1c and 4.1d) the less reliable the measure. Where there is very little random error (scatter) the measure is reliable.

Table 4.1 indicates the relationship between random error and systematic error and the concepts of reliability and validity.

Table 4.1   *Random and systematic error, and their relationship with reliability and validity*

		Random error	
		Low	High
Systematic error	Low	Valid and reliable	Valid but unreliable
	High	Invalid but reliable	Invalid and unreliable

Is a Valid Measure Always a Valid Measure?

When considering how to ascertain the validity of any measure three points should be borne in mind.

- A measure in itself is neither valid nor invalid. It is the *use to which a measure is put* that makes it valid or invalid. Scales are a valid measure of weight but not of health.
- The validity of a measure depends on how the concept is defined. A measure may be valid for a concept defined one way but invalid if the concept is defined differently.
- Validity will also be context-dependent. A measure may be valid in one context and with one sample but not another. An IQ test may be a valid measure of intelligence among western, middle-class people but not among people from a very different cultural background. Similarly, a measure may be valid for one age group but not for another, or for men but not for women.

How to Judge if a Question is Valid

There is no certain solution to the problem of establishing validity. This is especially so in the social sciences, where many of the concepts are abstract and many of the traditional methods are not very useful. In the final analysis we can test for validity in a number of ways, but no single way provides unambiguous evidence of validity. Validity has to be argued for: it is not proven.

Validity is traditionally tested using a number of methods including criterion, construct, content, convergent and discrimination methods.

What are Criterion Validity Methods?

This approach compares responses to a question with responses from a well-established (criterion) measure. If the responses on both the new and the established measure are highly correlated the new measure is considered to be valid.

There are two problems with this approach. First, it assumes that the criterion measure is valid. A low correlation between the new and an established measure could be because of problems with the established measure. Secondly, for many concepts in social sciences there are no well-established measures against which to check the new measure.

A related approach is to use to *criterion groups*. A measure designed to test subjective well-being might be given to people whom we believe would have high subjective well-being and to those we have good reason to believe would have low feelings of subjective well-being. If the measure matches the groups (i.e. the people we think would score high do so and those we expect would score low do score low) we have evidence of the measure's validity. Unfortunately, for many concepts, criterion groups are not readily available.

What is Content Validity?

Assessing content validity involves examining the extent to which the measure taps the different aspects of the concept. For example, a measure designed to gauge general health that confined itself to blood pressure would not adequately tap the concept of health – not, at least, as it would normally be understood. Health would usually be understood to be something much broader and more complex. Other aspects of physical health as well as, for example, psychological health would normally form part of a valid measure of health.

The validity of a test depends on the use to which it is put and not on the test *per se*. Whether we agree that a measure has content validity depends ultimately on how we define the concept it is designed to test. Given the disagreement about the 'content' of many social science concepts, it is difficult to develop measures whose validity would be widely accepted.

What is Construct Validity?

Construct validity refers to how the measures 'behave'. Do they behave as we would expect them to on the basis of both our theoretical understanding and knowledge of the concepts they were designed to measure?

One way to assess the validity of measures is to test whether they produce the results that we would expect on the basis of well-established theories. Suppose we have developed a new measure of alienation that we wish to evaluate. We might begin by saying, on the basis of theory, that social class will be related to alienation: the lower the class the higher the alienation. We administer alienation questions as well as questions to measure the social

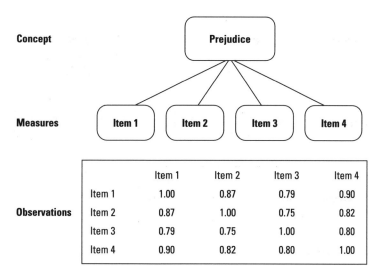

		Item 1	Item 2	Item 3	Item 4
	Item 1	1.00	0.87	0.79	0.90
Observations	Item 2	0.87	1.00	0.75	0.82
	Item 3	0.79	0.75	1.00	0.80
	Item 4	0.90	0.82	0.80	1.00

Figure 4.2   *Convergent validity*

class of our respondents. Suppose that alienation and social class are unrelated – contrary to theoretical expectations. Does this mean that the measure of alienation we were evaluating is invalid? Maybe, but other possibilities exist. The measure of the other concept (social class) could be faulty. The theory itself could be wrong or outmoded. There is a certain circularity in testing theories using measures that have been validated on the basis of the theory.

Another way of testing validity draws on the related concepts of *convergent* and *discriminant* validity. These two types of validity are subtypes of construct validity. This approach relies on having multiple, rather than single, measures of a concept; it can be best explained with an example.

What is Convergent Validity?

Suppose we have developed a four-item measure to gauge levels of prejudice. If all these items measure prejudice then, at the very least, they should each be highly correlated with each other. Where such items are highly intercorrelated (as in Figure 4.2) the measures are said to have convergent validity.

The major problem with testing validity simply with measures of convergent validity is that even though the four items are intercorrelated and may measure the same concept, this does not mean that they measure the concept that we claim they do.

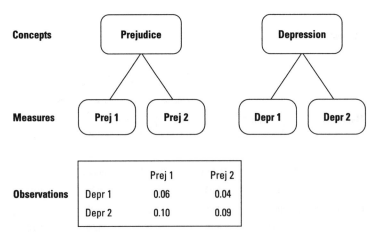

Figure 4.3   *Discriminant validity*

What is Discriminant Validity?

An alternative method is to measure discriminant validity. This approach is based on the argument that two different concepts should not correlate with one another. That is, if the concepts are really different then they will not correlate highly.

In Figure 4.3 the measures of depression are not correlated with the measures of prejudice. This is further evidence that the prejudice measures, as well as being correlated with each other, are distinct in that they are not correlated with other measures.

How to Combine Convergent and Discriminant Validity Methods

A stronger test of the validity of a set of measures is to look at the convergent and discriminant measures together. A measure is more likely to be valid if it has both discriminant and convergent validity than just one or the other.

Figure 4.4 provides an example of data in which both prejudice and depression have convergent validity. This convergent validity can be seen in the high correlations among the prejudice items and the high correlations among the depression items. Figure 4.4 also demonstrates discriminant validity. This is demonstrated by the very low correlations between the depression items on the one hand and the prejudice items on the other hand.

The evidence regarding convergent and discriminant validity provides support for the validity of the measures of the two concepts. However, the problem remains that although we may be confident that we have valid measures of two different concepts, we still cannot be sure that they measure the concepts we say they do.

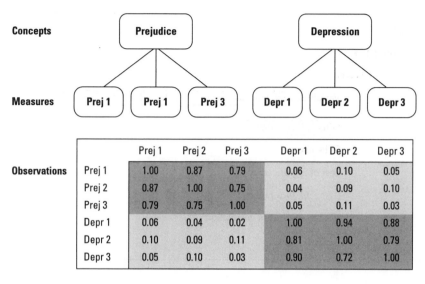

		Prej 1	Prej 2	Prej 3	Depr 1	Depr 2	Depr 3
Observations	Prej 1	1.00	0.87	0.79	0.06	0.10	0.05
	Prej 2	0.87	1.00	0.75	0.04	0.09	0.10
	Prej 3	0.79	0.75	1.00	0.05	0.11	0.03
	Depr 1	0.06	0.04	0.02	1.00	0.94	0.88
	Depr 2	0.10	0.09	0.11	0.81	1.00	0.79
	Depr 3	0.05	0.10	0.03	0.90	0.72	1.00

Figure 4.4   *Discriminant and convergent validity*

In the final analysis there is no sure way around this problem. All we can do is try to specify *which* concepts our measures are designed to measure. We may need to rely on some form of criterion group validity, theoretical confirmation or simply argue that the measures have face validity as judged by experts.

Other more complex methods of measuring construct validity have been developed. These include methods such as:

- multitrait–multimethod validity, developed by Campbell and Fiske (1959);
- pattern matching, as elaborated by Cook and Campbell (1979) and Trochim (2000b);
- factor analysis (Problem 19).

However, none of these overcomes the problem described here: proving that the measures gauge a particular concept. The task of the data analyst is to provide as much evidence one way or another for validity but to recognize that the validity of the use of any measure may always be contested.

Using SPSS

To test for convergent and discriminant validity, a correlation matrix of the variables being tested is required. The instructions below obtain correlations for interval-level variables (p. 41, 275).

Analyze ▾

   Correlate ▶

      Bivariate…

         Variables: | *Select variables to correlate: Depr 1, Depr 2, Depr 3,* |

         | *Prej 1, Prej 2, Prej 3* |

         ☑ Pearson

         Test of Significance

            ⊙ Two-tailed

         ☑ Flag significant correlations

         OK

5

How to Deal with Variables with Lots of Categories

What is the Problem?

A variable with a large number of categories can present two main problems for data analysis:

- A large number of categories can result in tables and graphs that are virtually unreadable. Figure 5.1 illustrates a graph of the relationship between frequency of church attendance (nine categories) and being politically left-wing or right-wing (seven categories). Since a separate line is drawn for each of the nine categories of church attendance, the graph becomes an unreadable tangle. Table 5.1 provides a crosstabulation of a relationship between the same two variables (Problem 32). This table not only requires a lot of space but also is very difficult to read and summarize.
- Depending on the sample size, a large number of categories can mean that some categories contain very few cases. Table 5.1 illustrates this problem of very small numbers in many cells. This can lead to distorted and unreliable statistics.

There are two main ways of handling variables with a large number of categories.

Do Nothing

Use methods of analysis that can handle and take advantage of a large number of categories and are unaffected by a small number of cases with a particular value. In the examples above we might avoid using graphs or tables and simply use a correlation coefficient such as gamma or Spearman' rho (Problem 36) to indicate the degree to which these two variables are related.

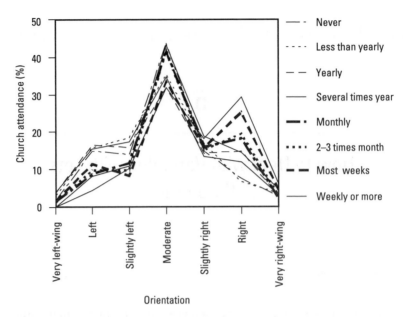

Figure 5.1   *Graph that is impossible to read because the variable has too many categories*
Source: Bean et al Australian Election Survey, 1998

If we were dealing with a single variable such as age or income, we might simply use a summary measure such as the mean age or income to provide a snapshot of the distribution rather than all the detail that a table or graph might provide (p. 219).

Reduce the Number of Categories

If we wanted to display the data in graphical or tabular form we could collapse categories of the variables to simplify the results. While collapsing categories can lead to a loss of detail, it can make it much easier to detect *patterns* in the data.

There are two main approaches to reducing the number of categories of a variable: the substantive approach and the distributional approach.

How to Reduce Categories by Substantive Recoding

This approach combines categories based on the *nature of the categories*. Thus we might collapse the categories of the variables in Table 5.1 as illustrated in Table 5.2. Here the categories have been collapsed so that categories which seem to belong together are combined. There is no set way in which to do

Table 5.1 *Political orientation by frequency of church attendance*

Orientation	Frequency of church attendance									Total
	Never	Less than yearly	Yearly	Several times yearly	Monthly	2–3 times a month	Most weeks	Weekly	More than weekly	
Very left-wing	9 4.0%	2 1.9%	6 3.1%	7 3.8%		2 1.5%	1 1.4%	4 1.6%		31 2.2%
Left	35 15.6%	16 15.0%	31 15.9%	30 16.5%	9 8.1%	12 8.8%	7 9.7%	29 11.4%	5 4.3%	174 12.4%
Slightly left	39 17.3%	15 14.0%	36 18.5%	29 15.9%	12 10.8%	16 11.7%	7 9.7%	21 8.3%	12 10.3%	187 13.4%
Moderate	78 34.7%	47 43.9%	69 35.4%	58 31.9%	48 43.2%	57 41.6%	30 41.7%	85 33.5%	37 31.9%	509 36.4%
Slightly right	30 13.3%	16 15.0%	33 16.9%	26 14.3%	21 18.9%	22 16.1%	11 15.3%	40 15.7%	21 18.1%	220 15.7%
Right	27 12.0%	8 7.5%	13 6.7%	27 14.8%	16 14.4%	25 18.2%	14 19.4%	64 25.2%	34 29.3%	228 16.3%
Very right-wing	7 3.1%	3 2.8%	7 3.6%	5 2.7%	5 4.5%	3 2.2%	2 2.8%	11 4.3%	7 6.0%	50 3.6%
Total	225 100.0%	107 100.0%	195 100.0%	182 100.0%	111 100.0%	137 100.0%	72 100.0%	254 100.0%	116 100.0%	1399 100.0%

Table 5.2   Substantive recoding

Orientation		Church attendance	
Original	Collapsed	Original	Collapsed
Very left-wing		Never	
Left	Left	Less than yearly	Infrequent
Slightly left		Yearly	
Moderate	Centre	Several times yearly	
Slightly right		Monthly	
Right	Right	2–3 times a month	
Very right-wing		Most weeks	Frequent
		Weekly	
		More than weekly	

Table 5.3   *Crosstabulation from Table 5.1 with fewer categories*

		Collapsed church attendance (%)	
		Infrequent	Frequent
Collapsed political	Left-wing	36	20
orientation	Centre	36	37
	Right-wing	28	43
Total		100	100

this. I have simply used my ideas about what belongs together. Someone else might have divided up the frequency of church attendance categories differently or included the slightly right and slightly left categories with those in the centre on the political orientation variable. Collapsing these variables in this way results in a crosstabulation as in Table 5.3 and the much more readable graph in Figure 5.2.

How to Reduce Categories Using Distributional Recoding

This approach to recoding creates categories by dividing a *distribution* into equal sizes – that is, each category will have approximately the same *number of cases*. This approach should only be used with ordinal and interval variables where the categories of the variable are at least ranked from low to high on some dimension (pp. 40–42).

Table 5.4 is a frequency table of annual income. Suppose we want to divide the income variable into four categories ranging from low to high. Using the substantive approach, we would have to decide what income level constitutes a low income and what constitutes a high income. Here we encounter

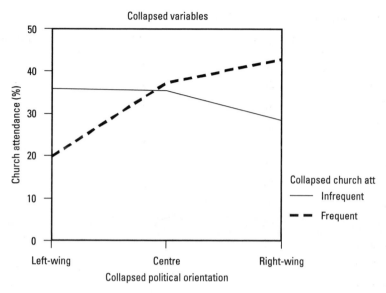

Figure 5.2   *Graph from Figure 5.1 with fewer categories*

a problem. My definition of a low income might be very different from yours and might be most inappropriate for this particular sample.

Using a distributional approach to recoding, we let the actual distribution of incomes in the sample define what is low and high income. Suppose that we want to divide income into four categories. The distributional approach to recoding involves dividing the sample into four equal groups. To accomplish this we have to look for the income *cutting points* to create four roughly equal-sized groups.

This is achieved by using the cumulative percentage column of the table (p. 198). This column indicates the percentage of cases in a given category *or below*. Thus the figure 12 means that 12 per cent of the sample earn $4999 *or less*. To divide the sample into four equal-sized groups we can look for cumulative percentage figures of 25, 50 and 75 per cent to indicate where the cutting points between the categories should be. Where there is not an exact figure, select the next percentage above the desired percentage.

In Table 5.4 the figure closest to the 25 per cent mark is 29 per cent . The income level that equates to this is $10 000–12 999. The bottom quarter of income earners (295 to be precise) earn $12 999 or less. The next cut-off point will correspond to the 54 per cent figure (i.e. $20 000–22 999) and the next cut-off corresponds to the 77 per cent figure ($30 000–34 999). This results in four income groups: lowest, up to $12 999; second lowest, between $13 000 and $22 999; second highest, between $$23 000 and $34 999; and highest, $35 000 and over.

Table 5.4 *Frequency table of annual income*

Income ($)	Frequency	Valid %	Cumulative %
< 1000	32	3	3
1000–2999	28	3	6
3000–3999	32	3	9
4000–4999	21	2	12
5000–5999	23	2	14
6000–6999	18	2	16
7000–7999	18	2	18
8000–9999	51	5	23
10 000–12 499	58	6	29
12 500–14 999	71	7	36
15 000–17 499	61	6	43
17 500–19 999	56	6	48
20 000–22 499	55	6	54
22 500–24 999	62	6	60
25 000–29 999	95	10	70
30 000–34 999	67	7	77
35 000–39 999	57	6	83
40 000–49 999	70	7	90
50 000–59 999	37	4	94
60 000–74 999	26	3	97
75 000+	32	3	100
Total	970	100	

An alternative method of finding cutting points for distributional recoding is to get a statistical analysis program such as SPSS to tell you what they are. When a sample is divided into four equal groups each group is called a *quartile*; five equal groups are called *quintiles*; ten equal groups are called *deciles*. In analysis programs you simply need to specify the number of groups and the cutting points will be provided in the output.

The key point here is that the cutting points are determined by the way the sample is distributed. The low-income group consists of *relatively* low income earners. The high-income group is *relatively* high. This approach to collapsing the categories of the variable allows the distribution to define what is high or low rather than the researcher imposing their own views as to what a low or high income is.

Using SPSS

Obtaining a Frequency Table and Cutting Points

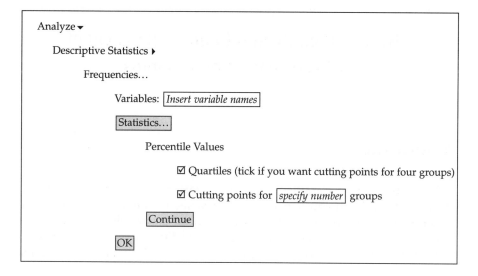

Analyze ▾

    Descriptive Statistics ▶

        Frequencies…

            Variables: *Insert variable names*

            Statistics…

                Percentile Values

                    ☑ Quartiles (tick if you want cutting points for four groups)

                    ☑ Cutting points for *specify number* groups

                Continue

        OK

Recoding a Variable

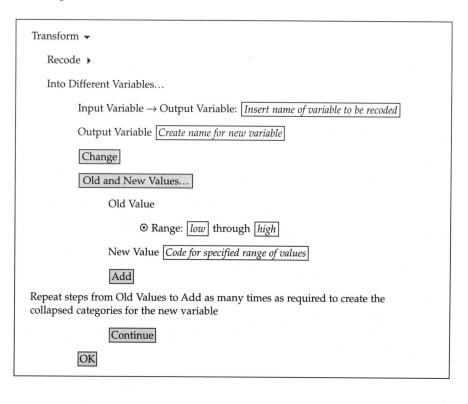

Transform ▾

    Recode ▶

    Into Different Variables…

        Input Variable → Output Variable: *Insert name of variable to be recoded*

        Output Variable *Create name for new variable*

        Change

        Old and New Values…

            Old Value

                ⊙ Range: *low* through *high*

            New Value *Code for specified range of values*

        Add

Repeat steps from Old Values to Add as many times as required to create the collapsed categories for the new variable

        Continue

    OK

6

How to Identify and Change the Level of Measurement of Variables

What is the Problem?

All variables can be classified as having a particular level of measurement. Many statistical techniques require that variables are measured at a particular level, so knowing the level of measurement of a variable is crucial when working out how to analyse the variable. Failing to correctly match the statistical method to a variable's level of measurement leads either to nonsense results or to potentially misleading results.

There are three key questions to resolve in relation to the level of measurement of variables:

- How can we work out the level of measurement of any variable?
- Which level of measurement is best?
- How fixed are the rules regarding level of measurement?

What does 'Level of Measurement' Mean?

The level of measurement of a variable refers to how the categories or values of the variable are arranged in relation to each other. There are four main levels of measurement: ratio, interval, ordinal and nominal. However, for the purpose of the statistical methods discussed in this book we do not need to distinguish between the ratio and interval levels. Accordingly I will use the term 'interval' level to include ratio-level variables. The level of measurement of a variable depends on whether:

- there are different categories;
- the categories can be rank-ordered;
- the differences or intervals between each category can be specified in a meaningful numerical sense.

Interval Level

An interval-level variable has all three characteristics and is therefore regarded as being at the highest level of measurement. An interval variable consists of values that can be expressed in *numerically meaningful* terms. For example, age, weight, height, income, and number of children in a family are all interval variables for which the numbers that represent the values of the variable are numerically meaningful (compared with codes of 1 and 2 to represent gender, where the codes have no numeric meaning). The numerical values of an interval level variable are organized in *order* – from the lowest to the highest value or vice versa. Finally, since the values of interval variables are numerically meaningful we can specify the *amount of difference* (or the interval) between cases with different values. Thus we can say that the difference between a person with a value of 20 and a person with a value of 15 on the age variable is 5 years.

Ordinal Level

An ordinal variable is one where we can rank-order categories from low to high. However, we cannot specify numerically *how much* difference there is between the categories. For example, when age has the categories 'child', 'adolescent', 'young adult', 'middle-aged' and 'elderly' it is measured at the ordinal level. The categories can be ordered from youngest to oldest, but we cannot specify precisely the age gap between people in different categories.

Nominal Level

A nominal variable is one where the different categories have no set rank order. For example, religious affiliation is a nominal variable where we can distinguish between categories of affiliation (e.g. Jewish, Roman Catholic, Orthodox, Protestant, Islamic, no religion) but cannot rank these categories as having an obvious *order*.

How to Work out a Variable's Level of Measurement

Figure 6.1 provides a summary of the distinction between levels of measurement. To work out the level of measurement of a variable, ask yourself how many of the characteristics in the first column of the figure your variable has.

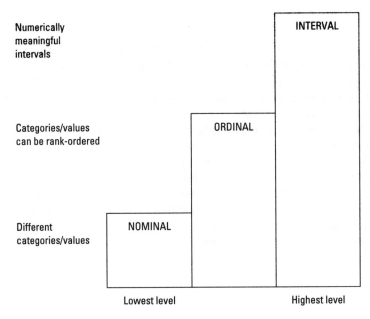

Figure 6.1 *Differences between levels of measurement*

Related Terms

There can be some confusion when reading texts and selecting statistics since some authors use terms other than nominal, ordinal and interval, while others use other sets of terms interchangeably with level-of-measurement terminology (see Table 6.1).

- *Qualitative and quantitative.* Qualitative variables are those where the codes have no inherent numerical meaning (as with nominal variables), while quantitative variables are those where the codes do have a numerical meaning (interval variables). This distinction does not recognize ordinal variables and thus makes it unclear how they are to be analysed.
- *Categorical and numeric.* This is equivalent to the qualitative–quantitative distinction.
- *Discrete and continuous.* A discrete variable is one with distinct categories, while a continuous variable will have a potentially unbroken set of values between the low and high values. Nominal and ordinal variables will normally have discrete categories and interval variables will frequently be continuous. Unfortunately this is not always the case, as some interval variables can be thought of as discrete variables. For example, the number of children a person has is an interval variable that is also discrete – the number of children a person has must be one of the discrete

Table 6.1   *Synonyms for different levels of measurement*

Level	Other terms
Nominal	Categorical; qualitative, discrete
Ordinal	Qualitative, discrete
Interval/ratio	Numerical, continuous, quantitative

values 0, 1, 2, 3, … ; it cannot be, for example, 1.23543. Dichotomous variables can also be regarded as discrete interval-level variables (see below).

Low and High Levels of Measurement

Nominal-level variables are regarded as having the lowest level of measurement. The codes of the variable contain the least information – they only indicate the existence of difference. Interval variables are regarded as being at the highest level of measurement since the codes contain at least three types of information about cases – existence of difference, order and the amount of difference between cases.

What is the Best Level of Measurement?

From a statistical perspective interval-level variables are the most desirable.

- An interval-level variable conveys much more information about cases and their relation to one another than does a nominal or ordinal variable. The more we know about cases the more powerful a variable should be in explaining phenomena.
- The most powerful statistical methods assume that variables are measured at the interval level. Using nominal or ordinal variables restricts the available methods of analysis.

However, statistical requirements are not the only consideration. Many social science variables simply are not interval and cannot be measured at the interval level (e.g. ethnicity, religious group, gender, family type). Furthermore, while interval-level measurements result in more *precise* data, these measurements are not necessarily more *accurate*. For example, if we ask people how many times they attended religious services in the last 12 months they may provide a precise number of times but this will not necessarily be correct. Sometimes the more precision we seek the greater the chance of obtaining inaccurate answers.

How Fixed are Level-of-Measurement 'Rules'?

Methods of analysis assume that variables are measured at a particular level. How hard and fast are these rules?

Can Higher-Level Variables be Treated at a Lower Level?

We can answer this question by stating two principles. The first is that *any statistic that can be used for a variable measured at a low level of measurement can be used for variables measured at a higher level.*

Variables measured at the higher level have all the characteristics of variables measured at the lower level of measurement. An ordinal variable has the characteristics of a nominal variable *plus* rank order. An interval variable has all the characteristics of an ordinal variable *plus* numerical values and intervals.

This means that any statistic that can be used with nominal variables also can be used with ordinal and interval variables. Any statistic that can be used with an ordinal variable can be used for an interval variable. However, this practice is not always desirable as it leads to a loss of information contained in the higher-level variables. A statistic that is appropriate for a low-level variable is not sensitive to all the information contained in a variable measured at a higher level (e.g. the order of categories and the numerical information contained in the intervals).

Our second principle is that *the reverse of our first principle is not true. Statistics designed specifically for higher levels of measurement should not be used to analyse variables measured at a lower level.*

Statistics designed specifically for interval variables should not be applied to ordinal or nominal variables. Statistics designed for use with ordinal variables should not be used with nominal variables. These principles are summarized in Table 6.2.

Does the Level of Measurement Depend on the Way a Variable is Used?

In some respects, the level of measurement of a variable is in the eye of the beholder. This applies in particular to the distinction between nominal and ordinal variables. The characteristic that distinguishes nominal and ordinal variables is that the categories of the ordinal variable can be ranked. But ranked in relation to what? Whether or not it makes sense to rank categories can depend on the use to which the variable is being put.

For example, suppose we have a variable indicating the university that people attended. Each category is the name of a particular university. These categories indicate difference (nominal) but can the categories be ranked? If so, on what criteria? The answer is yes – universities can be ranked by a

Table 6.2   *Use of statistics for variables measured at different levels*

		Statistic designed for		
		Nominal	Ordinal	Interval
Statistic can be used for	Nominal	✓	✗	✗
	Ordinal	?	✓	✗
	Interval	?	?	✓

✓ most suited.
? can be used but normally not the best choice.
✗ should not be used for variables at this level of measurement.

variety of criteria such as the age of the university, difficulty of obtaining admission, size, level of fees and quality of teaching. When the criterion used for ranking is relevant to the research question, it is appropriate to treat the variable as ordinal.

How to Convert Variables to the Interval Level

If interval variables are the most desirable type it makes sense to frame questionnaires so that interval-level data are collected. However, when the form in which data are collected is beyond our control, what can be done to maximize the level of measurement of variables?

TREAT ORDINAL DATA AS THOUGH THEY ARE INTERVAL   Many statisticians argue that some statistical techniques are 'robust' and that treating ordinal variables as though they were interval does not affect results. In practice, this relaxed approach is frequently adopted with scales and other ordinal variables with a large number of values.

CONVERT GROUPED NUMERICAL VARIABLES   Grouped numerical variables are those where the data could have been collected in a continuous interval-level form but were instead collected in bands of values. An example of grouped numerical data is age group where data were collected using the age bands 15–19, 20–29, 30–39, 40–49, 50–59, 60–64, 65–74 and 75 and over. As they stand, these categories are ordinal because we cannot specify the age gap between people in different categories. The age interval between a person in the 20–29 group and a person in the 30–39 group could be as little as a year or as much as 19 years.

To convert this grouped numerical variable to an interval variable we need to assume that people within any one category will be evenly spread across the category. The variable can then be converted to interval level in three steps:

1. Designate an upper cut-off point for any open-ended category (e.g. 75+).
2. Identify the numerical *midpoint* of each category (e.g. for the 20–29 age group the midpoint is 24.5).
3. Recode each category to this numerical midpoint (see below).

This recoding substitutes a person's age-group code for the average actual age of that age band. By assuming that people are distributed evenly in the age band and using the midpoint, the recoding should not lead to any distortions. If better information is available about the average age of people within an age band (e.g. from census data), then this information could be used instead of the midpoint.

CREATE DICHOTOMOUS VARIABLES As a general principle, if a variable has only two categories (i.e. is dichotomous) it can be treated as though it is an interval variable. This means that if we can convert a nominal or ordinal variable into a dichotomous variable or set of dichotomous variables, then for the purpose of selecting the method of analysis it often can be treated as an interval variable. There are several ways of obtaining dichotomous variables.

- *Collapse a variable to two categories.* For example, a variable indicating country of birth might include 100 categories reflecting different countries. This might be collapsed to 'born in this country' and 'born overseas'. Care is required not to lose so much information in the process that the variable hides more than it reveals.
- *Create dummy variables.* An ordinal or nominal variable with more than two categories can be converted into a series of dichotomous variables called *dummy* variables; these are used in some of the powerful multivariate analysis methods (pp. 368–9).

USE A DIFFERENT METHOD OF ANALYSIS Rather than converting variables, you can accept that the variable is measured at the nominal or ordinal level and select a method of analysis designed for this level of measurement. While these methods may be less powerful they are simpler to understand and communicate and may be preferable. Increasingly powerful analysis techniques are becoming available that can handle nominal and ordinal variables (see Problem 50).

Using SPSS

We can recode age bands to midpoints as follows:

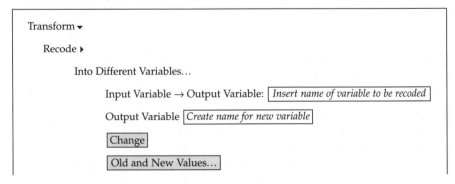

Old Value

⊙ Value: 2

New Value 24.5

Add

Repeat steps from Old Values to Add as many times as required to create the collapsed categories for the new variable

Continue

OK

7

How to Deal with Questions that Fail to Identify Real Differences between Cases

A questionnaire item that fails to identify real and relevant differences between cases on that variable is called a *non-discriminating* measure.

Why is the Failure to Discriminate a Problem?

Problems for Data Analysis

The variables in Table 7.1 illustrate variables that do not discriminate well. Ninety-five per cent believe that heroin should remain illegal, and on a nine-point marriage satisfaction scale 82 per cent rated their marriage at 7, 8 or 9. These types of distribution present a number of problems.

SKEWNESS   The skew in these distributions means that they introduce all the problems of skewness discussed in (pp. 224–6).

INFLATED CORRELATIONS   Non-discriminating dependent variables have the same effect as outliers with interval variables (Problem 13). A non-discriminating categorical variable can lead to inflated correlations. Rummel (1970) observes that in multivariate analysis a dichotomous variable with a very skewed distribution (e.g. 90–10 split) the 10 per cent act like outliers and have an undue effect on correlations. The same thing happens with simple bivariate analysis. Table 7.2 displays the relationship between gender and attitude to legalizing cocaine. Attitudes regarding legalization are very skewed, with a 95–5 split. The difference between males and females is only 6 percentage points – not much. However, the correlations indicate that the relationship is either strong (gamma = –0.62, $p < 0.002$) or at least moderate (Somers' $d = -0.32$, $p < 0.000$) (p. 268, 272).

Now let us suppose that the distribution on the dependent variable is much more even but the percentage differences between males and females are the same. In Table 7.3 the split on approving the legalization of cocaine is 51–49 but the percentage difference between male and female approval of

Table 7.1 *Two non-discriminating variables*

(a) Satisfaction with marriage

		Frequency	Valid percentage	Cumulative percentage
1	Terrible	11	1	1
2	Very unhappy	16	2	3
3	Unhappy	5	1	4
4	Mostly dissatisfied	1	0	4
5	Mixed feelings	29	4	8
6	Mostly satisfied	79	10	17
7	Pleased	118	14	32
8	Very pleased	289	35	67
9	Delighted	273	33	100
Total		821	100	

(b) Should heroin be made legal?

	Frequency	%
Legal	33	3
Don't know	27	2
Illegal	1168	95
Total	1228	100

Table 7.2 *Crosstabulation based on one poorly discriminating variable*

		Gender		Total
		Male	Female	
Legalization of cocaine	Illegal	(230) 92%	(245) 98%	(475) 95%
	Legal	(20) 8%	(5) 2%	(25) 5%
	Total	(250) 100%	(250) 100%	(500) 100%

Correlations	Value	Approx. Sig.
Somers' d	− 0.32	0.002
Gamma	− 0.62	0.002

legalization remains at 6 percentage points. With the more even distribution on the dependent variable the correlation between gender and attitude to legalization disappears. Gamma drops to 0.12 ($p = 0.18$) and Somers' d drops to 0.06 ($p = 0.18$).

Table 7.3   *Crosstabulation with two variables that discriminate*

		Gender		
		Male	Female	Total
Legalization of cocaine	Illegal	(135) 54%	(120) 48%	(255) 51%
	Legal	(115) 46%	(130) 52%	(245) 49%
	Total	(250) 100%	(250) 100%	(500) 100%

	Value	Approx. Sig.
Somers' *d*	0.06	0.18
Gamma	0.12	0.18

DEFLATED CORRELATIONS   Variables that fail to discriminate between cases where real differences exist make the sample appear homogeneous – they minimize variation. Many statistical measures are based on explaining variation in one variable in terms of variation in another variable. For example, we may try to explain variations in income levels in a sample as being due to the different levels of education (i.e. variance) among sample members (p. 267). However, if all members of the sample had identical education then income differences could not be due to educational differences.

When the sample is homogeneous in relation to the *independent variable,* any correlations between the homogeneous independent variable and any other variable will be deflated. This can be illustrated with the hypothetical and extreme example in Table 7.4. Despite quite substantial *percentage* differences between happy and unhappy people regarding their attitude to legalizing marijuana, the correlation coefficients are low and not statistically significant.

However, when we have the same sample size and the same percentage differences between happy and unhappy respondents *but a much better distribution on the happiness variable,* we obtain quite different correlation and significance statistics (Table 7.5).

The basic point is that if a variable has little variation (as will be the case with a non-discriminating variable) it will have less capacity to account for variation in the dependent variable.

Why do Some Variables Fail to Discriminate?

Variables fail to discriminate for three reasons:

• The data were collected in such a way that the questions and classification schemes were not able to identify the diversity that really existed in the sample.

Table 7.4 *Effect of a poorly distributed independent variable on correlations*

Legalization of marijuana	Respondent is:	
	Happy	Unhappy
Legalize	(100)	(1)
	51%	25%
Neither favour nor oppose	(60)	(1)
	31%	25%
Oppose legalization	(36)	(2)
	18%	50%
Total	(196)	(4)
	100%	100%

	Value	df	Sig.
Chi-square	2.60	2.00	0.26

	Value		Sig.
Kendall's tau-b	0.09		0.17
Somers'*d*	0.02		0.17

Table 7.5 *Effect of a well-distributed independent variable on correlations*

Legalization of marijuana	Respondent is:	
	Happy	Unhappy
Legalize	(50)	(25)
	50%	25%
Neither favour nor oppose	(30)	(25)
	30%	25%
Oppose legalization	(20)	(50)
	20%	50%
Total	(100)	(100)
	100%	100%

	Value	df	Sig.
Chi-square	21.60	2.00	0.00

	Value		Sig.
Somers'*d*	0.26		0.001
Kendall's tau-b	0.30		0.001

- The sample was homogeneous. Despite good questions, poor sampling may make it impossible to identify the variation that existed in the population (p. 151).
- Differences in the data were hidden by poor coding systems that did not allow for the differences to be recorded in the data file.

How to Deal with Non-discriminating Variables

There are three points in the research process where we can do something about poor question discrimination.

Avoiding the Problem at the Data Collection Stage

There are two points to note here. First, poor instrument design is a common cause of variables failing to discriminate. Questions may be so leading that they almost inevitably produce a particular response. Alternatively, the response categories may be so limited or unbalanced that there is little capacity for the question to detect genuinely different responses. Questions may suffer from a social desirability problem which, when compounded with particular data collection methods, can produce socially desirable but untrue responses.

The only way of avoiding this problem is by careful pilot testing. This should identify problems with response categories or other problems that constrain the range of responses.

Secondly, careful conceptualization is required. The classification system that is employed either in the questionnaire itself or at the coding stage needs to be properly thought through. Simply using a conventional system is of little use if the classification system has been shown to be outdated or empirically or theoretically confused.

Solving the Problem with Better Sample Design

Poor design can result in a sample that is much more homogeneous than the population. For example, samples of university students designed to represent young people (or all people for that matter) are likely to produce a homogeneous set of responses to some questions. Pilot testing and careful sample design are required to avoid this problem.

How to Deal with Non-discriminating Variables During Data Analysis

The options for dealing with non-discriminating variables at the data analysis stage are somewhat limited. If there is little variation in the data we cannot simply create variation during the data analysis. The best way of dealing with non-discriminating variables is to avoid them in the first place. At the data analysis stage we are limited to the following options:

- Do not use the variable. If the variable is not essential this may be the best option.
- Use the variable only in combination with other variables. Variables that do not discriminate much on their own can sometimes be very useful when used in conjunction with others. Some scaling techniques, such as Guttman scaling, rely on having a set of questions of increasing degrees of 'difficulty' – or 'tougher' tests of the underlying concept. For example, a Guttman scale designed to measure political activism might ask questions about a range of political activities in which the person has participated (e.g. voting, signing a petition, joining a political party, boycotting a product, participating in a lawful demonstration, participating in an unauthorized demonstration, occupying a building, damaging property, …). The first test (voting) is a relatively easy one and will only distinguish at a very crude level between activists and non-activists. However the 'tougher tests' such as occupying a building and damaging property will enable us to identify only the most active people. While these tough measures would not allow us to discriminate political activism on their own (they are too tough a test and most people would fall into the inactive category using just these measures), they enable much finer discrimination when used in conjunction with other variables that measure the same underlying concept.
- Adjust cutting points. This approach is only useful for non-discriminating variables that have a number of categories. The satisfaction with marriage question (Table 7.1a) is such an example. In this example 82 per cent of people rate their marriage on a nine-point scale at 7, 8 or 9. Recognizing the skew in this distribution, we might argue that since most people give a very high score, anything other than the highest score indicates reservations about their marriage. Relatively speaking those who rate their marriage as at 7 or below are indicating relative dissatisfaction. One way of analyzing this variable could be to recode it into three categories: most satisfied (the 33 per cent scoring 9), relatively satisfied (the 35 per cent scoring 8) and relatively dissatisfied (the 32 per cent scoring 1–7) (see pp. 36–38).

8

How to Rearrange the Categories of a Variable

The order of the categories can be important for a number of reasons. Here we will consider two types of misordered variable – those where the categories require rearranging, and those where they require reversing.

When to Rearrange Categories

There are two main difficulties that can arise from poorly ordered categories. First, the order of categories may make no logical or substantive sense. This problem, which is most likely with nominal variables, can result in variables and tables appearing messy and disorganized, and consequently more difficult to read. For reasons of presentation it is desirable to impose some coherent order on the categories. Table 8.1 provides an example of categories arranged without any coherent order.

Secondly, the order of the categories may lower the level of measurement of a variable. Since the level of measurement of a variable reflects the relationship between the categories (Problem 6), some reordering of the categories of nominal variables can transform the variables to ordinal ones. This can increase the range and power of statistical methods that can be applied to such variables.

In Table 8.2 the order of the categories means that the variable cannot be treated as an ordinal variable. The first four categories are rank-ordered from most in favour of legalization to most opposed. But the fifth category destroys the rank order of the categories since this final category does not constitute the highest level of opposition to legalization. As it stands, this variable must be treated as a nominal variable, which in turn restricts the way it can be analysed.

When to Reverse the Order of the Categories

Even though a variable may have rank-ordered categories; these categories might require reverse ordering. Reversing the order of categories or values may be required for either of two reasons.

Table 8.1 *Marital status with unordered categories*

	Frequency	Valid percentage	Cumulative percentage
1 Widowed	159	11	11
2 Married	745	50	61
3 Divorced	218	15	76
4 Never married	315	21	97
5 Separated	48	3	100
Total	1485	100	

Table 8.2 *Variable with categories that require reordering*

Should marijuana be legalized?	Frequency	Valid percentage	Cumulative percentage
Definitely legalize	220	12	12
Probably legalize	422	23	35
Probably not legalize	469	26	61
Definitely do not legalize	351	19	80
Can't decide	371	20	100
Total	1833	100	

To Create a Scale

When producing a scale or an index, the values of a number of variables are combined (Problem 17). A scale adds together a person's score on a number of different variables to arrive at an overall score on a broader concept. If we needed to develop a measure of social liberalism, we might ask individual questions about attitudes to abortion, capital punishment, censorship, euthanasia, etc. and 'score' answers on each variable. We could then combine the scores on each component into an overall measure of social liberalism.

Before such a composite measure can be created, each of the variables that contribute to the composite measure should be scored in the same direction. That is, a high score on each variable must mean the same thing. However, when constructing questionnaire items to be combined into a scale it is normal to mix up the direction of the statements to which people respond: some will be positive, while others will be negative. Table 8.3 provides an example of four variables designed to be combined into a single composite scale (pp. 121–2) where a low score does not consistently mean the same thing for each variable.

To Simplify the Interpretation of Results

Suppose we have two variables, highest qualification and annual income, coded as indicated in Table 8.4 where the code is indicated beside each category. The problem with the education variable is that the codes do not correspond well with the meaning of the categories. This lack of correspondence between the numerical value of the code and the 'quantity' implied by the

Table 8.3   *Inconsistent coding of variables designed for scaling*

Variable	Scores	Meaning
Abortion	1 = agrees, 5 = opposes	Low score = socially liberal
Voluntary euthanasia	1 = opposes, 5 = supports	Low score = socially conservative
Censorship	1 = supports, 5 = opposes	Low score = socially conservative
Capital punishment	1 = supports, 5 = opposes	Low score = socially conservative

Table 8.4   *Codes that do not match the 'quantity' implied by the categories*

Highest qualification	Income
1 Postgraduate	1 Less than $5000
2 Bachelor's degree	2 $5001 to $10 000
3 Undergraduate diploma	3 $10 001 to $15 000
4 Associate diploma	4 $15 001 to $20 000
5 Trade qualification	5 $20 001 to $25 000
6 Non-trade qualification	6 $25 001 to $30 000
	7 $30 001 to $35 000
	8 $35 001 to $40 000
	9 $40 001 to $45 000
	10 $45 001 to $50 000
	11 $50 001 to $60 000
	12 $60 001 to $70 000
	13 $70 001 to $80 000
	14 $80 001 to $90 000
	15 $90 001 to $100 000
	16 More than $100 000

categories of the variable can create considerable awkwardness in interpreting the analysis involving such a variable. This problem becomes especially pronounced when dealing with bivariate and multivariate statistics (pp. 272–3).

What Criteria to Use for Reordering

Creating Substantive Order

The type of substantively based reordering depends on the template you want to impose on the variable. Categories can be arranged according to a number of criteria.

THE NUMBER OF PEOPLE   Categories might be ordered according to how popular they are, as in Table 8.5.

Table 8.5   *Marital status ordered by frequency*

		Frequency	Valid percentage	Cumulative percentage
1	Married	745	50	50
2	Never married	315	21	71
3	Divorced	218	15	86
4	Widowed	159	11	97
5	Separated	48	3	100
	Total	1485	100	

Table 8.6   *Marital status (with categories arranged in substantive order)*

		Frequency	Valid percentage	Cumulative percentage
1	Never married	315	21	21
2	Married	745	50	50
3	Separated	48	3	3
4	Divorced	218	15	15
5	Widowed	159	11	11
	Total	1485	100	100

COMMONALITIES BETWEEN THE CATEGORIES Identifying what the categories have in common is largely up to you, but it will normally reflect the use to which the variable is being put. In Table 8.6 the categories of marital status have been ordered according to the order in which they are most likely to occur in the life cycle. In addition, the three categories that involve the ending of a marriage are arranged next to each other.

Another example concerns reordering countries into a coherent order. They might be ordered according to their geographical region, their size, level of development, main language, form of government, etc.

CHANGING ORDER APPROPRIATE TO THE FOCUS OF THE ANALYSIS We may have a variable indicating the industry in which a person works. Table 8.7a lists the initial order of industry categories. There is no obvious order to them. However, we might be undertaking analysis that is focusing on unionization and its impact on job satisfaction. For this analysis it might make sense to organize the industry categories according to the level of unionization of the industry. This would provide a logical order to the categories and probably make it easier to read tables later on. Table 8.7b indicates the way in which the variable might be recoded to reflect the unionization of the industry.

Creating Rank Order

Rather than ordering on the basis of the number of people in the category or placing similar categories next to one another, we can rearrange the

Table 8.7   *Rearranging categories into a logical order appropriate to the project*

(a) Original version

Code	Industry	Percentage in unions
1	Agriculture, forestry and fishing	15
2	Mining	54
3	Manufacturing	40
4	Electricity, gas and water	59
5	Construction	37
6	Wholesale and retail	18

(b) Revised version

New code	Industry	Percentage in unions
1	Agriculture, forestry and fishing	15
2	Wholesale and retail	18
3	Construction	37
4	Manufacturing	40
5	Mining	54
6	Electricity, gas and water	59

Table 8.8   *Categories reordered to produce an ordinal variable*

Should marijuana be legalized?	Frequency	Valid percentage	Cumulative percentage
1 Definitely legalize	220	12	12
2 Probably legalize	422	23	35
3 Can't decide	371	20	55
4 Probably not legalize	469	26	81
5 Definitely do not legalize	351	19	100
Total	1833	100	

categories so that they are rank-ordered. The earlier example of views about legalizing marijuana lends itself to this type of reordering. If we consider the 'can't decide' response as a middle position between opposition and support, we can convert the variable into an ordinal variable by rearranging the categories (see Table 8.8). Alternatively, we might decide not to include these responses at all, thus converting the variable to an ordinal variable with four ordered categories.

Why should Categories be Placed in Reverse Order?

Both the problems outlined earlier that arise when categories are in the *opposite* order to that which is required can readily be solved by reverse-coding the variables once data have been collected.

To Obtain Consistency for Scales

When variables need to be combined into an overall composite scale (Problem 17) they must first be coded in the same direction. Where they are not all coded in the same direction take the following steps:

1   Decide what a low and a high code on the scale will indicate.
2   Select individual variables where the direction of coding is *opposite* that which is required for the scale.
3   Reverse-code these selected variables.

In the social liberalism example (Table 8.3) we may decide that a low scale score will reflect social conservatism and a high score will indicate social liberalism. An examination of the direction of coding of the individual items indicates that all of the items except abortion are already coded in this direction. However, the abortion question is coded so that a low score indicates liberalism and a high score indicates conservatism. This variable needs to be reverse-coded.

To Assist Simpler Interpretation

Reverse coding only makes sense for variables with ordered categories – i.e., for ordinal and interval variables. The basic rule when coding ordinal variables is to allocate low numerical codes to categories that indicate a low 'quantity' of the variable and high codes to categories indicating a high 'quantity'.

The income variable in Table 8.4 follows this principle. However, the education variable is coded oddly – low codes are used for high qualifications while high codes are used for low qualifications. Reverse-coding the qualifications variable will enable us to make more common-sense statements about the relationship between qualifications and income.

How to reverse-code a variable

The logic of reverse coding is illustrated in Table 8.9. In this example the item has five values (1, 2, 3, 4, 5) that require reversing to the values indicated in the new code column. How this is done will differ between computer programs. However, the logic illustrated in the SPSS instructions below is the same as in other packages.

Table 8.9 *Reverse coding*

Original code	New code
1	5
2	4
3	3
4	2
5	1

Using SPSS

Reordering Categories

To reorder values of a variable simply create a new variable to reflect the new order of categories. To do this use the Transform procedures that allow you to create a new variable with the Recode function.

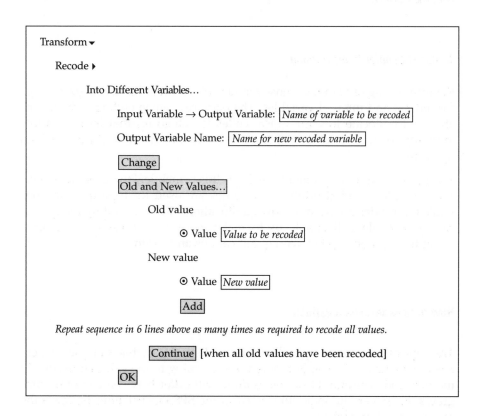

Transform ▾

  Recode ▸

    Into Different Variables…

      Input Variable → Output Variable: `Name of variable to be recoded`

      Output Variable Name: `Name for new recoded variable`

      Change

      Old and New Values…

        Old value

          ⊙ Value `Value to be recoded`

        New value

          ⊙ Value `New value`

        Add

Repeat sequence in 6 lines above as many times as required to recode all values.

        Continue [when all old values have been recoded]

    OK

Reversing Categories

A similar procedure is available to that for reordering categories:

Transform ▾

    Recode ▸

        Into Different Variables…

            Input Variable → Output Variable: *insert name of variable to be recoded*

            Output Variable *create name for reverse coded version*

            Change

            Old and New Values…

                Old Value

                    ⊙ Value: 1

                New Value 5

                Add

                Old Value

                    ⊙ Value: 2

                New Value 4

                Add

                Old Value

                    ⊙ Value: 3

                New Value 3

                Add

                Old Value

                    ⊙ Value: 4

                New Value 2

                Add

                Old Value

                    ⊙ Value: 5

                New Value 1

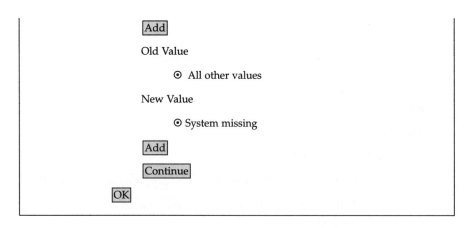

An easier method that for some people is less intuitive is to create a new variable using the Compute option.

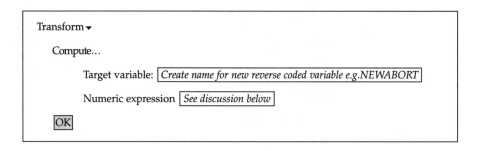

Here the numeric expression should take the general form:

$$(Highvalue\ of\ OLDVAR + 1) - OLDVAR$$

where *Highvalue* is the maximum possible valid code of the initial variable you are reverse-coding (e.g. 5), and *OLDVAR* is the name of the variable you are reverse-coding (e.g. ABORT).

For example:

$$Compute \quad NEWABORT = (5 + 1) - ABORT.$$

This transformation produces a new variable (NEWABORT) and a new value on the variable for each person. The value for each person is automatically computed by subtracting their code on the initial variable (ABORT) from 6 (i.e. *Highvalue* + 1). Thus all people with an initial code of 5 would obtain a new code of 1 (i.e. $(5 + 1) - 5 = 1$); those with an initial score of 4 would be recoded to a score of 2 (i.e. $6 - 4 = 2$) and so on.

This method can be used easily regardless of how many categories the initial variable has. For example, to reverse code a variable with 100 values the numeric expression would be:

$$101 - OLDVAR$$

In one simple step this would reverse code all 100 values of the original variable.

9

What to do with Gaps in the Data

Where do Data Gaps come from?

Gaps in a data set are called *missing values*. Missing values occur when we have either no response to a question or a non-valid response. A valid response is one where the respondent gives a substantive answer to the question. Missing values may occur because a respondent:

- is not required to answer the question;
- refuses to answer the question (privacy, etc.);
- provides illegible or ambiguous answers (e.g. ticked two boxes when only one was allowed);
- stops co-operating or begins to hurry;
- makes a mistake;
- gives a don't know or no opinion response.

Every person must have a code on every variable. Where responses are missing, respondents are given a missing-value code. The data analysis problem is whether to include cases with missing values in the analysis or to exclude them. If they are to be included how are they to be treated? There are potential problems with either approach.

Why are Missing Values a Problem?

Problems Caused by Including Cases with Missing Values

Including cases that have not answered a particular question presents data analysis problems for several reasons.

- It confuses real responses with non-responses.
- It can distort results. In Table 9.1 some respondents did not say whether life is exciting or dull. When these respondents are included in the calculation of percentages only 29 per cent say that life is exciting. When they

Table 9.1 *Frequency table illustrating the effect of including missing values*

Is life exciting or dull?	Frequency	Percentage	Valid percentage
1 Exciting	434	29	44
2 Routine	505	33	52
3 Dull	41	3	4
9 Missing	537	35	
Total	1517	100	100

are excluded from calculations (valid percentage column) 44 per cent say that life is exciting.

- The inclusion of cases with missing values can destroy the ordinal or interval character of any variable. Since a missing-value code cannot be ranked meaningfully, the categories of the variable are unrankable and the variable would need to be treated as a nominal variable.
- Including cases with missing values can inflate or deflate summary statistics such as the mean (p. 219). For example, in Table 9.2 the mean for the exciting life question varies considerably depending on how missing values are handled. In the first column missing values have been excluded and the mean is 1.6 (remember that 1 = exciting and 3 = dull, so a mean of 1.6 indicates that on average people were more towards the exciting end than the dull end). When missing values are included in the calculations the cases with missing values must have a code. If the code is, say, 9, this inflates the mean – in this case to 4.22, which is off the scale of meaningful values. If the missing values were coded as 0 the mean would be 1.03. Including missing values also alters the shape of the distribution, as indicated by the skewness statistics (pp. 224–6).
- Similarly, the inclusion of cases with missing values also inflates or deflates scale scores (p. 129).

Table 9.2 *Effect of missing values on summary statistics*

		Missing excluded	Missing coded as 9 and included	Missing coded as 0 and included
N	Valid	980	1517	1517
	Missing	537	0	0
Mean		1.60	4.22	1.03
Skewness		0.29	0.56	0.16

Problems Caused by Excluding Cases with Missing Values

Excluding cases who have not answered questions produces different sorts of data analysis problems:

- Cases with missing values may systematically differ from cases with valid values. Excluding these cases can lead to a biased sample and distort patterns. For example, women may be overrepresented among those who did not answer a question about income. Excluding those with missing values for income would bias the sample by excluding more women than men (Problem 21).
- If a large proportion of cases are excluded due to missing values the sample size can be reduced to unacceptable levels that may affect the precision of any sample-based estimates (Problem 27).
- Even if there are only a few missing cases on a particular variable this can add up to a large number of missing cases in multivariate analysis. For example, in Table 9.3 each variable has only one missing case. If the analysis includes all four variables then all cases will be excluded from the analysis.

Table 9.3   *Cumulative effect of missing values across cases*

	Var A	Var B	Var C	Var D	Total
Case 1		Missing			Missing
Case 2				Missing	Missing
Case 3	Missing				Missing
Case 4			Missing		Missing

How to Tell if Missing Values are a Problem

Before suggesting a way of dealing with missing data, we first need to establish whether missing values are a problem in any particular set of data. We only need to find a solution to the missing-data problem if it is a problem in the first place. There are two main checks.

1. Establish how much missing data there is. In the example in Table 9.1 there are a large number of cases with missing values. Where this loss of cases undermines the power of the analysis, the analysis can be completely compromised. In assessing the loss of cases attention needs to be given to both the missing values on individual variables and the cumulative loss of cases across a set of variables.
2. Check for missing-values bias (pp. 153–7).

What to do About Missing Values

Should the Cases be Dropped from the Analysis?

When certain codes are designated as missing-value codes, any cases assigned such codes are automatically dropped from any analysis of that particular variable (see the SPSS section below). In univariate or bivariate analysis this is straightforward. In bivariate analysis (e.g. crosstabulation, simple correlation, simple regression) any case with a missing value on *either* variable will be dropped from the analysis. In multivariate analysis there are two main approaches to deleting cases. These are:

- pairwise deletion;
- listwise deletion.

PAIRWISE DELETION   The pairwise method excludes a case that has a missing value on *either* of the pair of variables for which a relationship is being examined. Suppose we included the following six variables in an analysis: prejudice, political orientation, attitude to gun control, age, income and size of town. Part of the analysis involves examining the relationship between AGE and PREJUDICE. Any person who had a missing value on either of these two variables would be excluded from the analysis. If we examined the relationship between INCOME and PREJUDICE only those cases with a missing value from either variable would be excluded.

LISTWISE DELETION   The listwise method excludes a case if it has a missing value on *any* of the list of variables in the analysis. Thus, when calculating a correlation between AGE and PREJUDICE a case would be dropped if it had a missing value on any of the six variables even if the case had no missing values on the AGE and PREJUDICE variables.

More often than not the pairwise approach is taken – particularly in bivariate analysis. This is primarily because the pairwise method leads to fewer cases being discarded from analysis. Listwise deletion can cause a very serious loss of cases that can compromise the analysis, and probably should not be used if it leads to a loss of more than 10–15 per cent of cases. However, pairwise deletion methods can cause serious problems in some multivariate analyses, such as multiple regression, factor analysis and cluster analysis, that rely on what is called a 'true correlation matrix' – a matrix where all the correlations are based on exactly the same cases. Using pairwise deletion with these analyses requires care to ensure that missing data are distributed randomly.

Should the Variable be Dropped from the Analysis?

If missing values are concentrated in a variable which is not central to the analysis, consider dropping that variable from the analysis.

How to Impute a Value to Replace the Missing Values

A third alternative is to substitute a valid value for the missing value. This enables the retention of both the case and the variable for further analysis. Imputation involves calculating a best estimate of what the person's value would have been had they answered the question. Obviously 'making up' values is a risky business and must be done in the full knowledge of the implications of doing so. There are a number of different methods of imputing values.

SERIES-MEAN APPROACH This approach involves substituting the sample mean for the missing values of the variable. With ordinal variables the median can be used (p. 220). The problem with this approach is that the same value is given to all the cases. This reduces sample variability, which in turn reduces correlations (p. 272). In general, this is a crude method of dealing with missing values, and since computer packages allow for other better methods to be easily applied it is generally not recommended.

THE GROUP-MEANS APPROACH One way of overcoming the problem of reducing variability on the variable is to use *group* means rather than the overall sample mean. To do this the sample is divided into groups on a background variable (e.g. ethnicity, gender, education) that is well correlated with the variable for which missing values are being replaced. The mean on the variable is obtained for each category of the grouping background variable and these group-specific means replace the missing values for that variable for each group.

For example, when estimating income for people who refused to indicate their income the sample can be divided into age groups and then, within each age group, into males and females. The mean income for each group (e.g. for young men $35 000, for young women $32,000, etc.) is calculated and substituted for the missing income data for that specific subgroup.

The disadvantage of this approach is that it exaggerates the extent to which people in a group are similar to one another. This can inflate the correlations between variables when using the variable for which the missing data have been estimated.

MEAN ACROSS A SPAN To overcome the disadvantages of the two imputation methods already described, the mean of a random selection of cases can be used to replace missing values. This avoids the problems caused by reducing variance by replacing with a common value. Using the mean across a span involves selecting a set number of cases either side of the case with the missing value in the data set, calculating the mean or median of those cases and using this value.

LINEAR INTERPOLATION   This approach is similar to the previous method except that it examines the values across a span, identifies any pattern in the values and creates a substitute value for the missing value that conforms to that pattern.

REGRESSION ANALYSIS OR EXPECTATION–MAXIMIZATION (EM) METHODS   These methods are the most sophisticated and are generally recommended. They are an extension of the idea of using group means. They involve estimating what the missing value would be on the basis of regression methods (Problem 47). These estimates are based on any number of grouping variables and provide much better predictions than simply using a group mean for one or two group characteristics.

Using SPSS

Dropping Cases

SINGLE-VARIABLE ANALYSIS   Where a code has been designated as a missing-value code (p. 3), it must be activated by declaring that value as a missing value. This is achieved as follows:

- Select the Variable View (bottom Tab) with the Data Editor view.
- Select the row for the variable for which you want to activate the missing-value code.
- Select the missing-value column and click the missing value cell in the column that corresponds to your variable.

⊙ Discrete missing values: | *missing value code* | | *missing value code* |
  | *missing value code* |

[enter up to three different codes that you want to treat as missing. This can include codes for 'don't know' responses].

  OK

Note that for imputation methods or for pairwise and listwise options to take effect, the missing values for the variables must first have been declared and activated in this way.

PAIRWISE OR LISTWISE Most of the SPSS multivariate methods have options so that the user can select which method is required.

Imputation

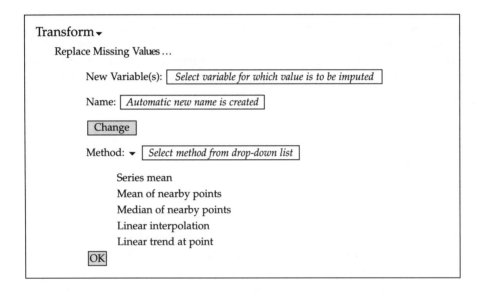

IMPUTATION BY REGRESSION OR EM This method is obtained using the Missing Values Analysis option in SPSS. Since this is an optional extra not all installations of SPSS will have this option available. A readable outline of this method is available online at http://www.social-research.org/Methods-resources/MissingP.pdf. Imputation using regression or EM methods can be accomplished with the following menu selections.

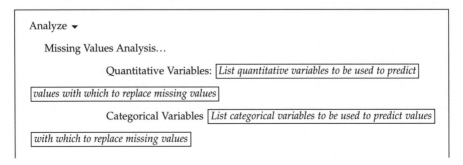

Estimation

☑ Regression

Variables ...

Variables

⊙ Select variables

Predicted variables: Insert variables for which missing values are to be predicted

Predictor variables: Select variables from which predictions will be made

Continue

Regression...

☑ Save completed data [this saves variable with imputed values in a separate file]

File

File name: Enter file name

Save

Continue

OK

10

What to do with People who 'Don't Know', 'Have no Opinion' or 'Can't Decide'

What's the Problem with Non-committal Responses?

It is generally recommended that respondents should be offered 'non-substantive' responses such as 'no opinion', 'don't know' or 'can't choose' when being asked attitude questions (Foddy, 1993; Sudman and Bradburn, 1982; Smith, 1984). However, there is generally little advice about how to treat these responses during data analysis.

The difficulty is knowing what these non-substantive answers mean. The research literature identifies a number of possible interpretations of 'don't know', 'no opinion' and 'can't choose' responses. Smith (1984) summarizes these as reflecting:

- *ambivalent attitudes* – an in-between or even neutral position between two sides of an attitude position;
- genuine *non-attitudes* – the person simply has no view on the matter;
- a *social desirability* effect – where a person holds an unacceptable view but hides this by giving a non-substantive response;
- failure to assert the true attitude due to lack of confidence, shyness, etc.;
- concealing the true attitude due to sense of privacy;
- stalling responses while the person considers the issue.

The evidence indicates that between a third and a half of non-substantive responses are in fact ambivalent attitudes, and that most of the other non-substantive responses reflect true non-attitudes.

The problem is how to handle these responses during data analysis. Since non-attitudes and ambivalent attitudes are very different things, they ideally need to be treated differently.

How to Handle Non-substantive Responses

How to Minimize the Number of Non-substantive Responses

This is a necessary approach, and there are three ways to go about it:

- Avoid offering non-substantive responses as alternatives (Schuman and Presser, 1981; Kalton et al., 1980). However, this raises the problem of forcing people who genuinely have no attitude, to take a position. This undermines the reliability and validity of questions.
- Use filter questions first to ascertain whether people have an opinion on a matter, and then ask only those with a view to say what that view is (Foddy, 1993; Smith, 1984).
- Explicitly offer a middle or ambivalent option to help distinguish between those holding such attitudes and those with non-attitudes.

Should Non-substantive Responses be Treated as a Middle Position?

If non-substantive responses reflect *ambivalent attitudes*, there is a reasonable argument for treating these responses as a middle position and including them in the analysis. Scores for these ambivalent responses should be between the pro and anti position scores for that attitude (e.g. 3 on a 1 to 5 scale).

For data that have already been collected, the problem is to distinguish non-substantive responses due to *ambivalent attitudes* from those due to *non-attitudes*. There are several approaches to this dilemma.

- Be conservative and treat the non-substantive response as missing data and *exclude the case* from the analysis of the variable. If the sample is large and there are not a lot of non-substantive responses this can be a reasonable approach.
- Treat the non-substantive response as missing data and *impute a score* to substitute for the non-substantive response (pp. 68–9). However, this can result in giving scores to people who have genuine non-attitudes. The effect of this will depend on the imputation method adopted.
- If the item on which the non-substantive response is given is to form part of a scale then treat the response as missing data and compute a scale score for the case but *exclude the variable* from the computation of the scale score. (See p. 129, 133 on how to do this.)

Should Non-substantive Responses be Treated as Missing Values?

This is a 'safe' method in that those with non-attitudes who have indicated a non-substantive response will not improperly be attributed with an attitude position. While the loss of cases can be a problem, there is little to be gained from maintaining sample size by incorrectly 'giving' attitude positions to some cases. The problem is that we may also exclude cases who have ambivalent attitudes and should justifiably be included in the analysis. If the sample is large enough the loss of cases may not be serious, but the loss of cases who have a particular 'position' on the attitude can bias results.

Dealing with Non-substantive Responses by Reconceptualizing the Variable

Cases with non-substantive responses can be included in the analysis legitimately by rethinking the focus of the analysis. For example, suppose we have seven questions designed to tap attitudes towards abortion (Table 10.1). Each question may have five responses, of which only two are substantive (yes and no). If our real interest is simply in the 'yes' position then we could reasonably combine the 'no' and the non-substantive responses. It does not matter whether these 'non-yes' responses reflect non-attitudes, ambivalent attitudes or 'no' responses.

Table 10.1   *Eliminating non-substantive responses by reconceptualizing the variable*

	Original response categories	Recoded categories
Please tell me whether or not you think it should be possible for a pregnant woman to obtain a legal abortion if:		
(i) there is a strong chance of a serious defect in the baby.	0 Not applicable 1 Yes	1 Yes 2 Other (no, don't know and no answer)
(ii) she is married and does not want any more children.	2 No 8 Don't know	
(iii) the woman's own health is seriously endangered by the pregnancy.	9 No answer	−1 Missing – not applicable
(iv) the family has a very low income and cannot afford any more children.		
(v) she became pregnant as a result of rape.		
(vi) she is not married and does not want to marry the man.		
(vii) the woman wants it for any reason.		

11

How to Tell if the Distribution is Normal

What is the Problem?

Many statistical tests assume that the distribution of particular variables approximates a *normal* distribution in the population.[1] These tests are based on what are called *parametric* statistics. The notion of a normal distribution only applies to interval-level variables. However, the assumption of a normal distribution applies to a fair number of widely used statistical methods such as Pearson's correlation, analysis of variance, *t* tests, multiple regression, discriminant analysis and factor analysis.

The assumption of normal distributions raises two problems for the data analyst:

- How can you tell whether the distribution is normal or not?
- What do you do if the distribution is not normal?

How to tell if a Distribution is Normal

1. Obtain a histogram and superimpose a normal curve. Figure 11.1 is a histogram of left-wing and right-wing political orientation. Simply looking at the bars indicates that the distribution has the rough shape of a normal distribution. The superimposed normal curve, however, shows that there is some deviation. The question is whether this deviation is small enough to say that the distribution is approximately normal.
2. Examine the skewness and kurtosis statistics for the distribution (pp. 224–7). A normal distribution is symmetrical. A non-symmetrical distribution is described as being either positively or negatively skewed. When a distribution is represented as a histogram (pp. 207–8) its skewness can be seen in the shape of the graph. A negatively skewed distribution is one in which the long tail of the distribution is to the left (towards the lower values on the horizontal axis). A positively skewed distribution has the long tail on the right side (high values) on the horizontal axis. The

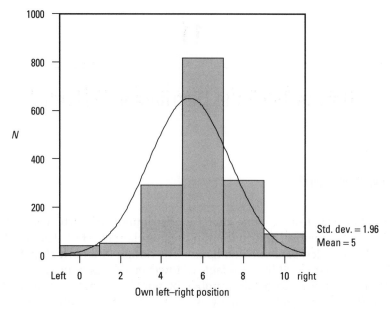

Figure 11.1   *Histogram with normal curve superimposed*

skewness statistic is negative if the distribution is negatively skewed, positive if positively skewed and zero if it is symmetrical. In a symmetrical distribution the mean will also be the same as the median (pp. 219–22). A normal distribution also has a kurtosis of 0^2 (the degree of peakedness or flatness of the distribution) (pp. 226–7). If a distribution meets the criteria of zero kurtosis and zero skewness it will have a normal distribution.

The relevant statistics for the political orientation variable displayed in the histogram in Figure 11.1 are provided in Table 11.1. This distribution appears symmetrical. Skewness is low (as a rule of thumb a skewness greater than 1.0 indicates a non-symmetrical distribution). However, the kurtosis is a little higher – something that might suggest that the distribution is not quite normal.

Table 11.1   *Statistics for Figure 11.1*

Mean	5.364
Median	5.000
Skewness	0.005
Kurtosis	0.839

A further test of normality is to use the *Kolmogorov–Smirnov Z* test. This test evaluates statistically whether the difference between the observed distribution and a theoretical normal distribution is small enough to be just due to chance. If it could be due to chance we would treat the distribution as being normal. If the difference between the actual distribution and the theoretical normal distribution is larger than is likely to be due to chance (sampling error) then we would treat the actual distribution as not being normal. If the *Kolmogorov–Smirnov Z* test yields a significance level of less than 0.05 it means that the distribution is probably not normal. In the case of the distribution in Figure 11.1 the *Kolmogorov–Smirnov Z* test indicates that this particular distribution is not normal (Table 11.2). It should be noted that with large samples even a very small deviation from normality can yield low significance levels, so a judgement still has to be made as to whether the departure from normality is large enough to matter.

Table 11.2   *Kolmogorov–Smirnov Z test of normality for the distribution in Figure 11.1*

	Statistic	df	Sig.
Own left–right position	0.21	1598	0.00

What to do if the Distribution is not Normal

Use a Nonparametric Statistic Instead

In many cases, if a distribution is not normal an alternative statistic will be available, especially for bivariate analyses such as correlations (Problem 35) or

Table 11.3   *Some nonparametric statistical tests*

Purpose of analysis	Normal distribution (parametric statistics)	Non-normal distribution (nonparametric statistics)
Differences between two independent groups	*t* test	Wald–Wolfowitz runs test Mann–Whitney *U* test Kolmogorov–Smirnov two-sample *Z* test
Differences between more than two independent groups	Analysis of variance and *F* test	Kruskal–Wallis analysis of ranks Median test
Differences between two related groups	*t* test for dependent samples	Sign test; Wilcoxon's matched pairs test; McNemar's chi-square test
Two variables measured in the same sample	Repeated measures ANOVA	Friedman's two-way analysis of variance; Cochran *Q* test
Relationships between variables	Pearson's r (for interval level variables)	Spearman's Rho, Kendall's tau, Gamma, Chi-square; Phi; Fisher's exact test

comparisons of means (Problem 38). These alternatives which do not require normal distributions are called *nonparametric* or distribution-free statistics. Some of these alternatives are listed in Table 11.3. They are covered in much more detail in Problem 39.

Table 11.4 *Ladder of powers for transformations for skewness*

To adjust for	Transformation	SPSS syntax
Severe positive skew	Negative reciprocal root[a]	Compute *newvar* = –1/sqrt (*oldvar*).
Moderate positive skew	Log[a]	Compute *newvar* = lg10(*oldvar*).
Minor to moderate positive skew	Square root[a]	Compute *newvar* = sqrt (*oldvar*).
Minor to moderate negative skew	Square	Compute *newvar* = (*oldvar*) * (*oldvar*).
Severe negative skew	Cube	Compute *newvar* = (*oldvar*) * (*oldvar*) * (*oldvar*).

[a] If a log or sqrt transformation is to be applied to values less than 1, add a constant to each value so that the minimum value is 1.
* *newvar* = enter a name for the transformed variable; *oldvar* = name of untransformed version of the variable.

Transform the Variable to Make it Normal

The shape of a distribution can be changed by expressing it in a different way statistically. This is referred to as *transforming* the distribution. Different types of transformations can be applied to 'normalize' the distribution. The type of transformation selected depends on the manner in which the distribution departs from normality. Table 11.4 indicates the types of transformations used to correct skewness.

Use a Parametric Statistic and do not Worry about the Non-normal Distribution

There are two reasons why one might decide to ignore the non-normal distribution and still use a parametric statistic.

- Statistical experimentation has demonstrated that violating the normality assumptions of tests has less severe effects than previously thought. Although there is little theoretical justification for ignoring the normality assumptions, in practice it does not seem to have a severe effect on results.

- The *central limit theorem* states the important principle that as the size of a random sample increases, its distribution approximates a normal distribution more closely. This means that even if the distribution of the variable in question is not normal and our sample size is large enough (e.g. 100 or more) it is reasonable to use statistics that assume a normal distribution. (see http://www.statsoft.com/textbook/graphics/an_sampl.gif for an interactive simulation of this principle).

Using SPSS

Histogram with a Normal Curve Superimposed

Graphs ▾

    Histogram

    Variable: | *Select variable for graph* |

    ☑ Display normal curve

        | Titles |

            Title/line 1: | *Enter title text* |

            | Continue |

      | OK |

Skewness and Kurtosis

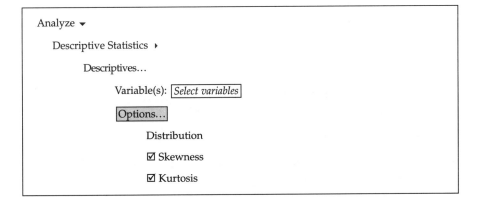

Analyze ▾

    Descriptive Statistics ▸

        Descriptives…

            Variable(s): | *Select variables* |

            | Options… |

                Distribution

                ☑ Skewness

                ☑ Kurtosis

Kolmogorov–Smirnov Z Test to Test Distribution Against Theoretical Normal Distribution

Analyze ▾

    Nonparametric Tests

        1-Sample K-S…

        Test Variable List: [*Insert variable name(s)*]

        Test Distribution

            ☑ Normal

    OK

Nonparametric Statistics

See Problem 39

Spearman's rho and Kendall's tau

Analyze ▾

    Correlate ▸

        Bivariate…

        Variables: [*Insert variables to correlate*]

        Correlation Coefficients

            ☑ Kendall's tau-b

            ☑ Spearman

        Test of Significance

            ⊙ Two-tailed

            ☑ Flag significant correlations

    OK

Gamma, Chi-square, Phi and Fisher's Exact Test

Analyze ▾

    Descriptive Statistics ▸

        Crosstabs…

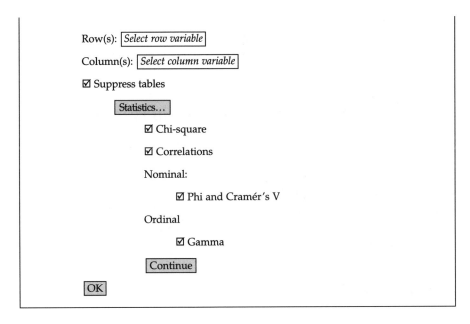

Transforming Variables

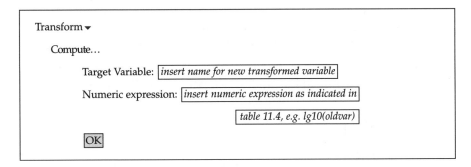

Notes

1 The term 'normal' is misleading, especially with social science variables where a normal distribution is relatively uncommon. A normal distribution is simply a distribution with particular statistical properties. The normal distribution is also called the *Gaussian* distribution.

2 Kurtosis is calculated in different ways in different computer packages. Strictly speaking kurtosis is 3 when the distribution is normal. However many people and packages adjust kurtosis so that it takes on a value of 0 when the distribution is normal.

12

How to Tell if the Relationship is Linear

Many methods of statistical analysis assume that variables are related in a linear fashion. It is therefore important to establish whether or not a relationship is linear and to know what to do in the event of discovering nonlinear relationships.

What is a Linear Relationship?

Linearity refers to the nature of the relationship between two interval-level variables (although relationships between ordinal variables are normally spoken of as being linear). A linear relationship is one in which a change in one variable is associated with a *constant* rate of change in the other variable. This is easily illustrated with a scatterplot (Figure 12.1).

Two variables can be related but in a nonlinear or curvilinear fashion (Figure 12.2). The nature of the nonlinear relationship can vary considerably.

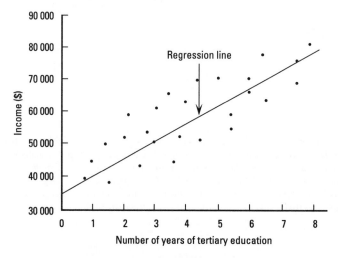

Figure 12.1   *Scatterplot indicating a linear relationship*

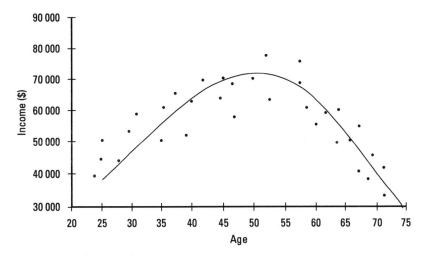

Figure 12.2 *A nonlinear relationship between two variables*

Why is Knowing about Linearity Important?

IT MAKES A DIFFERENCE TO THE WAY THE RELATIONSHIP IS DESCRIBED   A linear relationship between level of education and income is one where we say that as education increases income tends to increase. Such a statement is normally taken to mean that the effect of education has a fairly constant impact on income. If the effect of education only makes a difference up to a certain level, after which the impact of education either flattens out or reverses, then this nonlinearity needs to be made very clear.

SELECTION OF SUMMARY STATISTICS   Many summary statistics, including many correlation and regression coefficients (Problem 37), are only sensitive to linear relationships between variables. They say nothing at all about nonlinear relationships. A correlation or regression coefficient close to zero (p. 267) can give the mistaken impression that there is *no* relationship. All it means, however, is that there is no *linear* relationship.

SELECTING APPROPRIATE METHODS OF ANALYSIS AND MODIFYING DATA   Knowing that a relationship is nonlinear enables us to make adjustments to the variables (see below) or select analysis methods that will reflect the true relationship.

How to tell if the Relationship is Linear

Detecting the existence of nonlinear relationships should be undertaken early in the analysis – certainly before applying methods that assume linear relationships.

Table 12.1   *Crosstabulation indicating a linear relationship*

	Church attendance		
	Regular	Sometimes	Rarely/never
When should women be allowed to have an abortion?			
Whenever she wants one	20% →	46% →	72%
Only in special circumstances	60	43	27
Should not be allowed	20 ←	11 ←	2
N	327	201	1176

Use Crosstabulations

Crosstabulations are an appropriate method for detecting the nature of relationships between two ordinal variables which have only a small number of categories. If you are not familiar with crosstabulations, read (Problem 32) before proceeding to the discussion that follows.

Detecting linearity via a crosstabulation depends on the way in which the crosstabulation is constructed. In the example in Table 12.1, the independent variable (X) is placed across the top of the table and the dependent variable (Y) down the side. Accordingly, the figures are column percentages (i.e. percentages of all the cases in that column which have a specific characteristic of Y (pp. 240–1).

To detect *any* relationship in such a table, compare the column percentages *across* columns, *within* a row (Table 12.1). Differences between these percentages will suggest some relationship between the variables. The larger the percentage differences, the stronger the relationship.

In Table 12.1 a comparison of the percentages in the first row indicates a fairly constant rate *and* direction of change between the percentages. As we move across the columns in the first row the percentages increase by 26 per cent between each column. The reverse is true in the bottom row where the percentages decrease at a fairly constant rate. Given these two facts (constant *rate* of change and a constant *direction* of change within a row) we can conclude that the relationship between X and Y is linear.

Tables 12.2 and 12.3 illustrate nonlinear relationships. In Table 12.2 the percentages change in a constant direction within a row, but the rate of change is not at all consistent. In Table 12.3 the rate of change is consistent, but the direction of change *reverses* within the row.

Compare Group Means

When dealing with an interval dependent variable and an ordinal or interval independent variable (with relatively few categories) (Problem 38)

Table 12.2 *Crosstabulation indicating a nonlinear relationship: interest in politics by age group*

		Age group				
		18–29	30–39	40–49	50–59	60+
Interest in politics	A great deal	23% →	27% →	37% →	50% →	75%
	Some	15	38	42	37	16
	None	62 ←	35 ←	21 ←	13 ←	9
	N	267	346	398	321	417

Table 12.3 *Crosstabulation indicating a nonlinear relationship: income by age group*

		Age group				
		18–25	26–39	40–55	56–65	66+
Income category	Less than $35K	57% →	34% →	28% ←	55% ←	89%
	$36K–$50K	29	38	28	23	6
	$51K+	14 ←	28 ←	44 →	22 →	5
	N	152	417	575	242	235

we can compare the nature of changes in the means between groups (categories of the independent variable) to determine linearity (see Problem 38 for a detailed discussion).

Examine Graphs

Where there is a fairly strong relationship between two interval variables and there are not a very large number of cases, a scatterplot can provide a useful visual indication of whether the relationship between the two variables is linear or not (see Figures 12.1 and 12.2; see also pp. 252–4).

However, where the relationship is not strong and there are a large number of data points it can be very difficult to identify the nature of any relationship. Statistical summaries of the relationship provide a less error-prone way of assessing the nature of the relationship in such cases.

Compare Linear and Nonlinear Correlation Coefficients

If a linear measure of correlation is applied to a strongly nonlinear relationship it will produce very low correlations. If the relationship is curvilinear, a correlation coefficient that is sensitive to curvilinear relationships will result in higher correlations than will linear measures (p. 273). If there is uncertainty about whether the relationship between two variables is linear or nonlinear, obtain both linear and nonlinear measures of correlation. The selection and interpretation of nonlinear measures of correlation are discussed in Problem 35.

Analyse Residuals

In bivariate and multivariate correlation and regression an analysis of the residuals can indicate whether the relationship between the dependent variable and the independent variable(s) is linear or nonlinear. This is discussed in more detail in Problem 46.

Use Curve Estimation Programs

SPSS and other programs provide a simple means by which to estimate what type of line best fits the actual observations. SPSS will only do this for two variables at a time. It calculates R^2 for each type of line specified (linear, quadratic, logarithmic, cubic, etc.). A comparison of the R^2 values for each type of line indicates whether a curved line fits the distribution better than a straight line and which type of curved line fits best.

In Figure 12.3 several different types of curve have been fitted to the data. The straight line does not fit very well, and this is indicated by the R^2 of 0.05. The logarithmic curve does not fit much better ($R^2 = 0.09$). The quadratic curve fits the data better, but the cubic curve fits best ($R^2 = 0.22$). An inspection of the graph shows how the cubed line follows the data points best. An inspection of the type of curve that fits the data will indicate the type of transformation that should straighten the line (see p. 87).

What to do if the Relationship is not Linear

The approach that should be taken when a relationship is nonlinear will depend on the type and purpose of the analysis.

Use Tables and Graphs

If results are being presented in a crosstabulation, a set of means or a clear graph, there is no need to do anything. These forms of presentation should

Independent Variable: AGE
Dependent Variable: INCOME

Dependent	Method	R^2	d.f.	F	Sig. of F	b_0	b_1	b_2	b_3
INCOME	LINEAR	0.05	156	8.8	0.003	8.10	0.10		
INCOME	LOG	0.09	156	16.0	0.000	– 6.90	5.24		
INCOME	QUAD	0.19	155	18.1	0.000	– 7.56	0.89	– 0.01	
INCOME	CUBIC	0.22	154	14.0	0.000	– 23.61	2.09	– 0.04	0.002

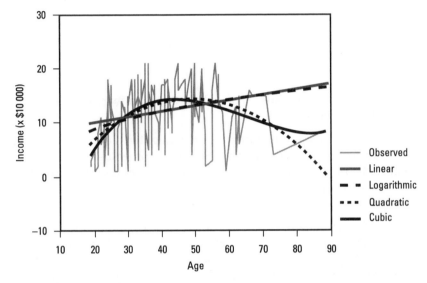

Figure 12.3   *Curve estimation*

make the linear or nonlinear form of the relationship obvious. When using scatterplots it is probably useful to include the best-fitting line. If this is a curved line it might be worth including it to indicate the nonlinear nature of the relationship.

Use a Coefficient that is Sensitive to Nonlinear Relationships

Many correlation coefficients that are used to summarize the extent to which two variables are related are only sensitive to linear relationships. If the relationship is nonlinear and a correlation coefficient is required to summarize it, then use a coefficient that is sensitive to nonlinear relationships.

Straighten the Curved Line: How to Transform a Curve

In Problem 11 we saw how to use transformations to change the distribution of a single variable to approximate a normal curve. Transformations can also

Table 12.4   *The ladder of powers*

Power	Expression	Name
⋮		
3	X^3	Cube
2	X^2	Square
1	X^1	Raw data
0.5	$\sqrt{X}$	Square root
0	X^0	?(log)
−0.5	$1/\sqrt{X}$	Reciprocal root
−1	$1/X$	Reciprocal
−2	$1/X^2$	Reciprocal square
⋮		

Source: Marsh (1988: 208).

be used to modify the shape of a line that summarizes a relationship between two variables.

The difficulty in using transformations to straighten a curve is working out which transformation is appropriate. Some experimentation is required, but Marsh (1988) provides a useful set of guidelines based on the principle of a ladder of powers (Table 12.4).

How can we use transformations to straighten a curved line? Any section of a curve can be visualized as part of a circle. At any point on the curve we can draw a tangent (a straight line touching the curve at that point only) as in Figure 12.4. Depending on the particular curve, we will use different transformations to straighten it. Normally a log transformation will be appropriate. Which particular log transformation will depend on the *degree* and *direction* of the curve. The greater the curve, the higher or lower we must go up or down the ladder of log powers, i.e. the 'stronger' the log required to straighten it. Table 12.4 provides a list of some of the log transformations arranged as a ladder of powers.

In Figure 12.4(1) we have to 'pull' the curve towards the tangent to straighten it. We have to 'pull' the top of the curve *up* the X axis to draw the points at this part of the curve towards the straight line. This would require transforming the X variable by going *up* the ladder of powers (Table 12.4), i.e. by squaring or cubing the X variable. This has the effect of 'spreading' the higher values of the X variable and straightening out the curve at the upper end. To straighten the bottom part of the curve we need drag the bottom values of the curve towards the straight line by dragging them *down* the Y axis. To do this we transform the Y variable by going *down* the ladder of powers, i.e. by using a log or square root transformation. Transformations down the ladder of powers 'spread' the lower values and thus straighten out the lower part of the curve.

The principle is if the data need to be pulled *up* on an axis towards the tangent we transform that variable (X or Y depending on the axis) by using

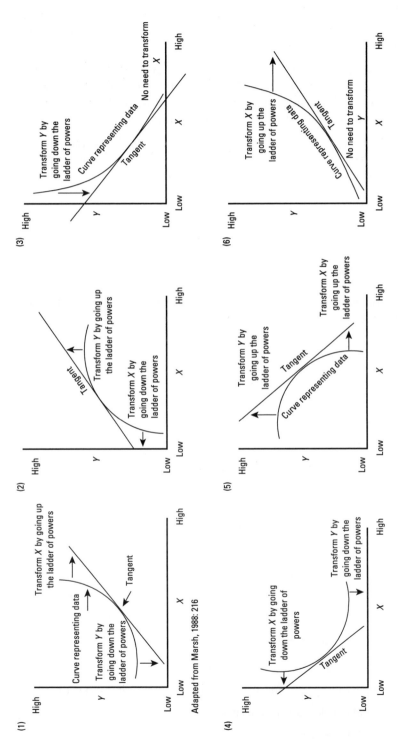

Figure 12.4 *Transformation guide to straightening curved lines*

a transformation *up* the ladder of powers. If data points need to be dragged *down* an axis we transform the variable for that axis by using a transformation *down* the ladder of powers.

The website *http://www.ruf.rice.edu/~lane/stat_sim/transformations/index.html* provides interactive simulations of the effect of applying different transformations to the X and Y axes on different types of distributions. It is worth experimenting with this simulation to see what these transformations do.

Having worked out which transformations work for the variables, new variables need to be created to reflect this transformation. The instructions to execute the transformations were provided in Table 11.4.

Using SPSS

Transforming Variables

See the numeric expressions for various transformations in SPSS in Table 11.4 and SPSS menus.

Curve Estimation

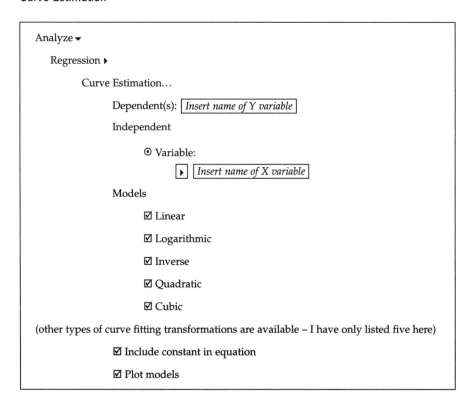

```
Analyze ▾
    Regression ▶
        Curve Estimation…
            Dependent(s): [ Insert name of Y variable ]
            Independent
                ⊙ Variable:
                    [▶] [ Insert name of X variable ]
            Models
                ☑ Linear
                ☑ Logarithmic
                ☑ Inverse
                ☑ Quadratic
                ☑ Cubic
    (other types of curve fitting transformations are available – I have only listed five here)
                ☑ Include constant in equation
                ☑ Plot models
```

Crosstabulations

To obtain crosstabulations in which the independent variable is placed across the top of the table and column percentages are provided, see Problem 32.

Simple Comparison of Means

See instructions in Problem 38.

Scatterplots

See instructions in Problem 33.

Analysis of Residuals

Analyze ▾

    Regression ▸

        Linear...

            Dependent: | *Insert Y variable* |

            Independent(s): | *Insert X variables* |

     | Plots... |

            Y: | *ZRESID |

            X: | *ZPRED |

          | Continue |

    | OK |

13

How to Tell if Outlier Cases are a Problem

What do Outliers do?

An outlier is a deviant case – it is an extreme numeric value in a distribution, and as such can have an undue influence on some statistics, especially parametric ones. Outliers can be a problem when using summary statistics to describe a distribution or a relationship between variables. Summaries, by their very nature, lose a certain amount of detail, and we can easily be misled when a small number of atypical cases distort the picture provided by the summary statistic.

When summarizing a *univariate* distribution, outliers can distort the mean and the standard deviation. Table 30.4 provides an illustration of how an extreme value distorts the mean.

Outliers can present a problem for *bivariate* Pearson's correlation and regression (p. 275, 280) and with *multivariate* methods. A single outlying case can change the slope of a regression line and the size of the correlation. Visiting the following websites will demonstrate this effect visually:

- *http://www.statsoft.com/textbook/graphics/anima3.gif*
- *http://www.statsoft.com/textbook/graphics/anima1.gif*

The following websites allow you to add an outlier to a distribution and to see the effect on the regression line and the regression and correlation coefficients:

- *http://www.math.csusb.edu/faculty/stanton/m262/regress/regress.html*
- *http://www.stat.sc.edu/~west/javahtml/Regression.html*

An outlier in bivariate analysis can be a case that is very atypical on a single variable, but more often is a case that has an unusual *combination* of values on both variables. Such cases can either inflate or deflate correlations and regression coefficients. For example, when examining the relationship between education and income the pattern will generally be that the higher a person's education the higher their income. However, a case of a person with a very high income (a millionaire) with no education at all would deflate the correlation between income and education.

How to Tell if there are Outliers

Use Means and Standard Deviations for Single Variables

The simplest way of detecting outliers on a single variable is to obtain the mean and standard deviation and to examine a frequency table (Problem 38). Measuring distance from the mean in terms of the standard deviation provides a way of evaluating how extreme the outlier cases are (pp. 222–4).

Selecting Statistical Tests for Bivariate and Multivariate Outliers

A simple visual method of detecting outliers is to obtain a scatterplot of the relationship between two interval variables. However, scatterplots can be more difficult to read with large samples and are not suitable for multivariate relationships.

A number of statistical methods are available for detecting outliers. These methods rely on analyzing the residuals in regression analysis (the third web address given above simulates the effects of outliers on residuals). There are a variety of methods of detecting outliers using residual analysis, but I will focus on four.

STANDARDIZED RESIDUALS An examination of standardized residuals can identify cases with strange combinations of values on both the independent and dependent variable. The residual of any case is the gap between the case's actual value on the dependent variable and its predicted value using the regression line (Figure 37.3). Cases with particularly large residuals are those that are furthest from the regression line. These cases are analogous to an outlier in univariate analysis being a long distance from the mean. An examination of standardized residuals can identify cases whose residual score (distance from the line) is a specified number of standard deviations from the mean of the residuals. Once such cases have been identified they can be examined more closely and perhaps dropped from the analysis.

MAHALANOBIS DISTANCE If a case does not have an unusual combination of values on two or more variables, an unusual value on the independent variable can still distort correlation and regression coefficients. A statistic called the Mahalanobis distance identifies cases that have an unusual value on the independent variable. Each case has a Mahalanobis distance, so we simply need to obtain a list of those with the highest Mahalanobis distance values. Once identified using Mahalanobis distance, the case can be examined more closely to see if it should be dropped from the analysis.

THE LEVERAGE STATISTIC This statistic, usually denoted by h and also called the hat-value, identifies cases which influence the regression model more than others. The leverage statistic varies from 0 (no influence on the model) to 1 (completely determines the model). A rule of thumb is that cases with leverage under 0.2 are not a problem, but if a case has leverage over 0.5 it has undue leverage and should be dropped from the analysis.

COOK'S DISTANCE Cook's distance, usually denoted by D, identifies cases with unusual values that have a considerable influence on the summary statistics. While an outlier can be identified, this does not mean that it is affecting the correlations much. In a large sample a single outlier will have little effect and we might safely leave it in the analysis. Cook's distance is calculated by examining what happens to all the residuals when the unusual case is eliminated. This is then compared to the residuals when the case is included. Each case has a Cook's distance value. Where the case makes a big difference the Cook's distance statistic is high, indicating that it should probably be dropped from further analysis. As a cut-off for detecting influential cases, Fox (1997) suggests a value of $4/(n - k - 1)$, where n is the number of cases and k is the number of independent variables.

What Defines an Outlier?

There is no precise statistical definition of an outlier. However, a common approach to defining outliers in univariate analysis is the number of standard deviations the case lies from the mean. In bivariate and multivariate analysis, statistics based on any of the four methods of the previous section can be used in the same way, by comparing the chosen statistic with the mean and standard deviation of the statistic for the relevant variable(s). Cases with values above a specified number of deviations of these distributions might be defined as outliers and deleted. Researchers vary in their use of ± 2 or ± 3 standard deviations as the cut-off point at which to define an outlier.

What to do if there are Outliers

- *Check data*. First, check the original data (if available) to see if the outlier is simply the result of a coding or data entry error.
- *Transform the variable*. Transforming the distribution of individual variables using the transformations described in Problems 11 and 12 can reduce outlier effects.
- *Change the score of the outlier case*. Tabachnick and Fidell (1983) argue that because much measurement is sometimes rather arbitrary the outlier values might be recoded to the value of the third standard deviation (or whatever cut-off point has been used to define outliers). This solution

keeps these cases in the analysis and retains at least some of their extreme effect, but moderates the impact on the correlations.

- *Delete the variable.* In multivariate analysis dichotomous variables with a very skewed split such as 90–10 can produce outlier effects. Rummel (1970) recommends that such variables be dropped from the analysis.
- *Drop the case.* The decision to drop a case from the analysis must be taken with care, and when cases are dropped this should be reported.

Using SPSS

Detecting Bivariate or Multivariate Outliers

SPSS requires that a syntax file is used to obtain the information required to use the statistics to identify outliers. Using a syntax file provides a different way of running a program. Instead of selecting options from menus, you type in and then execute a series of commands. These commands can be saved and easily rerun at another time.

To use a syntax file

Ensure that your data file is open. Then

File ▾

   New ▸

        Syntax

Then type the following syntax commands

Regression variables = | *List of dependent variable and independent variables* |

   /dependent = | *name of dependent variable for which outliers are located* |

   /method = enter

   /casewise = outliers (2) dependent ZRESID MAHAL COOK LEVER

   /save = ZRESID (Zresid_1) MAHAL (mahal_1) COOK (cook_1) LEVER (lev_1).

Then

Block out the commands using your mouse to execute your instructions
(in this case all of them).

Run ▾

   Selection

Table 13.1 *Case diagnostics for detecting outliers (cars with unusual fuel consumption) using regression procedures*

(a) Casewise diagnostics

Case number	Std. residual	Fuel consumption (miles per gallon)	Centred leverage value	Mahal. distance	Cook's distance
7	2.21	14.0	0.02	9.18	0.05
8	2.06	14.0	0.02	8.47	0.04
20	2.36	14.0	0.03	9.93	0.06
62	2.32	35.0	0.01	4.49	0.03
124	2.52	16.0	0.03	11.00	0.07
252	2.48	43.1	0.01	2.16	0.02
333	2.46	44.3	0.01	2.43	0.02
334	2.25	43.4	0.01	2.43	0.02
341	2.33	32.7	0.01	2.85	0.02
375	−2.67	17.6	0.01	1.86	0.02

(b) Residuals statistics

	Minimum	Maximum	Mean fuel consumption (MPG)	Std. deviation	N
Predicted value	3.65	34.31	23.45	6.46	392
Std. predicted value	−3.06	1.68	0.00	1.00	392
Mahal. distance	0.00	11.00	1.00	1.76	392
Cook's distance	0.00	0.07	0.00	0.01	392
Centred leverage value	0.00	0.03	0.01	0.01	392

The ZRESID keyword on the casewise subcommand identifies cases that are beyond ± 2 standard deviations from the mean of the residuals of the set of variables. The MAHAL, COOK and LEVER keywords will list cases that are beyond ± 2 standard deviations from the mean of these distances. The save command creates four new variables (Zresid_1, mahal_1, cook_1, lev_1) which contain, for each case, their scores on these variables.

Table 13.1 provides diagnostics for detecting outliers in a sample of cars and their fuel consumption. The diagnostics identify cases (cars) for which the fuel consumption is way out of the ordinary. By comparison with other outliers, case 124 seems to be the most serious problem, followed by case 20. However, none of the cases stands out as being generally problematic on the range of diagnostics (Table 13.1a).

Table 13.1b provides the summary statistics for the standardized residuals, Mahalanobis distance, Cook's distance and leverage values. Of most interest in these are the mean and standard deviations of these measures since they provide a sense of how far any case is from the mean.

Detecting the n Highest and Lowest Outliers

Analyze ▾

  Descriptive Statistics ▸

    Explore...

      Dependent List: | *Insert variable name for which extremes are sought* |

      Factor List: | *Enter nothing here* |

      Display

        ⊙ Statistics

     Statistics...

        ☑ Outliers

       Continue

    OK

Table 13.2 *Table of cases with extreme fuel consumption values*[a]

Fuel consumption (MPG)	Case number	Value
Highest	1 330	46.6
	2 337	44.6
	3 333	44.3
	4 403	44.0
	5 334	43.4
Lowest	1 35	9.0
	2 33	10.0
	3 32	10.0
	4 111	11.0
	5 46	−11.0

[a]Only a partial list of cases with the value 11 are shown in the table of lower extremes.

This set of selections will identify the five cases with the highest values and the five with the lowest values on the variable (Table 13.2). Examining the values of these extreme cases and the general characteristics of the distribution might help identify extremely unusual cases that might be dropped or checked further.

Dropping Cases

The normal way of removing outliers is to decide on criteria by which to define outliers (e.g. beyond ± 2 standard deviations) and then use these criteria to exclude the outliers. Supposing the criterion was beyond ± 2 standard deviations on any of the outlier tests (e.g. standaradized residuals, Cook's distance, etc.) the following SPSS syntax would identify outliers:

COMPUTE $\boxed{outlier}$ = 0.

IF   ($\boxed{zresid\_1}$ > 2.0) $\boxed{outlier}$ = 1.

IF   ($\boxed{zresid\_1}$ < –2.0) $\boxed{outlier}$ = 1.

IF   ($\boxed{mahal\_1}$ > 2 $\boxed{(s)}$) $\boxed{outlier}$ = 1.

IF   ($\boxed{mahal\_1}$ < – 2 $\boxed{(s)}$) $\boxed{outlier}$ = 1.

IF   ($\boxed{cook\_1}$ > 2 $\boxed{(s)}$) $\boxed{outlier}$ = 1.

IF   ($\boxed{cook\_1}$ < – 2 $\boxed{(s)}$) $\boxed{outlier}$ = 1.

IF   ($\boxed{lev\_1}$ > 2 $\boxed{(s)}$) $\boxed{outlier}$ = 1.

IF   ($\boxed{lev\_1}$ < – 2 $\boxed{(s)}$) $\boxed{outlier}$ = 1.

Note that the names z-resid_1, mahal_1,cook-1, lev_1 must have previously been created (see earlier syntax). Note also that (s) should be replaced with the actual value of the standard deviation for the relevant variables (e.g. for lev_1). These standard deviations are obtained from the output created by the earlier syntax (see Table 13.1b).

In subsequent analysis you can exclude the outliers by selecting only cases where the value for the newly created outlier variable is 0. This is achieved with the following menu selections:

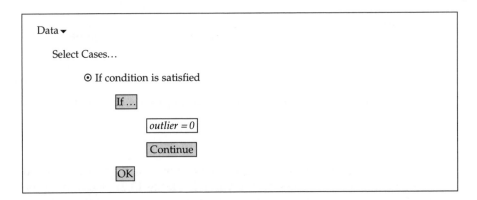

Data ▾

   Select Cases…

      ⊙ If condition is satisfied

         $\boxed{\text{If …}}$

            $\boxed{outlier = 0}$

            $\boxed{\text{Continue}}$

        $\boxed{\text{OK}}$

Note that the name of the variable entered in the panel after clicking the If… button must be exactly the name that you created with the previous set of syntax commands (i.e. Compute outlier = 0).

14

What to do if the Required Variable
is not Available

What is the Problem?

Often data are not collected in the form in which they are finally required. This situation can arise for several reasons.

- The data may have been collected by other people for other purposes. The great advantage of secondary analysis is that we can obtain large data sets with good samples at very low cost. The disadvantage is that they often do not have just the right variables. In such cases we have to make do, using the information in the data set to our best advantage.
- It may be easier and better, for good methodological reasons, to collect 'bits' of information from which we can produce the variables we need during the data analysis stage. The examples below provide illustrations of this. Collecting the 'bits' of information can be desirable for two reasons. First, it can reduce the burden on respondents, making it unnecessary, for example, for them to perform various calculations. Second, it provides greater flexibility. 'Bits' of information can be used in a variety of ways and for different purposes, while a summary or overview variable may only be suitable for a single purpose (see examples below).
- We may not anticipate the analysis that will be required. Although we are exhorted to know what our hypotheses and required variables are before collecting data, the reality is that data analysis is much more dynamic than this. We often get new ideas as we analyse the data and try to make sense of the patterns.

The problem of not having the right variables does not always have a solution. Even where there is a solution, it may be less than ideal. If we are to build a new variable from a data set we must have the building blocks of the required variable already in the data set. New variables can then be created by:

- either using information from a number of different questions (or variables) and producing a new, composite variable from the bits;
- or changing the form of a single variable.

Table 14.1 *Six income sources*

Source	Variable name
Wages and salary	INC
Social welfare or other government benefits	WINC
Income from business	BINC
Pension or superannuation	PINC
Dividends and interest	DINC
Other income	OINC

How to Create a New Variable from a Number of Individual Variables

There are two main approaches to combining information from a set of variables:

- arithmetical;
- satisfying logical conditions.

Using Arithmetical Methods

This approach is suitable when the original variables on which we want to base the new variable are interval-level variables with codes that make sense numerically (e.g. age, number of children, years of schooling, income). This approach can be illustrated with three examples.

TOTAL INCOME   The most reliable way to collect good income data in a questionnaire is to ask separate questions about individual income sources (see Table 14.1). Then, rather than asking an additional question on total income, we can save the respondent the computational effort and sum the income from the individual sources at the data analysis stage. Since each of the income source variables has numeric codes that give actual income values, we can simply get the computer to add up these values and create a new composite variable containing a value for each person that indicates the sum of their individual sources of income.

In SPSS the menu selections to create the new variable from the sum of the values of individual variables are:

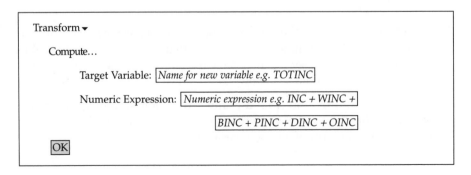

Transform ▾

Compute…

Target Variable: | *Name for new variable e.g. TOTINC* |

Numeric Expression: | *Numeric expression e.g. INC + WINC +* |

| *BINC + PINC + DINC + OINC* |

OK

The key part of this transformation is the numerical expression INC + WINC + BINC + PINC + DINC + OINC. This expression examines the value of each of these variables for a case (i.e. income from that source) and adds up the values of each variable to arrive at a total value. The total value becomes the value for that person on the 'target variable' TOTINC. Thereafter the new variable TOTINC would be used for the analysis of income.

AGE Suppose that we know a person's year of birth but do not have a variable that indicates their actual age. This can be calculated with a simple arithmetic operation in the same way as we would do in everyday circumstances. If I meet someone in the year 2002 and learn that they were born in 1950 I can easily calculate their age as being 52 (depending on their exact birthday). To arrive at this answer I have simply subtracted 1950 from 2002. A computer program such as SPSS can determine an age for each person by simply subtracting their year of birth [BIRTH_YR] from the current year (specified by the user in the instruction below as 2002). The SPSS menu selections to achieve this are:

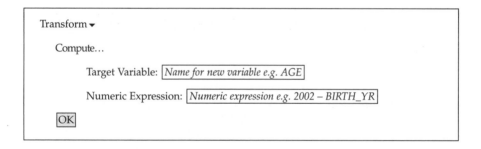

SOCIAL MARGINALIZATION This example represents a more complex process of variable creation. Suppose we need a variable to indicate social marginalization. We have no measures that directly measure social marginalization, so we have to create a proxy variable out of the information we have available. We decide that the best information we have is provided by whether people belong to groups that are traditionally more socially marginal. We have information regarding the six characteristics listed in Table 14.2 and define people belonging to certain categories as being more socially marginal.

One approach to measuring social marginalization would be simply to count the number of variables on which a person belongs to a socially marginalized category. The more marginalized categories a person belongs to, the more marginalized they are defined to be.

To create this variable in SPSS we would first recode each of the constituent variables into two categories with the values of 0 and 1, where the marginal categories are coded as 1 and non-marginal as 0. We could then use the following menu options:

Table 14.2 *Six variables indicating social marginalization*

Variable	Marginal categories	Variable name (recoded as 0 and 1)
Gender	Female	RSEX
Age	Young people (under 20)	RAGE
	Older people (65 or over)	
Race	Non-white	RRACE
Main language	Other than English	RLANG
Employment status	Unemployed	REMP
	Not in labour force	
Marital status	Other than married or cohabiting	RMAR

Transform ▾

 Compute…

  Target variable: | *Name for new variable, e.g. SOC_MARG* |

  Numeric expression: | *RSEX + RAGE + RRACE + RLANG + REMP + RMAR* |

 |OK|

Using this arithmetical operation, a person who belonged to all six marginal categories (e.g. not married, black, elderly, female, who is not in the labour force and does not speak English well) would obtain a code of 6 on the SOC_MARG variable. Those who belonged to none of these categories (e.g. middle aged, married, white, English-speaking, male, with a full-time job) would obtain a code of 0 and be regarded in subsequent analysis as the least marginalized.

Using Logical Conditions

Variables created in this way are based on individuals meeting a set of quite specific logical conditions. Rather than simply adding up codes, subtracting codes from a set value or some other arithmetical operation, this approach creates variables based on the specific attributes of cases. It can be best explained with some examples.

MIGRANT BACKGROUND Suppose that in our study a relevant variable is cultural background, and we need a variable that indicates something of the respondent's migrant background. Suppose that we have a variable that indicates whether or not the respondent was born overseas or locally. Suppose also that

Table 14.3 *Logical possibilities based on three dichotomous variables*

		Father born			
		Locally		Overseas	
		Mother born		Mother born	
		Locally	Overseas	Locally	Overseas
Respondent born	Locally	1	2	2	3
	Overseas	4	5	5	6

we feel that this is insufficient – that a good classification needs to take into account whether a person's parents were born locally or overseas. We want to create a variable that reflects this information. Suppose that we have three variables that reflect whether the respondent, their mother and father were born locally or overseas. These three sets of information provide eight logical possibilities, although I will only distinguish between six (see Table 14.3):

1. all born locally;
2. respondent locally born and only one overseas born parent;
3. respondent locally born and both parents born overseas;
4. respondent born overseas and both parents born locally;
5. respondent born overseas and only one overseas born parent;
6. all born overseas.

The particular categories that are defined will depend on what is required for the study. We could, for example, reduce the number of categories further by combining categories 2, 3, 4, 5 into a 'mixed' category. The central point is that the categories are defined according to particular characteristics of people, and the new variable is not simply an arithmetical combination of numerical values.

HOUSEHOLD FAMILY AND STAGE Suppose that you require a variable that indicates the nature of a person's family type (based on family members living in the household). Table 14.4 lists three variables that might be used to construct such a variable. We could construct a new variable from these four that classifies families into five types. The following list includes the codes that match the particular family types:

1. couple without children (PART = 1 and NKIDS = 0);
2. couple with dependent children in household (PART = 1, NKIDS = 1 and NDEP_KIDS = 1);
3. lone parent with dependent children (PART = 0, NKIDS = 1 and NDEP_KIDS = 1);
4. couple with only independent children in household (PART = 1, NKIDS = 1 and NDEP_KIDS = 0);

Table 14.4 *Three variables from which to construct a household type variable*

	SPSS variable name	Values
Does respondent have partner living in the household?	PART	0 = no partner 1 = partner
Number of children of respondent and/or partner living in household	NKIDS	0 = none 1 = one or more
No. of children in household financially dependent on respondent or partner	NDEP_KID	0 = none 1 = one or more

5. lone parent with only independent children in household (PART = 0, NKIDS = 1 and NDEP_KIDS = 0).

The SPSS menu selections below show how to create a new variable called FAMILY that defines each of these family types. The central part of these selections is the IF section. In this section we specify that IF a case meets particular conditions (e.g. coded 1 on the PART variable and 0 on the NKIDS variable) then they will be given a particular code (e.g. 1) on the new FAMILY variable. A separate IF sequence of selections is required to define the range of particular values on the new variable.

Transform ▾

  Compute...

      Target Variable: | *Name for new variable e.g. FAMILY* |

      | IF... |

            ⊙ Include if case satisfies condition:

              | *((PART eq 1) and (NKIDS eq 0))* | [enter in large panel]

              | Continue |

      Numeric Expression: | *Value for specified condition e.g. 1* |

      | IF... |

            ⊙ Include if case satisfies condition:

              | *((PART eq 1) and (NKIDS eq 1) and (NDEP_KID eq 1))* |

              | Continue |

      Numeric Expression: | 2 |

      | IF... |

            ⊙ Include if case satisfies condition:

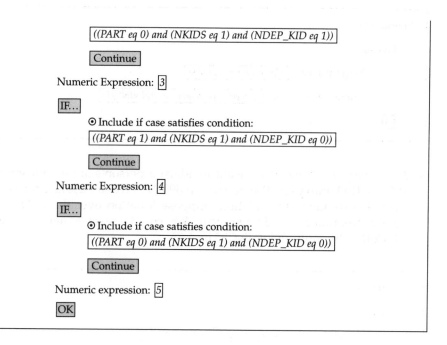

$((PART\ eq\ 0)\ and\ (NKIDS\ eq\ 1)\ and\ (NDEP\_KID\ eq\ 1))$

Continue

Numeric Expression: $\boxed{3}$

IF...

⊙ Include if case satisfies condition:

$((PART\ eq\ 1)\ and\ (NKIDS\ eq\ 1)\ and\ (NDEP\_KID\ eq\ 0))$

Continue

Numeric Expression: $\boxed{4}$

IF...

⊙ Include if case satisfies condition:

$((PART\ eq\ 0)\ and\ (NKIDS\ eq\ 1)\ and\ (NDEP\_KID\ eq\ 0))$

Continue

Numeric expression: $\boxed{5}$

OK

How to Change the Form of a Single Variable to Create the Required Variable

The examples above have used information from a number of variables to create one new variable. This is the most common way of constructing new variables. Sometimes, however, we can simply reconstruct a single variable so that it serves a different purpose than that for which it was originally intended. This reconstruction can be achieved either arithmetically or by reordering categories. The process of constructing new variables by reordering categories is discussed in Problem 8, so the discussion below is restricted to the use of arithmetic methods.

- *Dividing a variable by a value.* We may have collected information about a person's annual income, but for our particular analysis we need to know their weekly income. This can be obtained by creating a new variable simply by dividing annual income (ANNINC) by 52 (number of weeks in the year) to construct a new variable indicating weekly income (WEEKINC).

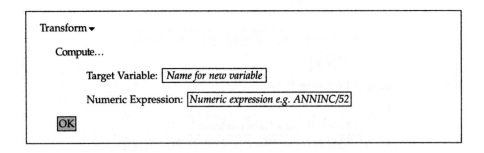

- *Multiplying a variable.* If we want to adjust a person's annual income in 1990 (INC90) into year 2000 dollars (ADJ90INC) we can use an arithmetic operation to adjust for inflation. Suppose inflation over the 1990–2000 period amounted to 35 per cent. We could create a new variable ADJ90INC by multiplying INC90 by 1.35.

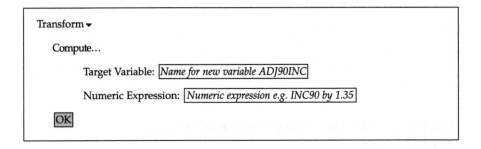

15

How to Compare Apples with Oranges: Comparing Scores on Different Variables

What is the Problem?

Attributes are often measured using items with different upper and lower limits. For example, we may have five measures of political orientation, each with a different range of values (Table 15.1). Each variable is measured in a different way. The measures have a different number of categories and the low and high scores on each measure are different.

Table 15.1   *Five measures of political orientation using different scales*

	Low score	High score	Variable name
Trust in government	1	10 (high trust)	TRUST
Political efficacy	0	4 (high efficacy)	POLEF
Feeling towards prime minister/president	0	100 (positive feeling)	LEAD
Alienation from politics	8	24 (not alienated)	ALIEN
Frequency of reading about politics each week	0	20 (frequent)	POLR

The different length measures on each measure present two important problems.

- It is very difficult to compare *across* these variables. The normal way of comparing across variables is to calculate the mean for each variable and to compare the means. However, since each of the variables is measured with a different length measure these means will be extremely difficult to compare. For example, the mean on trust in government might be 4. The mean for alienation might be 10. But because the scales are different length and have different starting points (Table 15.1) comparisons of means are very difficult. Since each question is measured in different units, it is like comparing apples with oranges.
- When creating multi-item scales (Problems 17 and 18), items that have different lower and upper points will contribute differently to the final

multi-item scale score if used in their raw form. This means that some items will count for more in the computation of a final score. Normally this is not what we want. It is similar to having three pieces of assessment to arrive at a final mark for a subject at university. One piece of work might be marked out of 80, another out of 10 and another out of 20. If we simply added up raw scores from each of these pieces of assessment then the piece of work marked out of 80 would count for much more in the final mark. If this is what was desired then all is well, but if each piece of work was meant to contribute equally to the final mark then we would need to adjust the items to equalize their contribution.

How to make Variables more Comparable

The solution to these problems is to convert the scales into a common measurement scale so that they can be compared. This can be achieved in two ways:

- converting each scale to have the same lower and upper levels.
- standardizing the variables and expressing scores as standard deviation units (z-scores).

How to Convert Variables to have the Same Lower and Upper Limits

This solution involves adjusting the scales on each variable, 'stretching' some measures and 'squeezing' others. For any numerical scale the conversion is achieved using the formula

$$Y = \left(\frac{X - X_{min}}{X_{range}} \right) n$$

where Y is the adjusted variable, X is the original variable, X_{min} is the minimum observed value on the original variable and X_{range} is the difference between the maximum observed score and the minimum observed score on the original variable and n is the upper limit of the rescaled variable. This conversion can be easily accomplished with a variable transformation in the main statistical analysis packages (see SPSS section below).

For example, suppose we want all variables converted to a scale of 0–10. Let us convert POLEF (see Table 15.1). From the table we see that the minimum observed score was 0, and the maximum observed score 4. The range is therefore 4. Our formula is thus

$$POLEFADJ = \left(\frac{POLEF - 0}{4} \right) \times 10$$

An individual with a score of 4 on POLEF would score $(4/4) \times 10 = 10$ on POLEFADJ; a score of 0 on POLEF would convert to $(0/4) \times 10 = 0$ on POLEFADJ, while a score of 2 on POLEF would become a POLEFADJ score of $(2/4) \times 10 = 5$.

Having converted all five variables to a range of 0–10, it becomes much easier to compare scores and averages across them.

How to Standardize Variables to Promote Comarability

Numeric variables can be expressed in terms of standard deviation units (p. 224). This gives each person's score in terms of the number of standard deviations it lies from the mean.

A score on a variable is standardized (z_i) by subtracting the mean for $(\bar{X})$ the variable from an individual's score on the variable (x_i) and then dividing the result by the standard deviation for the variable:

$$z_i = \frac{(x_i - \bar{X})}{s}.$$

A standardized variable will always have a mean of 0 and a standard deviation of 1. The full set of scores will range from negative to positive values (because on any variable some people obtain scores below the mean and some score above the mean).

Therefore the mean of a standardized variable is of little use in comparing the average score of a whole sample *across* standardized variables, since all the means will be zero. However, the means of standardized variables can usefully be compared across variables for subgroups (e.g. mean for males and mean for females).

Methods of Rescaling to Enhance Comparability

The values of a variable can be rescaled by *dividing* the values by a specific value. For example, rather than expressing a person's income in dollars or pounds, we can express it relative to the average income (Table 15.2). In this way we can compare the income in one year with that in another year, or income in one country with that in another country.

Alternatively, we can focus on categories rather than individuals. We can then compare groups relative to one another and overcome the problem of variables with different scales. For example, we may want to see whether the gender gap in income has changed between 1970 and 2000. The problem in comparing gender gaps in income is that inflation makes it difficult to interpret the gap in actual monetary terms. In Table 15.3 the dollar gap in male–female incomes is greater in 2000 than in 1970. But this may simply be due to inflation.

Table 15.2 *Rescaling income relative to a median of $600*

Case	Income ($)	Rescaled value
A	300	0.5
B	750	1.25
C	1000	1.67
D	450	0.75
E	650	1.08
...		

Table 15.3 *Female full-time annual earnings as a proportion of male full-time annual earnings*

Year	Column 1 Median, males ($)	Column 2 Median, females ($)	Column 3 Female as proportion of male (col 2/col 1)	Column 4 Absolute gap ($)
1970	5 000	3 400	0.68	−1600
1980	15 000	10 500	0.70	−4500
1990	25 000	18 000	0.72	−7000
2000	35 000	26 950	0.77	−8050

We can overcome this problem by rescaling female income in each year relative to male income. Columns 1 and 2 in Table 15.3 show the median income of males and females in the various years. Column 3 re-expresses average female income as a proportion of male average (median) income by simply dividing female median income by male median income. This overcomes the problem of the changed meaning of the monetary unit over the years. By rescaling we can compare the incomes over the years and, in this case, observe a narrowing of the gender gap, rather than a widening as the raw figures suggest.

Another way of rescaling is to *multiply* a variable by a specific value. For example, in comparing incomes over years we can re-express incomes in terms of a reference year by adjusting income in each other year for inflation. In Table 15.4, the sum of $1000 in 1990 is re-expressed in 1990 units for each subsequent year by adjusting for annual inflation. Thus, $1000 in 1991 is worth 8 per cent less than in 1990 because of inflation. We therefore multiply 1000 by 0.92 to adjust for the 8 per cent erosion in the value of the dollar. By making the relevant inflation adjustment each year, income can be compared across the years.

A similar exercise could be undertaken with incomes in different countries where the incomes in one country might be expressed in terms of a reference country (e.g. US dollars) and then compared. To do this we would simply convert the incomes in other countries by multiplying them by the exchange rate against the US dollar.

Table 15.4 *Income re-expressed in 1990 dollars*

	$	Inflation rate	1990 value ($)	
1990	1000	8	1000	
1991	1000	8	$920	year 1990 $1000 × 0.92 (i.e. 100–8%)
1992	1000	6	$846	year 1991 $920 × 0.92
1993	1000	8	$796	year 1992 $846 × 0.94 (i.e. 100–6%)
1994	1000	5	$732	year 1993 $796 × 0.92
1995	1000	4	$695	year 1994 $732 × 0.95
1996	1000	6	$668	year 1995 $695 × 0.96
1997	1000	3	$628	year 1996 $668 × 0.94
1998	1000	3	$609	year 1997 $628 × 0.97
1999	1000	2	$590	year 1998 $609 × 0.97
2000	1000	2	$579	year 1999 $590 × 0.98

There are many other ways in which variables might be re-expressed to make them comparable. The particular method of rescaling will depend on the nature of your variables and the purpose of the analysis.

Which Method of Improving Comparability to Use

Establishing uniform upper and lower limits has some advantages. These include:

- All the values are positive, and this may be more intuitively understandable than standardized scores to the consumers of the research.
- Standardized variables will have a mean of 0. Therefore rescaling variables to have comparable upper and lower limits may be preferable to standardizing when the analysis involves comparing the means of the standardized variables.

Standardized variables have the advantage that:

- they adjust scores for the different *distributions* of variables and thus can make comparisons more meaningful (see de Vaus, 2001a, Chapter 11);
- they have particular statistical properties that can be helpful for some forms of further analysis.

The rescaling methods are particularly useful when examining change in the one concept (e.g. income) over time or between countries.

The decision between the different approaches will depend on:

- which approach is most readily understandable to the data analyst and the research audience;
- the type of subsequent analysis that is required.

Using SPSS

Creating the Same Lower and Upper Limits for Variables

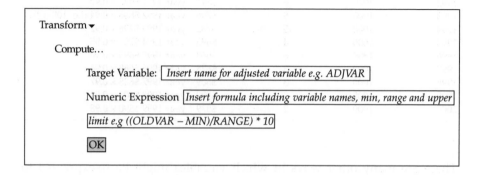

Transform ▾

Compute…

Target Variable: | *Insert name for adjusted variable e.g. ADJVAR* |

Numeric Expression | *Insert formula including variable names, min, range and upper* |

| *limit e.g ((OLDVAR – MIN)/RANGE) * 10* |

OK

Here OLDVAR is the name of the variable being changed, MIN is the minimum observed value of the OLDVAR, RANGE is the difference between the maximum and the minimum observed value of OLDVAR, and 10 is the upper limit you are setting for the transformed variable.

Standardizing Variables

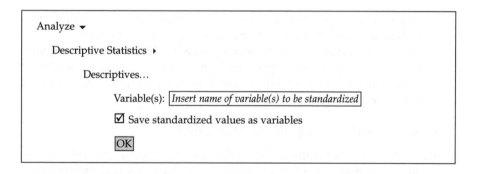

Analyze ▾

Descriptive Statistics ▸

Descriptives…

Variable(s): | *Insert name of variable(s) to be standardized* |

☑ Save standardized values as variables

OK

The Save option will create a new variable in the data file that is a standardized version of the variable listed on the variables instruction. The name of the standardized variable will be the same as the input variable except that it will be preceded by a 'z'.

Rescaling Variables

See Problem 14 on creating new variables from a single variable using arithmetic transformations.

Part Three How to Reduce the Amount of
Data to Analyse

16

How to Work Out which Variables to Use

What is the Problem?

Many data sets contain well over a thousand variables. Such complexity, the processing speed of contemporary desktop computers and the ease of use of the major statistical analysis packages can encourage lazy, ill-directed analysis. It is easy to generate a vast array of 'results' by throwing everything into the analysis just to see what turns up. Powerful multivariate techniques such as multiple regression make it easy to throw a very large number of variables into a model in the hope of maximizing the explanatory power of the model, as reflected in R^2 (p. 356). Factor analysis programs make it a simple task to throw every available variable into the analysis to see what factors emerge (pp. 134–7). With just 100 variables, it is a simple matter to produce 10 000 crosstabulations.

Why do Variables Need to be Selected before Analyzing the Data?

The thoughtless analysis of data is a problem for a number of reasons. It is easy to plunge into a data analysis without even thinking about what it is intended to achieve. Analysis without thinking will almost certainly produce barren results. The GIGO principle applies here – garbage in, garbage out.

A 'fruit salad' approach to analysis, where a bit of everything is thrown in, can produce misleading conclusions. Where significance tests (Problem 23) are used, 1 in 20 relationships will be statistically significant at the 5 per cent level by chance alone. That is, if we examine 20 relationships between variables where there really is no relationship, one of them will nevertheless emerge as statistically significant at the 5 per cent level. Again, with just 100 variables we can produce 10 000 correlations. Even if none of the variables are correlated in the population, we are likely to find in a sample that 500 of these correlations were statistically significant. If we try to make sense of these chance correlations we are liable to produce some pretty bizarre theories.

A similar problem applies with factor analysis (pp. 134–7). There is nothing to stop us factor-analyzing a random set of variables. Factor analysis will nearly always produce a 'solution'. However, it may well be a nonsense solution. Factor analysis is designed to identify sets of variables that are tapping the same underlying phenomenon. It does this by examining the patterns of correlations between variables. The assumption of factor analysis is that the variables that are identified as belonging to a factor are really measuring the same thing. The variables identified as belonging to the same underlying factor should not be *causally* related. Unfortunately factor analysis cannot distinguish between variables that are causally related and those that are non causally related. This can result in variables being grouped together when they should not be.

Unless the variables in a factor analysis are thoughtfully selected, meaningless factors can be produced. For example, if we included age and social class in a factor analysis with a number of religion and political orientation variables we might well emerge with two factors – a religion factor and a politics factor. Age might emerge as part of the religion factor, and class might appear to be part of the politics factor. This would occur because age and religiousness are correlated, as are social class and political views. But this does not mean that age and religion are really the same thing, or that class and political views are the same thing!

Regression analysis can include a large number of variables. Suppose that income is the dependent variable in a regression analysis and that the goal is to explain as much of the variation in income as possible. The extent to which income variation is explained is reflected in the value of R^2 – the higher this is the more income variation has been explained by the other variables in the model. In the hope of maximizing the R^2 we may be tempted to throw in as many variables as possible. Not only does such an approach produce 'explanations' that will generally be quite meaningless, it can also distort the R^2 (p. 356, 375).

How to Narrow Down the Choice of Variables

The selection of independent and dependent variables should be a function of the research question to which the data analysis is directed. Unless a clear research question is formulated, you will find no answers. See de Vaus (2001a) for some suggestions about how to focus research questions.

Before beginning to analyse the data, draw diagrams of the model you plan to evaluate. State what your dependent variable is (symbolized as Y).

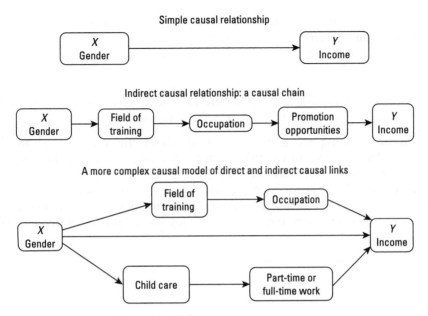

Figure 16.1 *Three types of causal model*

Specify the independent variable(s) (symbolized as X) and the likely mechanisms by which the independent and dependent variables might be related. Figure 16.1 illustrates three models, ranging from the very simple to the more complex. These models make some sort of sense and guide the selection of variables for further analysis.

Each of the links in any model should also make sense. In the case of Figure 16.1, you should be able to say why and in what way gender will affect income. Such arguments may derive from theories and explanations in the literature, from previous research, they may be popular lay explanations or they may simply be a reasonable hunch. Regardless of the source of your proposed models, you really do need them to guide your data analysis. These models assist in selecting which variables to use and provide guidance about the ways in which you might go about the analysis.

Another way of selecting variables to use in the analysis is to adopt the strategy used in elaboration analysis (Problem 41). Rather than developing a causal model before the analysis begins, elaboration analysis proceeds in steps. Initially we might examine the data to see if an expected relationship between gender and income exists. If it does exist, we might then seek to elaborate or understand what this relationship might be due to. We might ask:

- Why does this relationship exist? Is it due to more women than men working part-time?
- Is the relationship because of selective factors? (If so, which ones might it be due to?)

- Does the relationship between gender and income apply equally to blue-collar and white-collar workers?
- Are the gender differences in income just as large among younger men and women?

Questions such as these and our hunches about the answers can then guide our selection of variables to include in the data analysis.

When undertaking factor analysis, think about the variables involved. Before subjecting a set of variables to factor analyses you should have some idea of what they might have in common. You should make some attempt to include variables that might make sense together. You should also avoid including variables where any correlation is more likely to be due to causal relationships than due to the variables having something in common at the conceptual level.

17

How to Combine Information from a Set of Variables into a Single Measure

One common way of dealing with the problem of too much data is to reduce the number of variables by combining some measures into composite measures of concepts. One method of combining concepts is scaling, where a number of related variables are used to tap one underlying concept.

However, data reduction is not the only reason for combining measures into scales. In social research the concepts we seek to measure are often quite complex and cannot be adequately captured with a single question. Concepts such as social class, self-esteem, health, satisfaction, conservatism, prejudice and poverty require sets of questions to adequately measure them.

What are the Problems with Scaling Sets of Variables?

Developing multiple indicators of complex concepts results in several problems:

- Where each measure of a concept is treated individually in the analysis, both the researcher and the reader can drown in the resulting detail.
- Using a series of individual measures of a concept can produce conflicting sets of uninterpretable results.

The general solution to these problems is to combine the multiple measures into a single overall measure of the concept. If each measure taps an aspect of the concept then putting them together will provide a more rounded overall measure. An analogy is the way in which many university subjects are assessed using several pieces of work. These might include an essay, an examination, an oral presentation and a research report. The results from each of these individual indicators of ability are combined into a final mark which is assumed to be a more rounded indicator of ability than any single piece of work.

However this solution presents its own problems:

- How do you know whether it is reasonable to combine a set of variables? Do they really tap the same underlying concept?
- How do you choose between the range of different methods of producing these composite measures?

The discussion that follows outlines some of the factors to take into account when creating composite measures and briefly describes three common scaling methods.

What to Consider When Developing a Scale

What is the Difference between a Unidimensional and Multidimensional Scale?

Scales may be either *unidimensional* or *multidimensional*. The most common scaling methods aim to achieve unidimensional scales. The distinction between unidimensional and multidimensional scales can be explained with an example.

UNIDIMENSIONAL SCALES Unidimensional scales measure one underlying concept on a single continuum that ranges from low to high. Individual cases are placed along the continuum. Suppose we wish to develop a measure of conservatism. Since people can be conservative in different respects (e.g. economically, socially or politically) we may have items that tap different aspects of conservatism. Rather than combining all these measures into one scale that may confuse different dimensions of conservatism, we would create three separate measures each focusing on just one dimension (Figure 17.1).

MULTIDIMENSIONAL SCALES In some respects it is artificial to break up the concept of conservatism in this way. If the items measure separate dimensions, would it not be more valuable to develop a scale that combined these dimensions in some way so that we could distinguish between different *types* of conservatives?

Figure 17.2 illustrates a two-dimensional scale in which economic and social conservatism are included as separate dimensions. The horizontal axis represents social conservatism, while the vertical axis represents economic conservatism. The four quadrants represent different combinations of the two types of conservatism. The bottom left-hand quadrant represents social and economic liberals and the top right-hand quadrant represents the social and economic conservatives. The other two quadrants contain people who are conservative in one domain but liberal in the other.

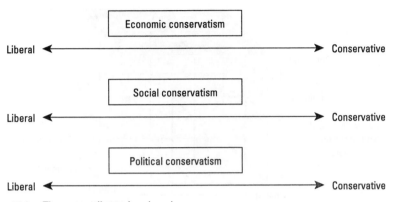

Figure 17.1 *Three one-dimensional scales*

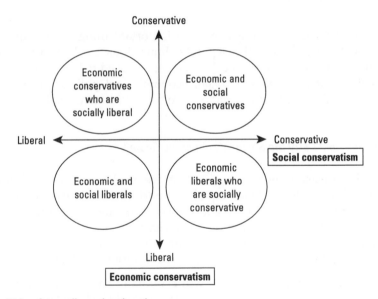

Figure 17.2 *A two-dimensional scale*

Figure 17.3 illustrates a three-dimensional scale incorporating social, economic and political dimensions. Each cube within the larger three-dimensional cube illustrates scale categories defined by the three dimensions. For the sake of simplicity each dimension has been classified as either liberal or conservative. In reality this would be a continuum. The highlighted cube represents cases who are socially, politically and economically conservative. Eight different types, or clusters, of conservatism are represented in this three-dimensional object.

The multidimensional version of the concept tries to place people on a multidimensional scale. Such a composite measure provides a more complex

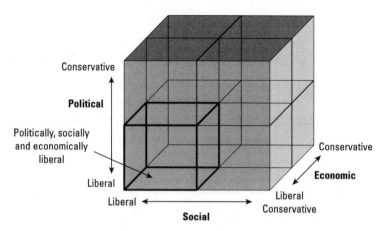

Figure 17.3   *A three-dimensional scale*

and rounded measurement system. The important thing to note in multi-dimensional scales is that the separate dimensions are kept apart to the extent that a person's score on each dimension is used to help classify them. This is different from having social, economic and political measures of conservatism all mixed up to yield a score on a unidimensional scale.

Should each Item Carry the Same Weight in the Scale?

Since scales consist of more than one item, we need to decide whether each item should be treated as being equally important. Should each measure in a scale be treated as an equally good measure of the underlying concept? Perhaps some items are much more powerful indicators of the concept and should count for more when calculating a final scale score. Methods of assigning weights to variables are discussed in Problems 18 and 19.

When building scales, each person will eventually have a scale score. This score summarizes their position on the scale and will be based on adding up their scores on each of the variables that make up the scale. This is comparable to a final grade in a university subject. The final grade consists of the marks for each piece of work. The final mark will probably differ depending on whether all pieces of work are worth the same number of marks or whether some are worth more than others.

What is the Difference between an Inductive and a Deductive Scale?

Scaling methods differ to some extent regarding their starting point. Some methods, which I will call *deductive* methods, *begin with a concept* and then develop or select items to tap the concept. The correlations between the

Table 17.1   *Items in a simple cumulative index*

Variable	Type of organization	Yes	No
1	Church or religious organization	1	0
2	Sport or recreation organization	1	0
3	Art, music or educational organization	1	0
4	Labour union	1	0
5	Political party	1	0
6	Environmental organization	1	0
7	Professional association	1	0
8	Charitable organization	1	0
9	Consumer group	1	0
10	Community service group	1	0

items are then examined to see which items can be combined to measure the inital concept.

Other, more *inductive,* methods *begin with a set of measures* and examine the pattern of responses to come up with a concept. These methods identify which items go together empirically. Once a set of items have been identified as being intercorrelated the researcher's task is to 'name' the concept of which these items are assumed to be a measure.

Are there Different Ways of Constructing Scales?

There are many methods of creating unidimensional and multidimensional scales. Only three unidimensional methods are outlined below. Two of these are discussed in detail in Problems 18 and 19.

Simple Cumulative Index

The simplest type of unidimensional scale is one that counts the number of items on which the respondent 'scores'. This scale is normally based on a set of items with simple yes/no answers where the items are selected according to their face validity. A scale or index score is produced for each person based on the number of items to which they give a 'yes' answer. An example of such an index is a survey in which respondents were asked which of a set of organizations they belonged to (listed in Table 17.1). The index score of any individual on this set of items indicated the number of organizations to which they belonged.

This simple index is designed to be unidimensional and each item is equally weighted by default, since respondents obtain 1 for membership and 0 for non-membership. If on some basis we thought that membership of some

Table 17.2   *A set of four Likert-style attitude items*

	Strongly agree	Agree	Neither agree nor disagree	Disagree	Strongly disagree
I almost always continue to work on a task until I am satisfied with the result.	1	2	3	4	5
I feel disappointed in myself when I don't accomplish my personal goals.	1	2	3	4	5
I like work so much that I often stay up late at night to finish it.	1	2	3	4	5
I make a lot of effort to live up to what my friends expect.	1	2	3	4	5

organizations was more important, then we could give people a double or triple score for that organization.

Likert Scales

This technique will be discussed in detail in Problem 18. At its simplest level it consists of a set of Likert-style questionnaire items (Table 17.2) in which respondents are presented with an attitude statement and asked to indicate how strongly they agree or disagree with it. Each respondent is given a scale score on the basis of their responses to each item. Although Likert-style items usually have either four or five response categories, there is nothing in principle to prevent the use of answering systems that have any number of categories.

Where all items in a Likert scale have the same number of categories an equal-weight scale will be produced by default. Where different items have a different number of categories an unequally weighted scale will result by default. This occurs because items with more categories are able to contribute higher scores to the overall scale score. A ten-point item will be scored 1 to 10. Strong agreement with such an item will give a person a score of 10, while strong agreement with a five-category item would only contribute five points to an overall score.

The process of building a Likert scale consists of a number of steps which involve assessing empirically which items from an initial set can be considered to belong to the scale. The outcome of this selection process should be a reliable and unidimensional scale.

Factor Analysis

Factor analysis will be covered in more detail in Problem 19. There are two general approaches: exploratory and confirmatory. Only exploratory approaches are dealt with here. Exploratory factor analysis is an inductive method of producing summary scales. It involves examining patterns in the way respondents have answered a set of items, and identifying whether the patterns can be represented by one or more underlying factors.

For example, we might have a number of questions that might tap the con-servatism of respondents. On the basis of the way people answered these questions, a factor analysis might see that there are three groupings of items: the way one set of items is answered is different from the way a second set is answered and different from the way a third set is answered. A factor analysis will identify these groupings of items that go together empirically. We can then examine the sets of items the factor analysis has extracted and see what these items have in common. We might find that one group of items are about social matters, another about economic matters and a third about political matters. This would suggest that there are three 'factors' identifiable from the responses to the pool of questions. Each factor so identified can be used to form a separate unidimensional scale.

Summary

Table 17.3 summarizes the main characteristics of the scaling methods outlined above.

Table 17.3   *Characteristics of some common unidimensional scaling methods*

Scale type	Weighted or unweighted?	Inductive or deductive?	Method of weighting	Measurement of items
Cumulative index	Unweighted	Deductive	None	Dichotomies
Likert	Can be either	Deductive	Automatic if variables have different number of categories	At least ordinal
Factor-based scales	Can be either	Inductive	Based on factor loadings	Interval
Factor scales	Weighted	Inductive	Based on factor scores	Interval

18

How to Build a Good Likert Scale

What Decisions must be made When Building a Likert Scale?

Likert scales are a simple and widely used method for constructing unidimensional scales (p. 118). However, combining items into a single measure cannot be arbitrary. The two central problems when creating Likert scales are identifying

- which items legitimately 'go together';
- the best way in which to combine them.

Dealing with these two matters involves attending to a number of subsidiary matters, including:

- how to identify a set of variables that *might* belong to the scale;
- how to tell whether an item belongs with the other items;
- how many items are required in a scale;
- whether items should be differently or equally weighted;
- if weighting is to be used, deciding on a weighting method;
- the use of items that have a different number of categories than other items;
- whether to include items that are negatively correlated with other items;
- dealing with cases that have missing values on one or more items.

Once a set of items have been selected for scaling, three tasks remain:

- evaluating the quality of the scale;
- comparing scores on different scales;
- interpreting scale scores.

How to Construct a Likert Scale

To illustrate the steps required to develop a good Likert scale we will refer to a set of questionnaire items (E1–E11 in Table 18.1) designed to measure support for environmentalism.

Table 18.1   *Eleven scale items designed to measure support for environmentalism*

Variable	Min.	Max.	No. of categories	High code	Missing cases	Mean	Skew	Standard deviation
E1	0	10	11	pro	182	4.4	−0.11	2.55
E2	1	3	3	anti	77	2.3	−0.48	0.66
E3	1	5	5	pro	53	3.1	0.03	1.16
E4	1	5	5	anti	43	4.2	−0.91	0.78
E5	1	5	5	pro	68	3.0	0.18	1.14
E6	1	5	5	anti	50	3.9	−0.70	0.88
E7	1	5	5	anti	40	4.4	−1.47	0.74
E8	1	5	5	anti	38	4.0	−0.75	0.84
E9	1	5	5	anti	53	3.2	0.06	1.10
E10	1	5	5	anti	51	3.69	−0.59	1.14
E11	1	8	8	pro	40	2.8	1.50	2.40

Deciding What is to be Measured

Before selecting items, you must specify the concept for which you are trying to create a scale. Assuming that you are building a unidimensional scale, decide what you want a high score and low score on the scale to indicate. In the example of Table 18.1 the concept is attitude to environmentalism. A high score on this scale will indicate a pro or supportive stance on environmental issues and groups.

Identify which Items to Select

The method of identifying potential scale items will depend on the data set you are using. If you are using a data set designed and collected by yourself, you will doubtless have included at the design stage a set of items to measure the concepts with which the research is concerned. If you are analyzing data collected by others, you will need to start with the concept for which you want a scale and then examine the variable set to see what items *might* tap this concept. In our example I have found 11 items that appear to reflect something about environmentalism.

What to Look for When Selecting Items

Before trying to scale the selected items, it is important to look at them individually. Check for the following:

- Are all the items coded in the same direction?
- How many categories does each item have?
- What is the minimum and maximum possible value of each item?
- How many cases have missing values on the item?

All these matters affect whether you need to modify variables before constructing the scale and the way in which you go about constructing the scale.

In the case of the variables in Table 18.1, the missing cases on each variable require some attention. Although no single variable has a large number of missing cases (except perhaps E1) there could be a large number of missing cases *cumulatively* (the missing-cases column adds up to 695). In fact, I know from other analysis that when all 11 items are combined that there are 296 cases (15.6 per cent) that have missing values on at least one variable. If we dropped cases with a missing value from the analysis we would lose 15.6 per cent of the sample, amounting to quite a loss.

How to Deal with Missing Values

If a particular variable is producing most of the missing values, it should be dropped from any further analysis. If, as in this case, the missing values are evenly spread across all the variables the problem of missing values will be dealt with when the scale is finally constructed (see below).

Is Reverse Coding Needed?

It is important that all variables are coded in the same direction. Since a high score on the final scale is meant to reflect a pro-environmentalist position, each of the items must reflect this. Variables E2, E4 and E6–E10 are all coded in the wrong direction and need to be reverse-coded. Variables must be reverse-coded before testing whether items belong to a scale (pp. 58–60).

Are all Items to Count the Same?

The concept of weighting items was discussed in Problem 17. Items E1, E2, and E11 all have a different number of categories than the other variables. Since E1 has a maximum score or value of 10 while most others have a maximum score of 5, E1 will automatically be weighted more heavily than most of the other items. E2 will carry the least weight of all the variables since it has a maximum score of 3. All variables can be transformed so that they are equally weighted. This is achieved by standardizing each variable (p. 109).

Another way of weighting variables is to weight them according to how strongly they are correlated with the sum of the other items in the scale. Items that are most strongly related to the rest can be weighted by their item–total correlation coefficient (see below). Any reweighting should be done before undertaking the statistical analysis of scale items.

Some people argue (McIver and Carmines, 1981) that weighting is not really necessary. They argue that in practice it rarely alters the general pattern of

Table 18.2   *Item–total statistics for scale items in Table 18.1*

Variable	Scale mean if item deleted	Scale variance if item deleted	**Corrected item–total correlation**	Squared multiple correlation	**Alpha if item deleted**
E1	34.69	36.68	**0.49**	0.30	**0.70**
E3	35.97	50.06	**0.43**	0.44	**0.70**
E5	36.05	48.81	**0.52**	0.60	**0.68**
E4	34.91	53.11	**0.41**	0.35	**0.70**
E6	35.19	51.80	**0.47**	0.51	**0.70**
E7	34.72	53.20	**0.45**	0.46	**0.70**
E9	35.89	47.29	**0.67**	0.62	**0.67**
E2	36.77	53.71	**0.47**	0.27	**0.70**
E10	35.38	49.23	**0.51**	0.34	**0.68**
E8	35.11	50.79	**0.59**	0.40	**0.69**
E11	36.32	50.46	**0.07**	0.02	**0.79**

Alpha = 0.72

results and that it is very difficult to establish relevant weights. They also argue that social science data are rarely so precise that weighting is really warranted. While these arguments have some merit, they do not convince me that we should not reweight items that have fewer or more categories than most of the other variables in the scale so that we achieve an equal-weight scale.

Do the Items Belong Together? How to Tell

Like any individual measure, a scale should be both reliable (Problem 3) and valid (Problem 4). Likert scales assess the reliability and validity of a scale with two statistics. *Cronbach's alpha* assesses reliability and *item–total correlations* assess whether the scale is unidimensional. A valid Likert scale should be unidimensional – it should measure only one concept, rather than a mixture of different concepts. Statistical packages that perform reliability analysis produce output containing both these statistics. This type of output (Table 18.2) is crucial in assessing the quality of the scale and the appropriateness of each item in the scale.

To be reliable, a scale should have as high an alpha coefficient as possible – at least 0.7. Here, with all items included, alpha (at the bottom of table) is 0.72. That is adequate, but it could be increased easily. The figures in the right-hand column indicate what the alpha would be if a particular item was omitted from the scale. If item E11 was dropped the alpha would increase to 0.79. This is a substantial increase and provides a good reason for redoing the scale without including E11.

The item–total correlations provide evidence for the unidimensionality of the scale. Items that do not correlate well with the rest of the items probably

Table 18.3   *Item–total statistics after dropping an item*

Variable	Scale mean if item deleted	Scale variance if item deleted	Corrected item–total correlation	Squared multiple correlation	Alpha if item deleted
E1	31.92	29.70	0.51	0.30	0.82
E3	33.18	42.56	0.44	0.44	0.78
E5	33.27	41.25	0.55	0.60	0.76
E4	32.13	45.54	0.41	0.33	0.78
E6	32.41	43.86	0.51	0.56	0.77
E7	31.94	45.31	0.48	0.45	0.78
E9	33.11	39.70	0.71	0.62	0.75
E2	33.99	45.83	0.48	0.28	0.78
E10	32.60	41.61	0.53	0.34	0.77
E8	32.33	42.98	0.63	0.49	0.76

Alpha = 0.79

do not belong to the scale since they are probably tapping a different concept. To remain in a scale an item should have an item–total correlation of at least 0.3. E11 is a problem on this count as well, with an item–total correlation of 0.07.

You should also check whether any of the alpha or item–total coefficients are negative. If so the variable probably requires reverse coding (pp. 58–60). If reverse coding is required, do this before dropping any items.

Once a problem item has been identified and dropped from the scale, the analysis in Table 18.2 should be repeated without the item. Table 18.3 reports the analysis after dropping item E11. Dropping E11 changes all the other coefficients. Alpha has increased to 0.79, but now we see that if we also drop E1 it would further increase to 0.82. This is a more marginal improvement in the alpha, but we might still consider dropping it.

Number of Items: How many Items to Aim for

The decision about whether to drop E1 would be affected by how high alpha was in the first place. If alpha was low, even marginal improvements may be worthwhile. The other factor to take into account is the number of items in the scale. A general rule is that the more items a scale contains, the more confidence we can have in the scale. The more items in a scale, the less impact a biased or less adequate item will have in the overall scale score.

Constructing the Final Scale

Establishing which items properly belong to a scale does not create a scale. To create a scale we have to create a new variable. Once created, the new variable will be used for subsequent analysis instead of the individual scale items.

The simplest way of creating the final scale is to create a new variable using a simple arithmetic operation (see Problem 14). A person's scale score will simply be the sum of their scores on the variables that make up the scale. If the variables have been transformed or reweighted, this will have been done before testing the scale's quality. If such reweighting has been applied, the reweighted variables will be used in computing final scale scores.

Create a 'Short' Version of the Scale Variable

Once a scale has been created it will have a fair number of values (see Table 18.4). This will make it impossible to use in certain types of analysis, such as crosstabulations (Problem 32). It is therefore worth creating a second version of the scale simply by collapsing the scaled variable into a small number of categories. A common way of doing this is to trichotomize the scale, that is, to divide it into three equal-sized groups (pp. 36–8). In our example this results in the classification of those obtaining a score of between 9 and 33 as being the least environmentalist, those with scores between 34 and 39 as moderates, and those between 40 and 53 as the most environmentally friendly respondents.

Adjusting Upper and Lower Scale Limits

It may be desirable to transform the final scale so that scores on this scale can be compared with scores on other scales. This can be achieved either by standardizing the scale or creating the same upper and lower limits for all scales. Methods of transforming scores to have set lower and upper limits are outlined in Problem 15.

How to Solve the Missing-value Problem in Scales

Before creating the scale, we need to decide what to do with cases that have missing values on any variable. If very few cases have missing values we could decide to do nothing. In our example, doing nothing would lead to a loss of over 15 per cent of the sample. To avoid this loss of cases we can construct the scale by computing a scale score for each person based only on the items to which they have responded.

Since this approach will automatically mean that those who have answered fewer questions will get a lower score on the scale, we need to adjust the scale score to reflect this. This adjustment is easily accomplished by dividing the scale score of each person by the number of items to which they gave a valid answer. In SPSS this averaging is accomplished by using a different numerical expression when constructing the final scale (see below).

Table 18.4 *Frequency distribution of scale scores and cut-off points for trichotomization*

	Scale score	Frequency	Valid percentage	Cumulative percentage
Anti	9	1	0.1	0.1
	12	1	0.1	0.1
	13	1	0.1	0.2
	15	1	0.1	0.2
	16	1	0.1	0.3
	19	4	0.2	0.6
	20	3	0.2	0.7
	21	12	0.7	1.5
	22	7	0.4	1.9
	23	13	0.8	2.7
	24	28	1.7	4.4
	25	21	1.3	5.7
	26	34	2.1	7.8
	27	51	3.1	11.0
	28	53	3.3	14.2
	29	54	3.3	17.5
	30	65	4.0	21.6
	31	72	4.4	26.0
	32	65	4.0	30.0
	33	81	5.0	35.0
	34	81	5.0	40.0
	35	100	6.2	46.1
	36	96	5.9	52.0
	37	94	5.8	57.8
	38	88	5.4	63.2
	39	76	4.7	67.9
	40	72	4.4	72.4
	41	72	4.4	76.8
	42	65	4.0	80.8
	43	49	3.0	83.8
	44	37	2.3	86.1
	45	38	2.3	88.4
	46	33	2.0	90.5
	47	31	1.9	92.4
	48	41	2.5	94.9
	49	25	1.5	96.4
	50	21	1.3	97.7
	51	21	1.3	99.0
	52	5	0.3	99.3
Pro Env	53	11	0.7	100.0
Total		1624	100.0	
Missing		273		

What do the Scale Scores Mean?

Scale scores are simply the sum (or the mean) of a person's 'score' on each item. Where the items have been transformed in some way (e.g. by

Table 18.5 *Case summaries of item scores and scale scores for 11 cases*

CASE	E1	E2	E10	E8	E3	E5	E4	E6	E7	E9	ENVIRO	ENVIRO2
1	5	2	5	4	3	5	5	4	5	4	42	4.2
2	9	3	5	5	1	2	5	5	5	2	42	4.2
3	1	2	2	3	2	2	3	3	3	3	24	2.4
4	5	2	3	3	3	3	3	3	3	3	31	3.1
5	5	1	5	5	5	5	5	5	5	5	46	4.6
6	5	2	4	4	5	5	5	4	4	4	42	4.2
7	5	2	4	4	5	4	4	3	4	3	38	3.8
8	7	3	5	5	3	5	4	1	1	5	39	3.9
9	5	3	2	5	1	1	5	5	5	1	33	3.3
10	0	2	.	.	.	.	.	.	.	.	.	1.0
11	5	2	5	5	3	5	5	4	4	4	42	4.2

standardizing or reweighting), the scale score will be the sum of these transformed item scores. Table 18.5 provides the scores on individual items and scale scores for our example. The scale score for ENVIRO is for the simple scale without any reweighting or inclusion of cases with missing data. Notice that case 10 has missing data on all but two variables (E1 and E2) and its scale score is also missing (indicated by a dot). The second version of the scale score is a version of the same scale in which the scale score is the average score on the answered items. Thus case 10 obtained a score of 2 from the two variables he or she answered. This results in a scale score of 1.

The scale scores themselves have no *absolute value*. To make sense of scale scores we need to know the 'length' of the scale. The lower limits of the scale can be worked out by calculating the score a person would obtain if they got the lowest score on each item. The upper limit is the score that would be obtained if the highest score was achieved on each item. This calculation should be done after items have been reverse-coded. In this case the lowest score would be 9 (one on nine items and zero on E1) and the highest would be 53 (ten on E1, three on E2 and five on the remaining eight items).

Once the range of the scale is known it is a little easier to make sense of individual scores. We can see where they lie relative to the upper and lower limits of the scale. However, people with the same scale score will not necessarily have answered each item in the same way. Cases 1, 2, 6 and 11 all obtained a score of 42 but answered individual questions differently (Table 18.4).

The only way to interpret scale scores is in a relative sense. That is, we can say that the higher the score the more pro-environment the attitude is. Those with a score of 53 are the most pro-environment on our measure and those with a score of 9 are the least sympathetic to the environmentalist position. However, we cannot say in any *absolute* sense those with a score of 53 are highly environmentalist. That depends on how well our set of items measures a highly pro-environment position.

Summary of Steps

1. Identify the concept to be scaled.
2. Select items to test for inclusion in the scale.
3. Examine the characteristics of each item.
4. Reverse-code and reweight items if required.
5. Obtain alpha and item–total coefficients for the items.
6. Identify any items that should be dropped.
7. Obtain alpha and item–total coefficients for the remaining items.
8. Repeat steps 6 and 7 as required.
9. Compute the scale (including cases with missing data if appropriate).
10. Obtain a frequency distribution of the scale and check that scale scores make sense.
11. Adjust the upper and lower limits to common values across all scales if required.
12. Create a 'spare' trichotomized version of the scale.

Using SPSS

Procedures for reverse-coding, and adjusting upper and lower limits have been outlined in Problems 8 and 15 and procedures for weighting are discussed at the end of Chapter 19. This section will describe the SPSS steps for:

- obtaining reliability statistics;
- computing the final scale.

Reliability

These menu selections will produce output similar to that in Table 18.2:

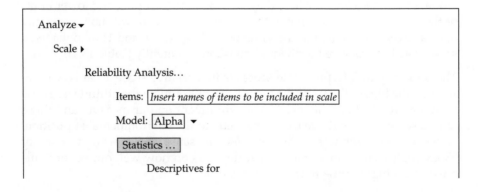

Analyze ▾

   Scale ▶

      Reliability Analysis...

         Items: *Insert names of items to be included in scale*

         Model: Alpha ▾

         Statistics ...

            Descriptives for

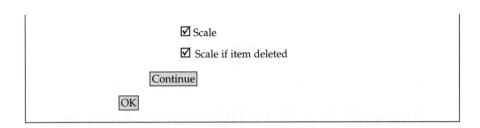

☑ Scale

☑ Scale if item deleted

Continue

OK

Building the Scale

Three different numerical transformations are described for building a scale. The first two do the same thing, while the third produces a mean score on the answered items, effectively adjusting scale scores for missing data.

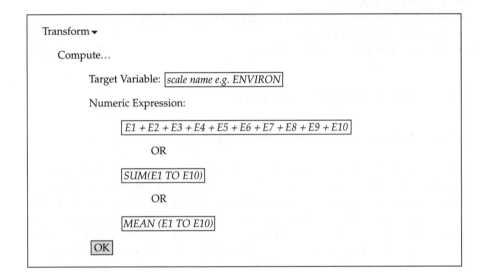

Transform ▾

Compute...

Target Variable: scale name e.g. ENVIRON

Numeric Expression:

E1 + E2 + E3 + E4 + E5 + E6 + E7 + E8 + E9 + E10

OR

SUM(E1 TO E10)

OR

MEAN (E1 TO E10)

OK

19

How to Build a Scale Using Factor Analysis

Factor analysis provides an inductive statistical method for creating scales (see Problem 17). This section explains how to:

- do a factor analysis;
- select among the different methods of factor analysis;
- read the statistical output;
- create scales from a factor analysis.

What is Involved in Doing a Factor Analysis?

How to Select Variables to Include in the Factor Analysis

The reasoning behind factor analysis is that the correlations between a set of selected variables occur because all the variables are caused by an underlying latent (not directly measured) factor, as indicated in Figure 19.1. The curved arrows connecting the items in the diagram indicate that these variables are correlated but *not* causally related. Since factor analysis is designed to identify the latent causal factor that explains the covariation among the items, it is important that the correlations between the items are not causal.

For example, suppose that we included gender and age among the set of environmentalist items in Table 19.1. Both these variables are correlated with attitudes to the environment and may 'work' in a factor analysis. However, any such correlation will be because age and gender affect environmentalist attitudes – not because they are the same thing as environmentalist attitudes. When selecting items to factor–analyse, ensure that you select only items that may measure a concept and avoid including variables that may be causally related to the items.

How to Know if Items Belong in the Factor Analysis

Once an initial set of factors have been selected, they need to be evaluated. There are several parts to such an evaluation. Table 19.1 lists the set of items initially selected for the example to be worked through below.

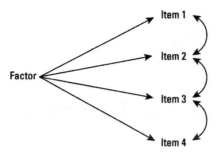

Figure 19.1 *The relationship between a factor and the component items*

Table 19.1 *Initial items for a factor analysis*

GREEN_ID	How strongly do you support the Greens (political party)?
NUC-NEC	Nuclear energy is a real necessity for the future.
NATURE	I cherish nature and preserve it as one of the most precious things in life.
URAN	Uranium should be mined.
SPEND+	Increase government spending to protect the environment.
POLLUT	Stronger measures should be taken to protect the environment against pollution.
ENV_GRP	Approve of groups campaigning to protect the environment.
URAN_GRP	Approve of groups concerned with stopping the mining and export of uranium.
NUCL_GRP	Approve of anti-war and anti-nuclear weapons movement.
GREENS	How do you feel about the Greens (political party)?
ENV_IMP	When you were deciding about how to vote, how important was the environment to you personally?

EXAMINE CORRELATIONS   The first step is to inspect a correlation matrix of the items to be analysed. This can show up items that are 'orphans' – that is, not correlated with anything much. Variable GREEN_ID looks like a problem, with only very weak or non-existent correlations (Table 19.2). While a number of other correlations are low, they are all statistically significant (Problem 23).

USE KMO VALUES   Another step in working out which variables to include in the analysis is to obtain KMO values for each variable. These statsitics provide a more formal way of assessing whether the set of variables overall, and each item in particular, is appropriate for a factor analysis. These values have been listed in Table 19.3.

As a guide to interpreting these figures, Kaiser (1974) has provided the guidelines in Table 19.4. On the basis of these KMO figures it appears that the set as a whole is suitable to try to factor-analyse. However, the 0.61 for GREEN_ID is cause for concern.

Table 19.2 *Bivariate correlation matrix of factor scale items*

	Green_id	Greens	Env_imp	Nuc-nec	Nature	Uran	Spend+	Pollut	Env_grp	Uran_grp	Nucl_grp
Green_id	1.00										
Greens	0.06	1.00									
Env_imp	0.00	0.33	1.00								
Nuc-nec	0.07	0.26	0.17	1.00							
Nature	0.05	0.22	0.33	0.06	1.00						
Uran	0.06	0.32	0.23	0.64	0.15	1.00					
Spend +	0.01	0.32	0.39	0.10	0.50	0.14	1.00				
Pollut	0.01	0.24	0.33	0.11	0.48	0.18	0.64	1.00			
Env_grp	0.00	0.44	0.41	0.21	0.42	0.27	0.53	0.48	1.00		
Uran_grp	0.06	0.45	0.31	0.49	0.26	0.67	0.30	0.29	0.47	1.00	
Nucl_grp	0.04	0.35	0.26	0.28	0.26	0.34	0.29	0.27	0.42	0.51	1.00

Note: Underlined coefficients are *not* statistically significant at the 0.05 level.

Table 19.3   *KMO values for factor analysis items*

Variable	KMO values	Variable	KMO values
GREEN_ID	0.61	ENV_GRP	0.90
NUC-NEC	0.80	URAN_GRP	0.83
NATURE	0.90	NUCL_GRP	0.91
URAN	0.73	GREENS	0.92
SPEND+	0.84	ENV_IMP	0.94
POLLUT	0.85	**Overall**	0.85

Table 19.4   *Interpretation of the magnitude of KMO values*

KMO value	Interpretation
0.90+	Marvellous
0.80–0.89	Meritorious
0.70–0.79	Middling
0.60–0.69	Mediocre
0.50–0.59	Miserable
Less than 0.50	Unacceptable

How to Obtain the Factors

Having determined that the set of variables is probably suitable for factor analysis, the next step is to identify (extract) the underlying factors. There are a number of different methods of doing this. Some guidelines for selecting between these methods will be discussed below. For the moment we will use the principal components method. (This method is sufficiently different from some of the other methods that it is often distinguished from true factor analysis. The term 'components' is used instead of 'factors'.)

This extraction phase will define as many components or factors as there are items in the analysis. However, most of these components are useless and can be ignored. Having extracted components, we have additional information that will help us decide which variables should be included in the final factor analysis.

EXAMINE COMMUNALITY   Each item being factor-analysed exhibits variance. The goal of factor analysis is to see how much of that variance is due to the causal influence of the latent factor(s) that have been extracted. Where the extracted factors explain a lot of the variance in an item, it means that the item should be retained for further analysis. The amount of variance in a variable that is explained by the extracted factors is called the *communality* – it is the variance in common between the factors and the item. Communality statistics

Table 19.5 *Communalities*

Item	Communality
GREENS	**0.39**
ENV_IMP	**0.39**
NUC-NEC	0.67
URAN	0.76
ENV_GRP	0.62
NUCL_GRP	0.44
NATURE	0.54
SPEND+	0.70
POLLUT	0.62
URAN_GRP	0.70
GREEN_ID	**0.02**

Extraction method: principal components analysis.

range from 0 to 1. The higher the figure, the better the fit of that variable in the analysis. Items with low communalities should be dropped from further analysis.

Not surprisingly, GREEN_ID has a low communality and should be dropped (Table 19.5). Two other variables show up as being possible candidates for dropping – GREENS and ENV_IMP have relatively low communalities.

Although factor analyses will allow as many components as there are items, only a few will be used. One of the goals of factor analysis is to reduce the number of variables with which we work. We seek to have fewer components than items.

SELECT THE NUMBER OF FACTORS: EIGENVALUES   We can control the number of components that are extracted and used in the computations of communality and other measures that indicate the power of the factor analysis. The most common method is to extract only the components that have an *eigenvalue* greater than 1. An eigenvalue is a statistic that relates to a factor or component. It indicates the amount of variance in the pool of initial items that that particular factor explains.

In Table 19.6 only two components have an eigenvalue greater than 1. This initial analysis therefore has resulted in a two-component solution. That is, these 11 items can be most simply reduced to two components. Each component will explain a particular amount of variance in the items. In this case component 1 explains 38.25 per cent and component 2 explains 15.31 per cent of the pooled variance. Together 53.56 per cent of variance in the pool of items is due to these two underlying components. Clearly the more variance that is explained by the components the better the factor solution – the more comfortable we can be in reducing the 11 initial items to two components.

Table 19.6 *Eigenvalues and explained variance for the initial factor items*

Component	Eigenvalue	Explained variance (%)	Cumulative (%)
1	**4.21**	**38.25**	**38.25**
2	**1.68**	**15.31**	**53.56**
3	1.00	9.09	62.64
4	0.79	7.20	69.84
5	0.72	6.50	76.34
6	0.62	5.60	81.94
7	0.53	4.83	86.76
8	0.43	3.94	90.71
9	0.42	3.84	94.54
10	0.36	3.29	97.83
11	0.24	2.17	100.00

Extraction method: principal components analysis.

What to do With the Initial Factors

Having extracted two components, we can see what each component looks like – which items belong to which component. When conducting a factor analysis the goal is to identify a set of items that uniquely belong to particular factors or components.

FACTOR LOADINGS Identifying which items 'belong' to which components or factors is done by examining the *factor loadings* in the component or factor matrix. These loadings are correlations between the item and the components. The higher the loading, the more that variable belongs to that components. Usually we expect a loading of at least 0.3 before the item is said to belong to the factor or component.

Where a variable has an acceptable loading on more than one component we will try to reduce one of these loadings (see rotation below) or say that it belongs to the component with the highest loading.

In Table 19.7 a confusing and unsatisfactory picture emerges. Six items load highly on both components. GREEN_ID loads on neither (this should not be surprising, since it has already been identified as a problem). Indeed this factor analysis does not really allow us to make much sense of the two components as there is so much overlap between them.

What is Rotation for?

At this point in the analysis it is common to *rotate* the solution to arrive at a clearer picture and to differentiate more clearly between the two components. Rotation is a procedure that often confuses people, and space precludes

Table 19.7   *Factor loadings on two unrotated factors*

	Component	
	1	2
GREENS	0.62	0.10
ENV_IMP	0.59	0.20
NUC-NEC	0.51	0.63
URAN	0.62	0.61
ENV_GRP	0.76	0.22
NUCL_GRP	0.65	0.14
NATURE	0.59	0.44
SPEND+	0.68	0.49
POLLUT	0.65	0.45
URAN_GRP	0.77	0.38
GREEN_ID	0.07	0.13

Extraction method: Principal components analysis.

Table 19.8   *Factor loadings on two rotated factors*

	Component	
	1	2
GREENS	0.44	0.45
ENV_IMP	0.60	0.19
NUC-NEC	0.04	0.82
URAN	0.14	0.86
ENV_GRP	0.74	0.27
NUCL_GRP	0.44	0.50
NATURE	0.73	0.00
SPEND+	0.83	0.01
POLLUT	0.78	0.02
URAN_GRP	0.40	0.77
GREEN_ID	−0.03	0.15

Extraction method: principal components analysis. Rotation method: varimax with Kaiser normalization.

a proper discussion of the concept here. There are a number of different methods of rotation and some guidance for selecting between these methods is provided below.

The effect of rotating should be to make some items load more clearly on one component than on the other and thus make the true content of the components more obvious. Table 19.8 provides the factor loadings for both the components after rotation. The solution is a little clearer, with some items clearly belonging to component 1 and some belonging to factor 2. However, other items are still loading on both components and item GREEN_ID loads on neither.

What to do if the Factor Analysis does not 'Work'

Since this is not a very satisfactory factor solution, the next step is to redo the factor analysis taking into account what we have learned in the initial factor analysis. Various tests have indicated that item GREEN_ID should be dropped. There is also a case for dropping GREENS and ENV_IMP, since both have relatively low communality figures.

After redoing the factor analysis without these three items, a much clearer and more satisfactory picture develops. Table 19.9 contains the results of the factor analysis without the three troublesome items. The KMO values for the set of variables and each item are acceptable (Table 19.9a). Two components are extracted. However, these two components explain more of the variance in the remaining pool of items (64.59 per cent, compared to 53.56 per cent in the initial run). This indicates that this is probably a better factor solution (Table 19.9b).

In this unrotated solution two components (factors) have been identified but they are difficult to interpret (Table 19.9c). Components are considered interpretable when some items load and some items do not load on the component. Furthermore, items should load more on one component than on another. Clearly the factor solution here is not all that interpretable.

A varimax rotation provides a much clearer picture (Table 19.9d). This rotated solution distinguishes between the two components. There is almost no cross-loading. An examination of the actual items that load on each component also shows that the components are interpretable. Component 1 loads on general environmental concerns such as pollution, spending more on the environment, loving nature and supporting environmental groups. It can be characterized as a CONSERVation factor. Component 2 loads on views regarding whether nuclear energy is a necessity, support for the mining of uranium, attitudes to anti-war and anti-nuclear groups, and attitudes to groups opposing the mining and export of uranium. This can be characterized as a NUCLEAR factor.

How to Produce Scales from a Factor Analysis

Having identified that the initial 11 items can be reduced to eight, and that these eight items can be represented by two components, the next step is to create two variables to represent these components. Once these two variables are created they will replace the individual items in any further analysis.

Three main types of scales can be produced from a factor analysis:

- equal weighted factor based scales;
- weighted factor based scales;
- factor scales or component scales.

Table 19.9 *Tables for revised factor analysis*

(a) KMO values

	KMO values
NUC_NEC	0.76
URAN	0.70
ENV_GRP	0.86
NUCL_GRP	0.88
NATURE	0.88
SPEND+	0.79
POLLUT	0.81
URAN_GRP	0.79
Overall	0.80

(b) Eigenvalues and expalined variance

Component	Eigenvalue	Explained variance (%)	Cumulative (%)
1	3.50	43.71	43.71
2	1.67	20.87	64.59
3	0.73	9.16	73.75
4	0.57	7.10	80.85
5	0.48	6.03	86.88
6	0.44	5.44	92.33
7	0.36	4.51	96.84
8	0.25	3.16	100.00

(c) Unrotated component matrix

	Component 1	Component 2
NUC-NEC	0.52	0.63
URAN	0.64	0.61
ENV_GRP	0.74	−0.23
NUCL_GRP	0.65	0.13
NATURE	0.59	−0.46
SPEND+	0.67	−0.51
POLLUT	0.66	−0.47
URAN_GRP	0.78	0.37

Extraction method: principal components analysis

(d) Rotated component matrix

	Component 1	Component 2
NUC-NEC	−0.04	0.82
URAN	0.06	0.88
ENV_GRP	0.70	0.33
NUCL_GRP	0.39	0.53
NATURE	0.75	0.05
SPEND+	0.84	0.08
POLLUT	0.81	0.10
URAN_GRP	0.32	0.80

Extraction method: principal components analysis. Rotation method: varimax with Kaiser normalization

Equal Weighted Factor Based Scales

Using this approach, we simply use the information about which items belong to each factor to construct the scales. Each scale is created simply by summing the codes of individuals on these variables in the same way as Likert scales are produced.

Weighted Factor Based Scales

Weighted factor based scales are produced in the same way as equal weighted scales *except* that the selected items are weighted by the rotated factor loadings for each item. Thus for the NUCLEAR scale we multiply each person's score on the relevant variable by the variable's factor loading. The numerical expression in the section on SPSS below shows how to create a weighted factor based scales for the items selected in our example factor analysis.

Factor or Component Scales

Factor analysis programs produce new variables on request. These new variables contain a scale score for each person on each extracted factor. In this case component scales would be produced that would code each person on the NUCLEAR and the CONSERV scales.

How to Choose Between the Different Extraction and Rotation Methods

A confusing variety of extraction methods are available. Principal components analysis (PCA), used above, is distinguished from other extraction methods but the steps involved are the same; see Kim and Mueller (1978) or Tabachnick and Fidell (1983) for an explanation of the difference between PCA and factor analysis.

The most important decision is whether to use PCA or one of the various methods of extraction provided by 'real' factor analysis. This decision depends largely on the purpose of the analysis. Where you are wanting a summary of the data set for the purposes of data reduction (it is in this context that the method has been discussed here) then PCA is the preferred choice. If inferred, hypothetical factor solutions are required then factor analysis is preferred (Tabachnick and Fidell, 1983). The choice between the particular factor analysis extraction techniques takes us too far from the focus of this section and will not be discussed here (Kim and Mueller, 1978; Tabachnick and Fidell, 1983).

The practical reality is that, whatever extraction method is used, similar results are obtained. Where there are differences, these usually disappear after rotating the solution. One approach is to begin with PCA extraction and then try some of the factor analysis extraction methods to see whether these improve on the PCA solution. More often than not, PCA will provide as good a solution for data reduction purposes.

Types of Rotation

There are two broad types of rotation: *orthogonal* and *oblique*. Orthogonal rotation methods are used when we want to minimize any correlation between the factors. Where there is reason to expect that the factors could be correlated, an oblique method can be used.

Varimax rotation (an orthogonal method) is the most common rotation method employed. It tries to produce factors that are as simple as possible by maximizing the variance of the loadings across the items within factors. This leads to high loadings becoming higher and lower loadings declining. This makes it easier to see the items that belong to the factor.

The selection between rotation methods will often be a process of trial and error. Many researchers will experiment with different rotation methods to find the set of factors and the best representation of factors to fit the data. When the goal is data reduction, the best starting point is PCA with varimax rotation. If this does not yield a reasonable solution, try varying the rotation methods and then the extraction methods to arrive at the best solution.

Using SPSS

Obtaning a Principal Components Analysis with Varimax Rotation

Analyze ▾

    Data Reduction ▸

        Factor...

            Variables: select variables for analysis

            Descriptives...

            Statistics

                ☑ Initial solution

            Correlation matrix

                ☑ Coefficients

                ☑ KMO and Bartlett's test of sphericity (KMO for pool of items)

                ☑ Anti-image (the diagonal on the bottom half of this provides the item-specific KMO values)

                Continue

            Extraction...

                Method: Principal components ▾

                Analyze

                  ⊙ Correlation matrix

                Display

                  ☑ Unrotated factor solution

                Extract:

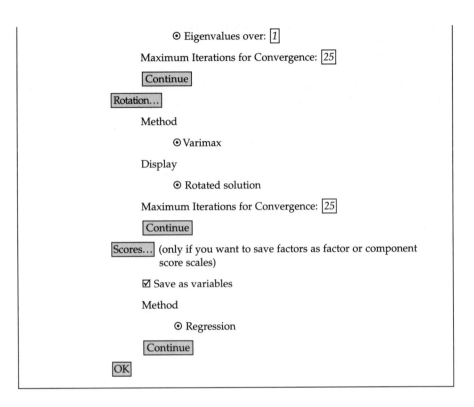

Constructing Scales

UNWEIGHTED FACTOR BASED SCALE (ASSUMING ALL ITEMS HAVE SAME NUMBER OF CATEGORIES)   Use the normal set of options to compute a new variable.

- The *target variable* will be the name of the new scale.
- The *numerical expression* will have the following form:

item1 + item2 + item3 + item4 + item5 ETC.

WEIGHTED FACTOR BASED SCALE   Use the normal set of options to compute a new variable.

- The *target variable* will be the name of the new scale.
- The *numerical expression* will have the following form:

(factor loading * item1) + (factor loading * item2) + (factor loading * item3) + (factor loading * item4) + (factor loading * item5) ETC.

For the NUCLEAR factor identified by the factor analysis the numerical expression would be

> (0.82 * NUC_NEC) + (0.88 * URAN) + (0.80 * URAN_GRP) + (0.52 * NUCL_GRP)

FACTOR/COMPONENT SCALES   Use the [Save] option in the menu selections when doing a factor analysis – see menus selections above.

20

What does it Mean to Generalize?

Nearly all social research is based on samples. Normally, sample-based research is used to make broader generalizations that are assumed to apply to people other than those cases included in the study. Some studies explicitly try to test whether the sample results can be generalized more widely, while others (by their failure to test whether results can be generalized) seem just to assume that the results apply more widely.

When we wish to generalize from a sample, four broad issues arise:

- What does it mean to generalize?
- Under what conditions can sample results be generalized beyond the sample?
- How broadly can sample results be generalized?
- How confidently can sample results be generalized?

There are two main types of generalization: statistical and theoretical.

What is the Difference Between Statistical and Theoretical Generalization?

What is Statistical Generalization?

Statistical generalization involves generalizing from a sample to a population. It relies on probability theory which enables us to estimate how likely patterns in a sample are to reflect real patterns in the population. Since statistical generalization is based on probability theory, it assumes that any sample from which such generalizations are made is a probability sample.

Inferential statistics are the tools used to establish whether sample results are likely to reflect patterns in the population. There are two broad types of inferential statistics used for this purpose: (1) point and interval estimates; and (2) tests of statistical significance.

POINT AND INTERVAL ESTIMATE STATISTICS   These estimate within what range of a sample estimate the true population parameter is likely to lie. This approach involves the use of sample errors, confidence intervals and confidence levels.

TESTS OF STATISTICAL SIGNIFICANCE   These tests provide a means of estimating how likely it is that the patterns in the sample are due simply to sampling error. We may find that two variables are correlated in a sample. Tests of significance help us estimate the chance that we would find such a relationship in a sample, even if there was no relationship between the variables in the population. There are many different tests of significance. Ways of selecting the appropriate tests are discussed in Problems 31 and 39.

What is Theoretical Generalization?

Theoretical generalization involves generalizing from a study to a theory, rather than to a population. It relies on the logic of replication. The logic of replication lies at the heart of experimental and case-study research (Yin, 1989; de Vaus, 2001b). Since experiments and case studies typically do not have randomly drawn samples or representative samples, they provide no *statistical* basis for generalizing to a wider population.

The logic of replication is that if the findings of an experiment or case study are found each time the experiment is repeated, then our confidence in the findings grows. If the patterns are repeated under a wide variety of conditions and with a wide variety of (non-probability) samples, then our confidence in the more general applicability of the results grows. By repeating the study we also discover the conditions and groups to which the results do not apply. Often the theory itself can alert us to the types of groups and conditions to which the findings will not apply. Replication under these conditions and finding that the theoretical predictions were correct provides further evidence in favour of the theory and helps define the scope of phenomena to which it applies.

In the remainder of this book, the discussion of generalization is limited to statistical generalization and assumes that results are based on probability samples.

What Factors Limit Statistical Generalization?

Two main factors limit the extent to which we can generalize beyond a sample.

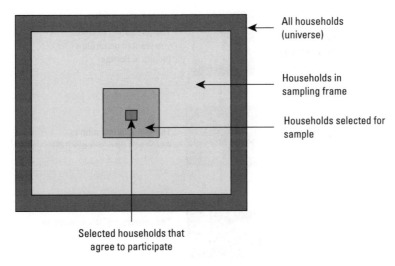

Figure 20.1 *An unbiased sample*

Sample Quality

The logic of statistical generalization requires that the:

- sample is *representative* of a wider *population*;
- wider population is properly defined;
- sample was drawn from the population using *probability sampling* methods.

Even where a sample is obtained using probability sampling methods, the ability of such sampling to produce a representative sample will depend on:

- the adequacy of the *sampling frame* from which the sample was drawn;
- any *bias* in response and non-response from selected *sample units*.

Figure 20.1 illustrates the concept of a representative sample. In this diagram the sampling frame (list of units in the population/universe) is unbiased – it has the same 'shape' as the population. The selected members of the sampling frame (sample units) are also an unbiased sample, and the participating sample members are representative of the selected sample units.

The sampling outcome in Figure 20.1 is the ideal. If each level were an exact mirror of the other levels, then generalization would be straightforward. If the final sample was an exact mirror of the population/universe then whatever patterns were found in the sample would reflect the patterns in the population.

However, the sample is extremely unlikely to be an exact mirror of the population because:

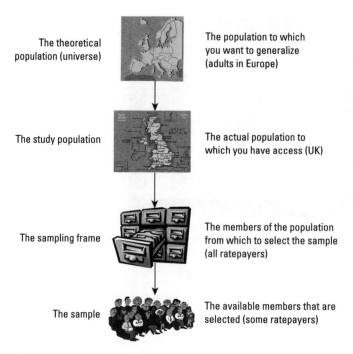

The theoretical population (universe) — The population to which you want to generalize (adults in Europe)

The study population — The actual population to which you have access (UK)

The sampling frame — The members of the population from which to select the sample (all ratepayers)

The sample — The available members that are selected (some ratepayers)

Figure 20.2 *From population to sample*

- bias will occur to the extent that the sample frame is not a good representation of the universe;
- sample units may not be correctly drawn from the sampling frame;
- refusals by sampling units may further bias the sample;
- even if the sampling frame were perfect, the sample were drawn correctly from the sampling frame and all selected units agreed to participate, the sample would still be subject to *sampling error*.

To the extent that sampling error occurs this must affect the capacity to generalize from the sample. We must acknowledge the likely margin of error to which any sample-based estimates are subject.

Sampling error is a function of two matters:

- The absolute size of the sample. Smaller samples are liable to greater sampling error.
- The degree of diversity in the population regarding the matter about which we wish to generalize. If the population were unanimous on some issue then any sample would reflect this and we could generalize accurately from a sample of one person. Where there is considerable population diversity the chances of sampling error increase, so any generalizations must acknowledge the likely margin of error.

Population

Since generalizing is all about extrapolating from sample patterns to population patterns, we must be clear about what is meant by *population*.

In sampling terms a population is the group to which the sample results are meant to apply. The population should be defined *before* drawing the sample. Figure 20.2 illustrates the steps in moving from a theoretical population or universe via a study population and a sampling frame to a sample. Inadequacies at any of these steps can limit the capacity to generalize backwards from the sample.

To generalize we must specify the characteristics of the population. This includes specifying the units in the population that are being sampled. Is it individuals, companies, families, households, institutions (e.g. schools)? Once the sampling unit is specified, we also need to spell out which of these units are included and excluded from the population definition. There are a number of questions that can help in this specification (Sudman, 1983). The following questions simply illustrate some of the matters that can help specify a population and thus define the boundaries of generalization:

- What are the geographical limits of the population?
- Assuming individuals are the sampling unit, what ages are included/ excluded?
- What demographic groups are excluded from the population definition?
- Does the population exclude non-citizens? Non-voters? Those living in institutions?...
- If families are the sampling unit, what is defined as a family?

21

How to Judge the Extent and Effect of Sample Bias

Why is Sample Bias a Problem?

Sample bias is always a potential problem in any sample-based research. Bias occurs when the characteristics of a sample are systematically different from those of the population. For example, if the sample is older, wealthier or healthier than the population then the sample has an age, wealth or health bias.

Bias is a problem because it:

- introduces errors when population estimates are being made from the sample;
- can distort relationships between variables within a sample.

Sample bias arises for one or more of the following reasons:

- selecting a study population that is not an adequate reflection of the theoretical population;
- having a biased sampling frame;
- biased non-response patterns. Certain types of people (e.g. poorer, less educated, the elderly) may decline to participate in the study or be uncontactable (*unit non-response*). Of those who do participate some types of people may decline to answer particular types of question (*item non-response*).

Since bias is always a possibility we need to establish at the data analysis stage whether:

- there is bias;
- any bias is affecting the results;
- any effect of bias can be eliminated.

How to Tell if the Sample is Biased

Establishing sample bias is not simply a matter of working out whether the sample is biased. It is a matter of testing for *particular* biases. A sample may be biased in some regards (e.g. age) but not others (e.g. gender).

Bias only exists in relation to a defined population. It is not an absolute. Therefore, sample bias can only be *established* by comparing the sample with characteristics of the sample's population. For general population surveys the best population figures will be obtained from census figures. Where these are out of date, estimates based on regular government surveys may be helpful.

For special samples population figures are sometimes available. The population census may be appropriate for subgroups (e.g. students, people in a particular geographic location). Other official records can provide population parameters. For example, a sample of students could be compared to official government statistics about the characteristics of students. If the survey was of students in a specific institution, the characteristics of that population of students may be available from official records.

However, it is not always possible to make population comparisons. Unfortunately, the population is often inadequately specified. But even when the population has been specified properly, its exact characteristics will be unknown. For example, if we had a sample of regular churchgoers, how would we know whether it was an unbiased sample? Unless we know the population characteristics of regular churchgoers (the distribution of gender, age, class, education, etc.) we cannot test for sample bias.

How to Tell if the Bias Matters

Where bias is identified and where it is suspected but cannot be established, we need to:

- work out whether the suspected bias affects results;
- take steps to reduce any such effect.

The simplest way to establish whether a possible bias on one sample characteristic is affecting results is to introduce the 'bias variable' into the analysis. This can be done in a variety of ways. The following discussion, which outlines how to test for the effect of possible bias, draws on concepts and methods that are discussed later in this book (problems 41 and 42). If the methods outlined below are difficult to follow at this stage, it may be better to return to this discussion when you are more familiar with these methods.

Table 21.1 *Gender distribution indicating sample bias*

	Frequency	(%)
Male	921	39.4
Female	1416	60.6
Total	2337	100.0

Table 21.2 *Attitudes to abortion*

		Frequency	(%)
Feelings about abortion	Whenever they want one	1138	49.9
	Only in special circumstances	920	40.3
	Should not be allowed	107	4.7
	Don't know	118	5.1
Total		2283	100.0

Table 21.3 *Approval of abortion by gender*

		Males (%)	Females (%)
Feelings about abortion	Whenever they want one	51.8	48.6
	Only in special circumstances	38.4	41.5
	Should not be allowed	4.2	5.0
	Don't know	5.6	4.9
Total		899	1384
		100.0%	100.0%

How to Test for the Effect of Bias on a Single Variable

Suppose that we have a sample in which there is a gender bias, as indicated in Table 21.1. Suppose that one of the purposes of a study is to report on attitudes to abortion, and we find that there is a higher level of support for abortion than we expected. We may be surprised at how few people say that abortion should not be allowed under any circumstances (Table 21.2).

Knowing that there is a gender bias in the sample, we hypothesize that the relatively pro-abortion stance of the sample is due to the overrepresentation of women. The implicit assumption here is that women are more pro-abortion than men. We can test whether the gender bias in the sample is responsible for the pro-abortion response pattern by examining the attitudes of men and women separately. Table 21.3 indicates that the attitudes of men and women are very similar, and thus the gender sample bias is not responsible

Table 21.4   *Church attendance by gender*

		Gender	
		Male	Female
Church	Irregular	74.3%	83.7%
attendance	Regular	25.7	16.3
N		1500	1500
		100%	100%

for the higher than expected level of support for abortion. Since men and women have similar attitudes regarding abortion, the gender bias simply does not matter for this part of the analysis.

How to Test for the Effect of Bias on a Relationship between Variables

A similar logic applies when examining relationships between variables. We can examine the simple relationship between two variables. If we suspect that the relationship might be due to a sample bias, we should proceed as follows:

1. Examine the relationship between the two variables (X and Y).
2. Select the biasing factor (call it variable Z) that we think might be influencing the relationship between X and Y.
3. Examine the relationship between X and Y within each category of the biasing variable.

The results of analysis to test for bias can be interpreted as follows:

- If the relationship between X and Y *remains* within each category of Z then the bias variable is *not* affecting the X–Y relationship.
- If the relationship between X and Y *disappears* within each category of Z then the bias variable *is* affecting the X–Y relationship.
- If the relationship between X and Y *declines but does not disappear* or it *increases* within each category of Z then the bias variable is *partly* affecting the X–Y relationship.

This can be illustrated with an example. Table 21.4 indicates that males are more regular church attenders than females (25.7% regular compared with 16.3% of females). This pattern seems odd because most research indicates that woman are either more or at least equally religious as men but never less religious. We suspect that this odd result might be due to a sample bias. We may have observed in some earlier analysis that there seem to be a lot

Table 21.5   *Church attendance by Gender by Age group*

			Gender	
			Male	Female
Young	Church attendance	Irregular	93.0%	93.0%
		Regular	7.0	7.0
	N		500	1000
			100%	100%
Elderly	Church attendance	Irregular	65.0%	65.0%
		Regular	35.0%	35.0%
	N		1000	500
			100%	100%

more older men than older women on the one hand and a lot more younger women than younger men. For some reason our sample seems to have a bias towards younger women and older men. We also know that in general older people seem to be more religious than younger people. We suspect, therefore that the surprising result of men being more religious than women might have something to do with the bias towards older men and younger women.

We can test this hypothesis by examining the relationship between church attendance and gender among just the young people and then just among the older people. If the original relationship between gender and church attendance is because a large proportion of the women are young (and therefore less religious) then if we just look at young men and women we should find the normal pattern (either no gender difference or women being more religious). Similarly, if the greater religiousness of men is just because there is an overrepresentation of older men in the sample then if we just look at older people there will be no gender difference in church attendance (or women will be more regular attenders).

Table 21.5 reports this analysis. The top part of the table is restricted to the younger members of the sample. Among this subset there are no gender differences in church attendance. The bottom part of the table shows the same analysis but for older people. Again, among older people, there is no gender difference in church attendance.

In other words, the original pattern reported in Table 21.4 is due to the overrepresentation of older men and of younger women. If these biases are removed by controlling for age (i.e. just looking at people of a similar age at the one time) the gender diffference in church attendance disappears.

Since the bias in this sample is affecting the results we would need to use methods of removing the influence of this bias from subsequent analysis. Methods of doing this are discussed in later sections (Problem 22 and the sections describing multivariate methods of analysis).

Partial Correlations

When dealing with interval-level variables (or dichotomous variables) the same logic can be pursued even more simply by using partial correlations. Partial correlations allow us to examine a relationship between two variables X and Y with the influence of a third variable removed. Partial correlations and their interpretation are discussed at length in Problems 41, 43 and 45.

The steps in using partial correlations to assess the effect of any potentially biasing variable are:

1. Obtain the simple correlation between X and Y (called a *zero-order correlation*).
2. Select the bias variable, the influence of which you want to evaluate.
3. Obtain the partial correlation between X and Y, controlling (partialling out) the effect of Z.
4. Compare the partial correlation with the initial zero-order correlation.

Once you have the two correlations it is a simple matter to interpret them:

- If the zero-order and partial correlation are much the same the bias variable is *not* responsible for the X–Y relationship.
- If the partial correlation is 0 (or close to 0) then the bias variable was responsible for the initial zero-order correlation between X and Y.
- If the partial correlation is substantially lower or higher than the zero-order correlation then the bias variable was affecting the initial relationship.

Multivariate Analysis

The same general logic can be applied in multivariate analysis. Where we suspect that particular sample biases may influence the core relationships we want to examine, we can remove these effects by statistically controlling for these variables and thus removing their effect from the analysis. These techniques are discussed in Problems 41–45, 47 and 49.

Using SPSS

Comparing Sample Characteristics with Population Characteristics

To compare against a single population characteristic use a frequency distribution:

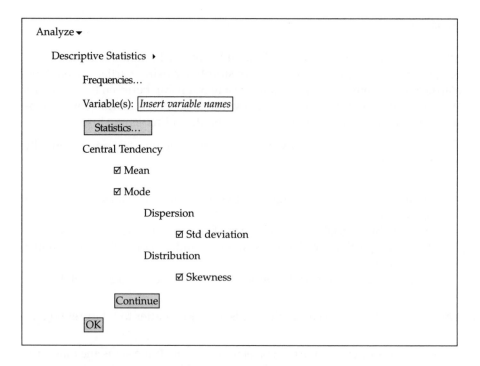

Testing for the Effect of a Bias Variable on a Relationship Between Two Variables

Two separate steps are required. First, examine the initial relationship between X and Y:

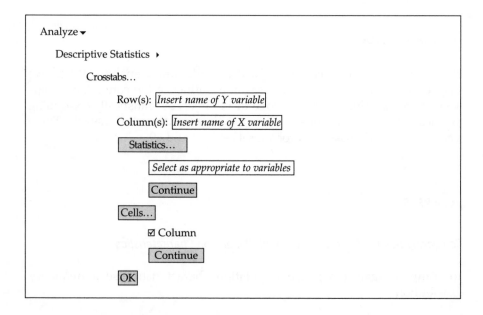

Then, examine the *X–Y* relationship separately within each category of the bias variable (Z).

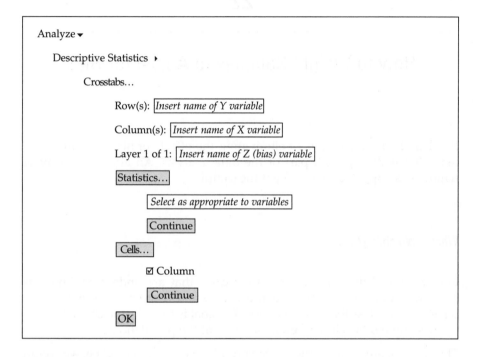

Partial Correlations

See Problem 45.

22

How to Weight Samples to Adjust for Bias

Problem 21 outlined ways of eliminating the effects of bias by statistically removing it during each part of the data analysis. An alternative way of removing sample bias is to weight the sample.

What is Weighting?

In effect, weighting involves counting cases that are underrepresented as being the equivalent of more than one case and counting overrepresented cases as worth less than a whole case. The goal is to make the characteristics of the sample more closely resemble those of the populations.

Thus if there are more women in the sample than there should be, we would count each woman as equivalent to less than one case for the purpose of any calculations. We would also count each man as equivalent to more than one case. This solution to sample bias assumes that men in the sample are representative of men in the population and that making each man count for more than one case will not introduce other biases.

There are different methods of weighting a sample, depending on whether we are weighting for a single variable or for several variables.

How to Weight to Adjust for Bias on a Single Variable

There are four main steps to weighting for a single variable:

1. Obtain the frequency distribution of the relevant variable for both the sample and the population. In the example in Table 22.1 we have a sample involving almost twice as many women as men, from a population in which men and women are equally represented.

Table 22.1 *Sample and population proportions for one variable*

	Sample	Population
Male	35%	50%
Female	65%	50%

2. Calculate weights for each category of the variable. Weights are obtained by:

$$\text{weight} = \frac{\text{Population}\%}{\text{Sample}\%}$$

For the variable in Table 22.1, males will be weighted by 50/35 = 1.43, and the corresponding weight for females will be 50/65 = 0.77.

3. Create a weight variable. The methods for creating the weight variable will vary between computer packages. Instructions for creating a variable called WT1 in SPSS are provided at the end of this section.
4. When running the data analysis apply the weight variable to give effect to the weighting. (See SPSS section for menu selections).

How to Weight for More than One Variable

There are two approaches to applying multiple weights:

- iterative weighting;
- one-step multiple weighting.

Using Iterative Weighting

Iterative weighting involves weighting for each variable sequentially. The weight for the first variable is applied, followed by the second, then the third and so on. In the following discussion two variables will be weighted. The procedure can easily be extended for additional variables simply by applying the same logic.

The steps for iterative weighting are as follows:

1. Calculate and apply the weight for the first variable as outlined above.
2. Select the second weighting factor (e.g. age) and obtain the relevant sample and population percentages for the categories of this variable (e.g. percentage under 40 and percentage aged 40 and over). The percentages for the sample should be obtained from the sample *after* the first weight has been applied.
3. Calculate the weights for the second variable in the same way as described earlier.

Table 22.2   *Sample and population proportions on three variables*

Sample (using total percentages)

	Male		Female	
	Young	Old	Young	Old
Low education	10%	20%	10%	15%
High education	15%	10%	10%	10%

Population (using total percentages)

	Male		Female	
	Young	Old	Young	Old
Low education	15%	10%	15%	10%
High education	15%	10%	15%	10%

4. Create a second weight variable (e.g. WT2). The instructions for creating this variable using SPSS are provided at the end of this section.

It is worth checking the outcome of any multiple reweighting to ensure that it has achieved the desired outcomes. One easy way of doing this is to crosstabulate the weighted variables (e.g. age and gender) and compare these with a crosstabulation of the same variables from the populations. The percentages in the crosstabulation of the sample should be very similar to those in the population crosstabulation.

Using One-step Multiple Weights

When reasonably large samples are available, multiple weighting can be accomplished in a single step. The more variables that are weighted for, the larger the sample needs to be.

One-step multiple weighting can be illustrated with the same two variables as used above plus a third variable (education level). For the sake of simplicity, each of the three variables has been dichotomized.

1. Obtain a crosstabulation of the three variables for which reweighting is required for both the sample and the population (see Table 22.2). These crosstabulations should use total percentages (i.e. the number of cases in each cell is expressed as a percentage of the whole sample) (p. 240).
2. Calculate weights for each cell by dividing the population percentage by the equivalent sample percentage:

Table 22.3   *Weights based on three variables*

	Male		Female	
	Young	Old	Young	Old
Low education	1.5	0.5	1.5	0.67
High education	1.0	1.0	1.5	1.0

$$\text{weight} = \frac{\text{Population\%}}{\text{Sample\%}}$$

This results in the weights in Table 22.3.

3. Create a weight variable (WT) in which the weights are applied (see SPSS section for SPSS instructions).
4. Apply the WT variable to weight the sample before using the sample (see below for SPSS instructions).

Using SPSS

Creating a Weight Variable to Weight for a Single Variable

Since the menu-based method of creating a weight variable can be tedious, I have provided the SPSS syntax commands instead. To use syntax commands, proceed as follows.

1. Create a new syntax file:

```
File ▾
   New ▸
        Syntax
```

2. Enter the syntax commands below (adapt according to your variables:

```
COMPUTE WT1 = 0.
IF (GENDER = 1) WT1 = 1.43.   (assumes that male is coded as 1)
IF (GENDER = 2) WT1 = 0.77.   (assumes that female is coded as 2)
```

When creating the WT1 variable it is initially set to 0 for all cases. The subsequent IF statements will convert this 0 to either 1.43 or 0.77 depending on the case's code for gender. All cases for whom we do not know their gender will automatically be given a weight of 0 and will effectively be dropped from the sample.

3. Block out the commands with the mouse. Then:

```
Run ▾
    Selection
```

Iterative Weighting for Multiple Variables

To weight for two variables using the iterative method:

1. Create and apply the weights using the first variable (e.g. gender).
2. Create a second weight variable which incorporates the first weight variable and then add weights for a second characteristic (e.g. age). The SPSS syntax commands to create the WT2 variable are:

```
COMPUTE WT2 = WT1.
IF (AGE = 1) WT2 = (WT1 * the weight that was calculated above for those under
40 years old). (1 = under 40).
IF (AGE = 2) WT2 = (WT1 * the weight that was calculated above for those aged
40 or over). (2 = 40 and over).
```

This second weight variable for age (WT2) should incorporate the WT1 (gender) and its weightings. It may help to explain what the IF statements are doing by explaining the logic of the first IF statement above.

*   The statement intially selects people under the age of 40 [IF (AGE = 1)].
*   Then, for each person, it initially assigns their weight on gender – the first weight variable (WT1) to the new weight variable (WT2). This is achieved with the WT2 = WT1 part of the statement. At this point all cases aged under 40 have a weight on WT2 that is the same as their weight on WT1.
*   This *initial* WT2 weight is then multiplied by the weight previously calculated for those aged under 40. This is achieved with the section of the IF statement that reads WT2 = WT1* *weight for under 40 year olds.*

The same steps are repeated for those aged 40 or over.

3. Run the syntax commands (see above).

Creating a One-step Multiple Weight

The following steps will create a weight variable for the Gender/Age/ Education example in Table 22.2.

1. Open a new syntax file (see above).
2. Type in the commands below (using the correct variable names and appropriate codes):

IF ((gender = *male*) and (age = *young*) and (educ = *low*)) WT = 1.5.
IF ((gender = *male*) and (age = *young*) and (educ = *high*)) WT = 1.
IF ((gender = *male*) and (age = *old*) and (educ = *low*)) WT = 0.5.
IF ((gender = *male*) and (age = *old*) and (educ = *high*)) WT = 1.
IF ((gender = *female*) and (age = *young*) and (educ = *low*)) WT = 1.5.
IF ((gender = *female*) and (age = *young*) and (educ = *high*)) WT = 1.5.
IF ((gender = *female*) and (age = *old*) and (educ = *low*)) WT = 0.67.
IF ((gender = *female*) and (age = *old*) and (educ = *high*)) WT = 1.

In this syntax the italicized values would be replaced with the numeric codes for these categories.

3. Run these commands (see above).

Applying the Weight

First create the weight variable using the instructions above. Then use the following menu selections:

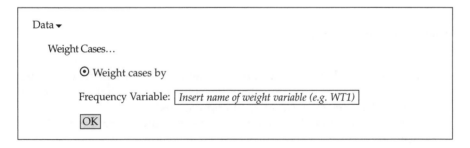

Data ▾

  Weight Cases…

    ⦿ Weight cases by

    Frequency Variable: | *Insert name of weight variable (e.g. WT1)* |

    OK

23

What are Tests of Significance?

What Problem are Significance Tests Designed to Address?

Typically the goal of research is to generalize results beyond the particular cases participating in the study. But how do we know when we can extrapolate from our sample? If 52 per cent of a sample indicate that they intend to vote for a particular political party, can we confidently say that 52 per cent of the population will vote this way? If the males in a sample earn $5000 more than the females, is this likely to be true of the population? How confidently can we apply our sample findings to the population?

Tests of statistical significance are a widely used method for addressing these questions. However, the method is not without its problems. Problems 24 and 25 examine some of the criticisms of tests of significance and ways of avoiding these misuses.

However, a clear understanding of the logic of significance tests is required before the criticisms and solutions make much sense.

What are Significance Tests?

- Tests of statistical significance are a subset of a wider category of statistics called *inferential statistics*. Inferential statistics are designed to assist in making inferences from samples to populations.
- Inferential statistics tell us *nothing* about the nature of patterns within a sample.
- Significance tests indicate the probability that results found in a sample are due to sampling error, or reflect patterns in the population from which the sample is drawn.

There is a wide range of tests of significance. Later sections will explain the difference between the different tests and when to use one rather than another (Problem 39).

What is a Null Hypothesis and how does it Relate to Significance Tests?

To make sense of tests of significance, you have to understand the concept of the null hypothesis. In some respects the null hypothesis is a bizarre concept that appears to be based on double negatives and designed to confuse people. In fact the logic of using null hypotheses reflects a conservative approach to scientific generalization.

In brief, a null hypothesis is:

- a statement of a pattern we *assume* exists in the population;
- a hypothesis that we seek to *reject*.
- normally the converse of the *substantive hypothesis* – the pattern we *expect*.

The logic of null hypothesis testing requires that we begin by *assuming* a particular pattern in the population. This pattern will be the opposite to that which we *expect* (on the basis of theory, etc.) to find.

Normally this assumption will be that variables are unrelated in the population – that groups do *not* differ from one another, that two variables are not related, etc. When we expect the absence of patterns, differences or relationships this is presented symbolically as $H_0 = 0$.[1]

With this starting point in mind, data are collected from a sample. These sample data are analysed with a view to checking whether the null hypothesis of no relationship fits the sample. Suppose we wanted to see if gender is related to marital satisfaction. Marital satisfaction is measured on a scale of 0 to 10, where a high score indicates a high level of marital satisfaction. Are men more satisfied with their marriage than are women? We can calculate the average level of marital satisfaction of men and of women.

The null hypothesis would be that there is no difference in the levels of marital satisfaction of men and women. That is, the difference in the male and female means will be 0. On analyzing the data from a sample we learn that men have an average of 7.5 on the scale, while women average 6.3. That is, the difference in means is 1.2.

We now have a 'problem'. We *assumed* a difference between men and women of 0, but have *observed* a difference of 1.2. How can we account for this discrepancy? There seem to be two options:

- *The sample data are wrong.* These data are misleading and do not provide any basis to revise our original assumption that the difference in satisfaction is 0.
- *The initial assumption is wrong.* The difference between male and female marital satisfaction means in the population is *not* zero.

If the first explanation is accepted, the reasoning is that the nature of the sample is such that sampling error (chance) could produce a misleading sample. By attributing the discrepancy between the null hypothesis of a zero difference and an observed sample difference of 1.2 to sampling error we *fail to reject the null hypothesis*. We continue to work on the *assumption* that the mean difference in the population is 0.

We must be very clear what it means to fail to reject the null hypothesis (forgive the confusing use of double and triple negatives, but this is the language of null hypothesis testing). Failing to reject the null hypothesis does *not* mean that:

- the null hypothesis is *proven*;
- the opposite to the null hypothesis (the substantive hypothesis that the sample difference of 1.2 reflects a real difference between men and women in the population) is wrong.

Failure to reject the null hypothesis simply means that we cannot rule out the chance that the differences between men and women in the sample could be due to sampling error.

If the second explanation is correct (i.e. the assumption of no difference is wrong) we should reject the null hypothesis. Since the null hypothesis is that $H_0 = 0$, rejecting it means that there is a good chance that in the population the male–female difference in marital satisfaction is something other than zero. Indeed, there is a good chance that a difference as great as we have observed in the sample exists in the population.

How to Decide to Accept or Reject the Null Hypothesis

Which of these alternative explanations should we accept? The choice is traditionally made on the basis of probability theory. When a probability sample is drawn from a population it is possible to estimate the probability of obtaining a discrepant sample – that is, a sample that does not mirror population patterns. Thus we can estimate the chance of obtaining a sample in which there *is* a difference between men and women even though they exhibit *no* difference in the population. For example, if the men and women in the population have the same level of marital satisfaction how many samples from that population would produce a male–female difference of at least 1.2?

For many years a magical cut-off point has been used to decide at what point the null hypothesis is rejected. Traditionally researchers have said that the null hypothesis should only be rejected if very few samples would produce the observed results because of sampling error. The precise cut-off point has varied a little but the 5 per cent (0.05) level is frequently applied. In larger samples the 1 per cent level often is applied.

What does it mean to apply the 5 per cent level? Using the example above of a difference of 1.2 points, if 100 samples were drawn from the same population in which there was *no* difference, how many samples would nevertheless produce a difference of at least 1.2 points? The 5 per cent level means that five out of 100 comparable samples could result in such a misleading finding of at least 1.2 points' difference. If our sample has found a difference of 1.2 it *could* be one of those five misleading samples.

When we say that a sample could produce a pattern that does not exist in its population we are describing *sampling error*. Clearly, the less likely it is that sampling error is responsible for the observed sample pattern the more confident we can be that the sample finding reflects something real in the population – the more confidently we can reject the null hypothesis.

As indicated earlier, researchers have traditionally used the 5 per cent or 1 per cent levels for rejecting the null hypothesis. If the probability (of sampling error) is *less* than this critical point, then researchers have taken their chances that their sample is probably not one of the faulty samples – there is at least a 95 per cent (or 99 per cent) chance that their sample reflects something real from the population.

- If we observed a difference of 1.2 points in a sample and the likelihood of this being due to sampling error was one in 100 we would report this mean difference of 1.2 points as being *statistically significant* at the 1 per cent level. The null hypothesis of no difference would be rejected.
- If there was a chance of four in 100, we would report the correlation as being statistically significant at the 4 per cent level. The null hypothesis would be rejected (assuming 5 per cent the critical cut–off).
- If there was a six in 100 chance of sampling error, the difference between male and female means would be reported as not statistically significant and the null hypothesis would *not* be rejected.

Using these probabilities is a cautious approach to research. All that failing to reject the null hypothesis means is that we cannot rule out the chance that the correlation we have observed *could* be due to sampling error. Unless we can very confidently rule out sampling error as an explanation of the sample findings we will assume that there is insufficient support for the substantive hypothesis.

The Use of Tests of Significance

The only use of a test of significance is to provide an estimate of the likelihood that a particular sample result differs from an assumed population level due to sampling error. The significance test provides an estimate of the probability of sampling error. Where the probability of sampling error is *less* than a set level (e.g. 5 per cent or 1 per cent) the probability of sampling error is usually considered too low to worry about so the null hypothesis (of no relationship in the population) is rejected.

The rejection of a null hypothesis lends support to the substantive hypothesis – that a difference between groups, a correlation or some other pattern at least as substantial as found in the sample, is likely to exist in the population.

Should One-tailed or Two-tailed Significance Tests be Used?

Tests of significance come in two flavours: one-tailed and two-tailed. Since many statistics packages provide the option it is important to know what the difference is.

Choosing between one- and two-tailed tests depends on the nature of the substantive hypothesis being tested. We can distinguish between directional and non-directional hypotheses.

Non-Directional Hypotheses

Non-directional hypotheses predict that the sample value will simply be statistically different from a particular value. For example, we might anticipate that men and women will have different levels of marital satisfaction without predicting in which direction the difference will be – whether men or women will be more satisfied. We might predict that age and prejudice will be correlated without knowing whether older people will be less or more prejudiced than younger people. When your substantive hypothesis is non-directional, use a two-tailed test.

Directional Hypotheses

A directional hypothesis predicts an effect (correlation, difference between means of groups, etc.) *and* states the nature of the difference – that the correlation will be positive, that group A will have a higher mean than group B (or whatever the predicted direction is). One-tailed tests are used for testing directional hypotheses.

Notes

1 The null hypothesis does not have to be that $H_0 = 0$. As Cohen (1994) points out, we could begin with a proposition derived from a theory or previous research that specifies a correlation of a particular size and direction. In the Popperian tradition of trying to falsify a theory, this hypothesis would be the null hypothesis that we tried to reject.

24

Should Tests of Significance be Used?

In Problem 23 I outlined the logic and purpose of tests of statistical significance. These tests are widely used, but are not without their problems. Indeed, the problems with and misuse of these tests have given rise to considerable debate and led to calls to abandon the use of tests of significance altogether (Labovitz, 1970, 1971; Selvin, 1957; Carver, 1978; Morrison and Henkel, 1970).

Here I will highlight some of the problems with using tests of significance, to encourage you to use and interpret them appropriately.

What to Check for Before Using Significance Tests

Is the Sample a Probability Sample?

Earlier I described the links between samples and populations (p. 151). This distinction is important since tests of significance are designed to help generalize from samples to populations.

Tests of significance allow us to generalize from a sample to a population by providing estimates of the probability that a sample result is due to sampling error. These estimates of sampling error are only possible if the samples are drawn using probability sampling methods.

It makes no sense to use tests of significance when using non-probability samples. Since sampling error cannot be estimated for a non-probability sample, it is not possible to calculate the likelihood of a sample result from a non-probability sample being due to sampling error. Where non-probability samples are used, researchers should rely on the logic of replication, rather than on statistical generalization using significance tests (pp. 147–8), (Cohen, 1994; Carver, 1993; Kirk, 1996). Despite this, the journals – especially psychology journals – are full of articles reporting results from studies that use non-probability samples. It is hardly any wonder, therefore, that some of the most trenchant critics of the use of tests of significance have come from psychological researchers who see such widespread misuse of these tests (Cohen 1990, 1994; Carver, 1978, 1993; Rozeboom, 1960).

Table 24.1   *Defining Type I and Type II error*

		Population	
		H_0 is true	H_0 is not true
Decision	Accept H_0		**Incorrectly fail to reject H_0** **TYPE II ERROR**
	Reject H_0	**Incorrectly reject H_0** **TYPE I ERROR**	

Are the Data from a Sample or a Census?

A census collects data from a complete population rather than from a sample of the population. Since significance tests are designed to estimate whether sample estimates are likely to reflect population patterns, it makes no sense to use tests of significance when using population data. Whether the population is the population of a country or a much more limited population (club, organization, occupational group, school, etc.), a study that is a census of that population should not use tests of statistical significance.

Can 'Significant' Results Obtained from Data Dredging be Relied On?

A significance level of 5 per cent in a sample does *not* mean that the two variables are related in the population. It simply means that it is *likely*. There is still a 5 per cent chance that the sample is misleading. Five out of 100 samples could still produce a result that does not hold in the population. Suppose we had 100 variables, and none of them were related in the population. If we correlated these 100 variables with each other we would obtain 10 000 correlations. Scanning through these 10 000 correlations, 500 would show up as statistically significant simply due to sampling error.

This fact warns against data dredging analysis – simply looking for statistically significant results and then trying to make something of them.

If an analysis of the relationship between two variables, on the basis of a sample, produces a significant result at the 5 per cent level, it does *not* mean that the two variables are related for the population. It simply means that this is *likely*.

What Type of Error to Avoid: Type I or Type II?

Using cut-off points such as 5 per cent or 1 per cent to reject the null hypothesis is conventional but arbitrary. Whatever cut-off point is used, we are always in danger of making one of two types of error. These two types of error have quite imaginatively been designated Type I and Type II (Table 24.1).

TYPE I ERRORS   Rejecting the null hypothesis means that the sample patterns are strong enough for us to reject the assumption of no difference or no relationship in the population. In other words, we accept that the sample figures are telling us about something real rather than simply being sampling error noise.

However, we may be mistaken in rejecting the null hypothesis and accept the reliability of the sample figures too readily. We may mistakenly reject the null hypothesis when in fact it is true. To mistakenly reject the null hypothesis is called a *Type I error*. Type I errors can occur when we set a high cut-off point (often called the *alpha level*). Thus if we set the critical cut-off point at 5 per cent rather than 1 per cent, there would be a greater chance of making a Type I error.

The way to avoid mistakenly rejecting the null hypothesis is to set a tougher cut-off point – for example, 1 per cent rather than 5 per cent. If we set the cut-off point at 0.1 per cent (one chance in 1000) we would all but eliminate the danger of a Type I error.

TYPE II ERRORS   The problem with the strategy of setting a very tough alpha level is that we run into the opposite problem – we *fail* to reject the null hypothesis when we should reject it. That is, we continue to assume that the null hypothesis (i.e. no relationship) holds when, in reality there is a relationship in the population. Too tough an alpha level can deafen us to the message that the sample is sending us.

We may miss important findings by being too tough. Failing to reject (i.e. accepting) the null hypothesis when we should have rejected it is a *Type II error*. Type II error is caused by being too ready to attribute sample findings to sample error – by having too low a cut-off point for rejecting the null hypothesis.

What Cut-off Point to Use

One reason why tests of statistical significance have been roundly criticized is the rigid use of cut-off points. The use of 5 per cent or 1 per cent levels to decide whether two variables are related, two groups are different, etc. uses the concept of sampling error in a very black and white way. Why do we say that a 5 per cent chance of sampling error is acceptable but a 6 per cent chance is not? These cut-off points are purely conventional and ought to be used with judgment. There seems to be a strong case for treating significance levels as a continuum rather than in terms of a simple significant/not significant dichotomy. It makes more sense to report the actual significance level so that the reader can make a judgment based on the probability of sampling error. An alternative is not to use significance levels at all but to report confidence intervals instead (Problem 27).

What does Significance Mean?

It is unfortunate that the word 'significance' has been linked to the process of testing for the probability that results may be due to sampling error. Naming these tests has led to their widespread abuse. *Statistical* significance is widely taken to mean *substantive* significance or importance.

Statistical significance simply tells us something about the likelihood of results being attributable to sampling error. The likelihood of sampling error is substantially (but not solely) a function of sample size. In large samples it is quite common to obtain statistically significant results for very trivial relationships (pp. 175–8). The fact that a relationship is strong and statistically significant does not mean that it is important. Problem 25 discusses these matters in more detail, but the key point to stress at this stage is that the significance level of a finding tells us *nothing* about its strength, importance or anything other than the likelihood of sampling error.

Whenever you use significance tests, take care always to use the term *statistical significance*, and avoid shortening it to *significance*. Whenever anyone reports that something had a significant effect, always ask *how much* effect it had.

Some Guidelines

The solution to the misuse of significance tests is not to abandon them but to use them properly. They are a useful *guide* in the task of generalization which, in the end, is the goal of research. The following guidelines can help reduce some of the dangers of using tests of statistical significance.

- Limit their use to probability samples.
- Use the term *statistical* significance, rather than just significance, when referring to the results of tests of significance.
- Always use tests of statistical significance together with appropriate descriptive statistics that provide an indication of the magnitude of an effect (p. 178).
- Take note of and report sample size when using tests of significance (p. 178–9).
- Use low significance levels (such as 1 per cent or 0.1 per cent) for large samples to avoid meaningless and trivial results being statistically significant. This should reduce the problem of Type I errors when using large samples.
- Do not blindly rely on critical cut-off levels such as 5 per cent. Report the actual probability level and consider using confidence intervals (Problem 27).
- Avoid data dredging analysis where all possible relationships are examined in the hope of some significant relationships turning up.
- Most of all, do not let tests of statistical significance substitute for *thinking* about and *looking* at results thoroughly.

25

What Factors Affect Significance Levels?

Do Significance Levels Indicate Anything about the Strength of Relationships?

Researchers often use tests of significance to make claims about the nature of a relationship, the extent of differences between groups or the magnitude of an effect. That is, tests of significance have been used to *describe* patterns in the sample rather than to *infer* from the sample to the population. It is still not uncommon to come across studies that report significance levels of 0.01 per cent and conclude mistakenly from this very low significance level that there exists a strong relationship or a substantial effect of one variable on another.

Tests of significance provide an estimate of the probability that a pattern in a sample is due to sampling error. They tell us *nothing* more than this, and certainly indicate nothing about the nature of relationships.

The probability levels of any sample result are a function of three main factors:

- the sample size;
- the diversity within the population;
- the 'effect magnitude'.

Since the probability level is affected by *three* factors it is not possible to draw unambiguous conclusions about the *nature* of any correlation, difference between groups or effect from the probability level alone. The only thing that a low probability level indicates is that whatever effect has been found in the sample is substantial enough to be not due to sampling error. Low probability levels indicate nothing about the strength, direction or importance of any relationship. To be useful, probability levels need to be used in conjunction with descriptive statistics such as correlation coefficients so that we can get a sense of the nature and extent of the relationship.

What do Correlations Reveal about Significance Levels?

On the other hand, the size of a correlation coefficient only tells us about the relationship between two variables *in a sample*. A correlation of 0 means that the two variables are unrelated and a correlation of 1.0 means that the two variables are perfectly related (p. 272). The higher the correlation, the stronger the relationship. On its own a correlation coefficient indicates *nothing* about the existence of the relationship in the population. Tests of significance and the associated probability levels are required to make such inferences. To be useful, a correlation coefficient needs to be accompanied by a test of statistical significance.

It is also important to know the sample size on which any correlation coefficient is based since sample size provides an important context in which to 'read' a correlation. There are three reasons why knowing the sample size is useful:

- Strong correlations are easier to obtain in small samples than in large samples.
- Strong correlations will often not be statistically significant in small samples.
- A strong correlation in a small sample may be statistically non-significant, while a much weaker correlation in a large sample may be statistically significant.

Table 25.1 enables us to explore the links between probability levels, the size of correlations and the sample size. This table provides correlations between a number of variables and reports the correlations for the same variables from four random samples consisting of 1500, 60, 30 and 15 cases. It illustrates a number of points about the interrelationship of sample size, correlation size and probability levels.

- The correlations in the large sample of 1500 are nearly all statistically significant.
- Almost no relationships in the small samples were statistically significant. This is because small samples are subject to high degrees of sampling error.
- In the large sample even very low correlations (as low as 0.06) are statistically significant.
- Similar sized correlations that are statistically significant with the large sample are not significant for the smaller samples. This is because with smaller samples the likelihood of sampling error is higher. For example, the correlation between education and church attendance is 0.08 for samples of size 1500 and 30. The correlation is statistically significant in the large sample but not in the small sample.

Table 25.1 *Effect of sample size on Pearson correlations and significance levels*

	Gender				Income				Freq. of church attendance			
	1500	60	30	15	1500	60	30	15	1500	60	30	15
Education					0.38^{***}	0.47^{**}	0.44^{ns}	0.80^{*}	0.08^{**}	-0.06^{ns}	-0.08^{ns}	0.23^{ns}
Age	0.08^{**}	0.11^{ns}	-0.25^{ns}	-0.09^{ns}	0.18^{***}	0.25^{ns}	0.62^{**}	-0.14^{ns}	0.13^{**}	0.12^{ns}	0.08^{ns}	0.24^{ns}
Job prestige	0.01^{ns}	-0.11^{ns}	-0.03^{ns}	-0.35^{ns}	0.41^{***}	0.46^{**}	0.51^{*}	0.50^{ns}	0.06^{*}	-0.08^{ns}	-0.16^{ns}	0.30^{ns}

*** = significant at < 0.001 level; ** = significant at < 0.01 level; * = significant at < 0.05 level; ^{ns} = not significant at 0.05 level

Table 25.2   *Relationship between correlation strength, significance level and sample size*

		Correlation is	
		Low	High
Relationship may be statistically	Not significant	Sample could be either small or large	
	Significant	Large sample	Sample could be either small or large

- A high correlation in a small sample may not be statistically significant, while a low correlation in a large sample may be significant. For example, the correlation between church attendance and job prestige is 0.06 in the sample of 1500 and 0.30 in the sample of 15. The weak correlation of 0.06 is statistically significant, while the stronger one of 0.30 is not significant.
- There is a tendency to find higher correlations among the smaller samples than among the larger samples.

What Information to Report when Using Significance Levels

What conclusions can be drawn from these observations about the inter-relationships between sample size, correlation size and probability levels?

The most important conclusion is that all three figures should be reported together. Probability levels need to be read in the context of sample size and the strength of the correlation. Correlation coefficients must be read in the context of the sample size and the significance level. Table 25.2 shows how the three sets of information – correlation, significance level and sample size – can interact.

The critics of significance tests have called for the reporting of *effect sizes* or *effect magnitude statistics* with significance tests. This is excellent advice. Reporting effect sizes and probability levels together helps avoid the confusion between statistical significance and substantive significance (p. 174). The effect size will indicate whether or not the statistically significant relationship is trivial or substantial.

For those not familiar with effect sizes and effect magnitude statistics, these terms are simply different labels for those descriptive statistics that indicate the extent and nature of differences between groups, correlations between variables and so forth. Many different measures of effect magnitude are available (Kirk, 1996; Wilkinson and Task Force on Statistical Inference, 1999). The common correlation coefficients such as Pearson's correlation (reported in Table 25.1), gamma, Cramér's *V*, and Spearman's correlation are correlational versions of effect magnitude (Problem 36). Regression coefficients indicate effect magnitude by reporting the strength and direction of any effect (Problem 37). Mean differences are measures of effect magnitude. Cohen's *d* and many other statistics are available and outlined in Kirk (1996).

Summary

A number of generalizations can be made about the links between sample size, probability level and effect magnitude.

- The larger the sample, the less the sampling error. Other things being equal, a lower probability level will be obtained as the sample size increases.
- The greater the effect magnitude in the sample (e.g. the higher the correlation), the less likely this effect will be due to sampling error. Other things being equal, weak correlations are more likely than stronger correlations to be due to sampling error.
- A strong effect magnitude in a large sample is relatively unlikely to be due to sampling error. This is because obtaining a strong correlation in the sample when there is no correlation in the population requires a very large degree of sampling error. Substantial sampling error is unlikely in large samples.
- A strong effect magnitude in a small sample could be due to sampling error. This is because there is a considerable chance of substantial sampling error in small samples.
- A very weak effect in a large sample often will not be attributable to sampling error. This is because large samples are subject to low sampling error. Therefore if the chance of sampling error is very low then even the slightest effect may not be attributable to sampling error.
- A weak effect in a small sample is likely to result in statistical significance.

26

Is the Sample Large Enough to Achieve Statistical Significance?

Problem 25 identified three important matters regarding the links between sample size, the size of relationships and statistical significance:

- It is more difficult to obtain statistically significant relationships with small samples than with larger samples.
- Even substantial relationships can be statistically non-significant in small samples.
- Trivial relationships can be statistically significant in large samples.

These observations create practical problems for the researcher. If we only anticipate a modest relationship, this may be attributed to sampling error in a small sample even though it might actually exist in the population. A study must be *capable* of detecting a relationship. A study that has too small a sample to detect the expected relationship lacks *power* and is pretty much pointless.

Suppose that we had reason to expect that men will, on average, score two points higher than women on a marital satisfaction scale that ranges from 0 to 10. If we conducted a study based on 30 cases and found that we were correct – men did score two points higher than women – would the difference be statistically significant? Or would the tests of significance attribute this observed difference to sampling error?

What is needed is a way of determining how large a sample needs to be to give us a reasonable chance of detecting a relationship in the population, should one exist. Power analysis provides a way of calculating the sample size that would be required in order to achieve statistical significance if a hypothesized effect[1] is found in the sample. That is, we ask the question: *if* X and Y really do have a correlation of Z (or group 1 and group 2 differ by Z), then how large a sample would be required for such a result to be reasonably likely to be statistically significant (i.e. not due to sampling error)?

What Factors Affect Achieving Statistical Significance?

Although I have emphasized the importance of sample size, there are five factors that affect whether a particular finding will be statistically significant:

- The sample size.
- The effect size.
- The significance level that is set.
- Whether a one-tailed or two-tailed test (p. 170) is used.
- The level of variation in the population. The greater the variation, the larger the sample needs to be to avoid sampling error.

How to Achieve a Balance between Type I and Type II Errors

One function of power analysis is to ensure that the sample size is large enough to avoid Type II errors (failing to reject an incorrect null hypothesis). However, avoiding Type II errors by increasing the sample size exposes us to Type I errors – rejecting a correct null hypothesis (pp. 172–3). This is more likely in large samples where even the most trivial effects are statistically significant.

This means that the goal of a power analysis must be to establish a sample size that is large enough, but not too large. We must establish the optimal power of a study – to establish a reasonable chance of detecting effects (rejecting H_0) but not of detecting trivial effects and not committing a Type I error (rejecting H_0 when we should not have done so).

Achieving this optimal balance is done by specifying a power for the study. This can be set anywhere between 0 and 1. If it is set at 1 then any result would be statistically significant. Normally the power of a study will be set between 0.8 and 0.9. This means that there will be an 80–90 per cent chance of finding a relationship if there really is one. Setting the power of the study much higher exposes us too much to Type I error.

How to Conduct a Power Analysis

Power analysis should be conducted before collecting data, or at least before analyzing the data. To calculate the desirable sample size using power analysis, a number of pieces of information are required:

- the expected effect size;
- the degree of variance in the population;
- the required power of the study;
- a specified significance level;
- the directional or non-directional nature of the anticipated effect.

The first two of these – expected effect size and population variance – often are unknown.

How to Specify the Effect Size in the Population

There are three main ways of estimating a population effect size for the purposes of power analysis.

- Rely on previous research and use this as the best estimate.
- Undertake a pilot study.
- Establish what effect would be substantively or theoretically worth detecting. The analysis then focuses on developing a study that can detect an effect of that level *if it exists in the population*.

The simplest way of explaining how to conduct a power analysis is to use examples. In the two examples below I have varied the elements that affect the required sample size so that the impact of these factors becomes clear. The calculations below were obtained using a specially designed computer package called PASS (see below).

Role of Effect Size and Variation on Sample Size

Research question: Do men and women express different levels of marital satisfaction?

Null hypothesis: Men and women express the same levels of marital satisfaction.

Substantive hypothesis: (two-tailed): Men and women express different levels of marital satisfaction.

Substantive hypothesis (one-tailed): Men express greater marital satisfaction than women.

Scale: Marital satisfaction is measured on a scale of 0 to 10. The more satisfied with marriage, the higher the score.

Analysis: Test for mean *differences* between men and women on the 0 to 10 marital satisfaction scale. This will involve a two-sample *t* test (pp. 296–7).

The results of a power analysis of this scenario are provided in Table 26.1:

- I have assumed that the mean for women will be 7, and then asked for estimates of samples size required if men had a mean of 7.5, 8.0 or 8.5.
- In each case I have set a power of 0.8, an alpha of .05 and a standard deviation in each group of 1.
- The columns N1 and N2 report on the sample size required to detect male–female differences of 0.5, 1 and 1.5, respectively.

Table 26.1 *Power analysis of mean differences*

Two-Sample T-Test Power Analysis

1 = female;

- n1 = female sample size,
- Mean1 = female mean on marital satisfaction,
- s2 = female standard deviation on marital satisfaction scale]

2 = male;

- n2 = male sample size,
- Mean2 = male mean on marital satisfaction,
- s2 = male standard deviation on marital satisfaction scale]

Numeric Results for Two-Sample T-Test

- Null Hypothesis: Mean1 = Mean2.
- Substantive Hypothesis: Mean1 < > Mean2 [i.e. two tailed test]
- The standard deviations were assumed to be known and equal.

Power	N1	N2	Alpha	Beta[a]	Mean1	Mean2	S1	S2
0.801	63	63	0.05	0.20	7.0	7.5	1.0	1.0
0.807	16	16	0.05	0.20	7.0	8.0	1.0	1.0
0.801	7	7	0.05	0.20	7.0	8.5	1.0	1.0

[a] Beta = 1-power

- Given these parameters, the results indicate that we would need only 7 males and 7 females to have an 80 per cent chance of detecting a difference as large as 1.5 points *if such a difference existed in the population.*
- If the male–female difference in marital satisfaction were only 0.5, a sample of 63 males and 63 females would be able to detect such a difference *if it existed in the population.*
- A larger sample size is required to detect a smaller effect.
- S1 and S2 are the population standard deviations (p. 224). These statistics represent the variability in the populations. The more variability on the variable being measured (marital satisfaction) the larger the sample required (see below).

The statistics provided in Table 26.1 can also be displayed as graphs (Figure 26.1).

THE EFFECT OF VARIANCE Figure 26.2 provides the same type of analysis as Figure 26.1 except that scenarios have been included for different amounts of variation. This figure shows how the required sample size increases when the assumed population variation (indicated by the standard deviation) increases. For a small effect size of 0.5 points and a high degree of variation (3 standard deviations) a sample of 566 is required for each group (i.e. 566 males and 566 females) to provide a power of 0.80. However, if the variation is assumed to be 2 standard deviations the required sample size for each group drops to about 250 per group. Under the assumption of a relative homogeneity in

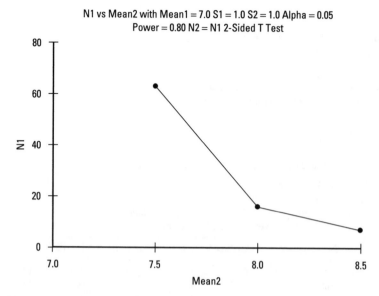

Figure 26.1 *Power analysis for mean differences using the same parameters as Table 26.1*

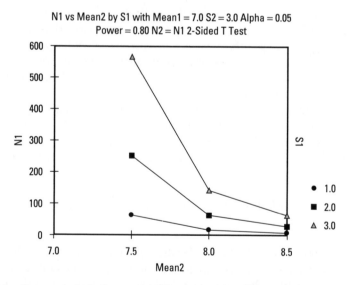

Figure 26.2 *Power analysis for mean differences using different variation assumptions*

the population (1 standard deviation) the required sample size for each group drops to 63.

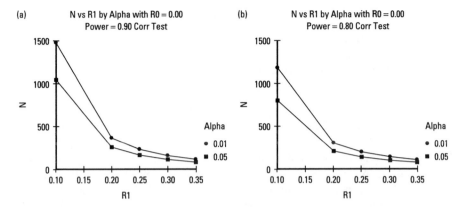

Figure 26.3   *Sample sizes under different conditions of power, significance levels and effect sizes: (a) power = 0.9; (b) power = 0.8*

The Effect of Power, Significance Level and Effect Size on Sample Size

Research question: Is age related to happiness?
Null hypothesis: There is no linear relationship ($r = 0$).
Substantive hypothesis: There is a linear relationship between happiness and age.

Figure 26.3 indicates the required sample sizes under different conditions. Figure 26.3a indicates the sample size required for a power of 0.9, and Figure 26.3b indicates the same estimates to achieve a power of 0.8. In each diagram, sample sizes are calculated according to alpha levels of 5 per cent and 1 per cent and for different effect sizes (r varies from 0.1 to 0.35.)

These charts illustrate that:

- the weaker the effect (correlation), the larger the sample size required to detect it (compare across the bottom axis in each graph);
- a larger sample size is required for equivalent conditions when the power is set at higher levels (compare 0.9 and 0.8);
- a larger sample size is required when alpha is more stringent (1 per cent).

Putting these three factors together, we see that the *smallest* sample size (61) is required when:

- power is 0.8 (lower power);
- r is 0.35 (stronger effect);
- alpha is 0.05 (higher significance level).

The *largest* sample size (1481) is required when:

- power is 0.9 (high power);
- *r* is 0.10 (weak effect);
- alpha is 0.01 (low significance level).

Software for Power Analysis

The power analysis provided above has been computed with a special software package. A number of such packages are available. The best that I have seen are *PASS* and *Power and Precision* (also marketed as Sample Power). PASS is downloadable for evaluation from *http://www.icw.com/ncss/pass.html*. Power and Precision can be downloaded for evaluation from *http://www. power-analysis.com/*.

Neither package is cheap. An extensive list of power analysis software is available from *http://www.forestry.ubc.ca/conservation/power/index.html*.

Notes

1 In the language of power analysis, these patterns in the population are called *effects*. These effects might simply be a difference in means between two groups, the existence of a correlation between two variables, percentage differences between groups, etc. In experimental designs these differences do reflect effects of an experimental intervention. In other research designs (e.g. survey research) we cannot assume that differences or correlations reflect causal effects. However, in the discussion below the term effect is used, but it should not be read to mean *causal* effect.

27

Should Confidence Intervals be Used?

One of the problems with using tests of significance is that black and white cut-off points such as 5 per cent or 1 per cent are artificial and difficult to justify (p. 173). Furthermore, significance tests on their own indicate nothing about the nature or magnitude of any effect to which they apply. One way of avoiding both these problems, recommended by the critics of significance tests, is to use confidence intervals.

What is a Confidence Interval?

Any sample-based findings that are used to generalize to a population are subject to sampling error. One way of dealing with sampling error is to ignore results if there is a given likelihood that they could be due to sampling error. This is the approach adopted with significance tests, where sample results are treated as being zero if there is more than a 5 per cent or 1 per cent chance of their being produced by sampling error.

Confidence intervals provide a useful alternative to significance tests. Instead of deciding whether or not to accept or reject the sample figure (called the *sample estimate*) as applying to the population, we can take a less cut and dried approach. We can take the sample estimate as the starting point for estimating the equivalent population figure (called the *population parameter*). Confidence intervals can then be calculated to estimate how close the true population parameter is likely to be to the sample estimate. The confidence interval takes into account the sample size and the degree of variation in the population, and estimates the likely margin of error of the sample estimate.

For example, we might find in a sample that 52 per cent of respondents say that they intend to vote for Party X at the next election. This figure is the sample estimate. Since this figure is based on a sample in which there inevitably will be some sampling error, we must allow a margin of error when predicting the actual percentage vote in the population. Using the confidence interval we can estimate the *range* within which the population parameter is likely to lie.

This approach also avoids the confusing logic of null hypothesis testing and the simplistic significant/not significant dichotomy of significance testing. Confidence intervals are a form of inferential analysis and can be used with a wide range of different types of descriptive statistics such as percentages, percentage differences between groups, correlation coefficients and regression coefficients. Like tests of significance, confidence intervals assume that the sample estimates are based on a *simple random sample*. It is inappropriate to use these statistics on data from non-probability samples.

How to Read a Confidence Interval

The simplest way of explaining how to use and interpret confidence intervals is to provide a number of examples.

How are Confidence Intervals Calculated for Percentages?

The monthly unemployment figures provided by most governments are based on sample surveys. The released figures are not the actual unemployment levels based on a complete census of all unemployed people. Instead, monthly surveys ask a sample of respondents about their labour force participation. These samples are used to estimate the actual number of unemployed in the population. The figures we see, however, are the sample figures applied as though they are population parameters. We normally only see a single figure (e.g. unemployment is 6.2 per cent). This single figure is called a *point estimate*. However, since it is based on a sample and is subject to sampling error it would be useful if we knew how much error that point estimate is likely to contain. How close is the real population figure likely to be to the sample estimate?

We can work this out (see below) and come up with an *interval* within which we can be pretty confident that the real population parameter will lie. This interval is called a *confidence interval*. The range within which we can be confident that the real population unemployment figure lies is a function of the estimated degree of sampling error.

Different confidence intervals can be calculated depending on how confident we want to be about our estimate of the true population value. The degree of confidence we want to have in our population estimates is called the *confidence level*. The confidence *level* is used when calculating a confidence *interval*. The confidence interval is calculated by applying two rules derived from probability theory:

- There is a 68 per cent probability that the population parameter will lie within ± 1 standard error unit of the sample estimate.

- There is a 95 per cent probability that the population parameter will lie within ± 1.96 standard error unit of the sample estimate.

The calculations are carried out by the following steps:

1. Obtain the sample estimate.
2. Calculate the *standard error* as a measure of sampling error.
3. Decide how confident you want to be in estimating population para-meters (i.e. specifying a confidence level). Usually the 95 per cent confidence level is used.
4. Calculate a confidence interval by applying the appropriate rule for the selected confidence level.

Suppose, then, that we have obtained a sample estimate of 6.2 per cent for unemployment, with a calculated standard error of 0.15 per cent. We have decided on a confidence level of 95 per cent. Since there is a 95 per cent chance that the population parameter will lie within ± 2 standard errors of the sample estimate, we can be 95 per cent confident that the true population unemployment level is 6.2 per cent ± 0.29 per cent (i.e. 1.96 x 0.15 = 0.29 per cent), i.e. the real unemployment level is almost certainly somewhere between 5.91 per cent and 6.49 per cent.

How to Interpret Confidence Intervals for Means

The figures in Table 27.1 were obtained for the average income of males and females in a survey in 1998. How much better do males do than females in the income stakes? The sample estimate, based on 1698 respondents, is that males, on average, earn $5299 more than females ($44 640 – $39 341). What is the dif-ference between males and females likely to be in the population? The table indicates this difference in the sample ($5299) and provides the standard error of this difference ($1422). Applying the 95 per cent rule, the table also displays the confidence interval: we can be 95 per cent confident that the real male–female income difference in the population is between $2509 and $8088.

Can Confidence Intervals be Used With Correlation Coefficients?

In a probability sample of 969 cases the correlation between education and income was calculated as 0.38. What is the true correlation in the population likely to be? By calculating and applying the standard error, we can estimate that in the population the correlation between education and income is somewhere between 0.32 and 0.43 (at the 95 per cent confidence level). You can easily calculate the confidence interval for Pearson's correlation (p. 275) by using the web-based calculator located at *http://ebook.stat.ucla.edu/textbook/ bivariables/correlation/rci.html*.

Table 27.1 *Sample estimates and standard errors for income by gender*

Gender	N	Mean	Std. deviation	Std. error of the mean
Male	860	**$44 640**	$30 288	$1033
Female	838	**$39 341**	$28 248	$976

Mean difference	Std. error of the difference	95% confidence interval of the difference	
		Lower	Upper
$5299	$1422	$2509	$8088

What does it Mean when the Confidence Interval Spans Zero?

Suppose that the correlation between two variables, X and Y, is 0.07 in a sample of 500 cases. In this case the confidence interval is from –0.02 to +0.16 (calculated at the website above). In this case the confidence interval includes zero. A correlation of zero means that two variables are completely unrelated (p. 267). When the confidence interval of a correlation coefficient includes zero it means that the population correlation *could* be zero. If a test of statistical significance were applied to the same data it would result in a significance level greater than 0.05 (i.e. we could not confidently reject the null hypothesis of zero correlation). The confidence interval tells us this too, but provides considerably more information. The correlation *could* be as high as 0.16.

What does it Mean when Confidence Intervals do not Overlap?

Returning to the income example above, we can calculate the confidence intervals for the two groups separately and see whether the confidence intervals overlap.

- If the confidence intervals for groups overlap we cannot be confident that the group means really differ.
- If they do not overlap we can be pretty certain that in the population the means really are different.

Using the information in Table 27.1, we can calculate the 95 per cent confidence intervals for males and females as follows. For males, the confidence interval (at 95 per cent confidence level) for average income was $44 640 ± $ 2025, or between $42 615 and $46 665 (i.e. $44 640 ± (1.96 × $1033)). For females, the confidence interval (at 95 per cent confidence level) for average income was $39 341 ± $1913, or between $37 428 and $41 254 (i.e. $39 341 ±

(1.96 × \$976)). Since the male and female confidence intervals do *not* overlap we can be 95 per cent confident that the real mean incomes are different for men and women. There is only a 5 per cent chance we are wrong.

Should Confidence Intervals or Tests of Significance be Used?

Although tests of significance are more widely used than are confidence intervals, there are a number of reasons for preferring confidence intervals over tests of significance when they are available. These reasons include:

- Confidence intervals provide all the information that a test of statistical significance provides and more. If, at the 95 per cent confidence level, a confidence interval for an effect includes 0 then the test of significance would also indicate that the sample estimate was not significant at the 5 per cent level.
- The confidence interval provides a sense of the magnitude of any effect. The figures in a confidence interval are expressed in terms of the descriptive statistic to which they apply (percentage, correlation, regression, etc.). Since the confidence interval, by its very nature, provides a sense of the strength of an effect it automatically provides the information that is missing when a test of significance is used on its own. Thus in our income example the interval estimate for the difference between male and female average incomes was between \$2509 and \$8088. This gives a sense of roughly what the actual difference is and also of the margin of error of any such difference.
- Since confidence intervals avoid the term 'significance' they avoid the misleading interpretation given when statistically significant results are described as being significant.
- Confidence intervals, by their nature, remind us that any estimates are subject to error and that we cannot provide any estimate with absolute precision.

What Determines the Width of the Confidence Interval?

A narrow confidence interval enables more precise population estimates. The width of the confidence interval is a function of two factors:

- the confidence level;
- the degree of sampling error.

The greater the confidence level, the wider the confidence interval. If we assume the confidence level is fixed, the only way to obtain more precise population estimates by narrowing the confidence interval is to minimize the sampling error. Sampling error is measured by the *standard error* statistic. The size of the standard error is due to two factors:

- the sample size;
- the degree of variation in the population.

There is nothing that we can do about changing the degree of variation in the population, so the only thing we can do to reduce the sampling error and thus narrow the confidence interval is to increase the sample size. As a general guide, to halve the standard error the sample size needs to be quadrupled. To obtain very precise population estimates with little margin for error, large sample sizes are required. Surveys designed to measure unemployment levels are much larger than normal surveys since precise unemployment estimates are required. However, in the more typical surveys where such precision is not required there is a point where the gain in precision is not worth the cost of increasing the size of the sample.

What Sort of Analysis can Confidence Intervals be Used for?

As we shall see later in this book, confidence intervals can be used in univariate, bivariate and multivariate analysis. They can be applied to a wide range of statistical methods.

The standard error is the basis for calculating confidence intervals. Where the standard error can be calculated for a statistic then confidence intervals can also be calculated. Most statistics packages routinely provide standard error estimates for a wide range of statistics so, with one exception, there is no need to outline how to compute the standard error.

All that we need to know is how to interpret the standard error figure in the context in which it is provided. The key to reading a standard error statistic is that the standard error is expressed in the units of the variable or statistic to which it applies. This is the case for interval variables, mean differences, regression coefficients, correlation coefficients, and percentages. For income in dollars (an interval variable) or for mean differences in dollar income, the standard error will be expressed in dollars. The standard error of a correlation coefficient is expressed in terms of the coefficient; so, if a correlation is 0.40 and its standard error is 0.025 then at the 95 per cent level we estimate the true correlation to be between approximately 0.35 and 0.45.

The standard error of a percentage will also be a percentage. However, most computer packages, including SPSS, do not supply this figure. To obtain the standard error of any percentage figure use the following simple equation:

$$S_B = \sqrt{\frac{PQ}{N}},$$

where

P is the percentage figure for which the standard error is to be computed, Q is the sum of all the other percentagess and N is the sample size. Thus if $N = 500$ and $P = 45\%$, then $Q = 55\%$ and

$$S_B = \sqrt{\frac{45 \times 55}{500}} = \sqrt{4.95} = 2.2\%.$$

28

How to Use Tables Effectively to Display the Distribution of a Single Variable

Tables can contain a great deal of information but they also take up a lot of space and overwhelm readers with detail. How should tables be presented to provide necessary information in a manner that can be easily understood?

Why Consider Using Tables?

Tables contain far more information than summary statistics (Problem 30) can provide. Where this extra detail is useful, frequency tables can provide a good way of presenting it. Where a report is likely to become a reference source for a study, the detail provided by frequency tables can be invaluable.

In general, frequency tables are best used for variables that have relatively few categories. Table 28.1 presents tables for variables with different numbers of categories. The frequency table for age (Table 28.1c), which has a large number of categories, is cumbersome and extremely difficult to read. In contrast, the tables with just a few categories (Tables 28.1a and 28.1b) are easier to read and interpret.

Variables with a large number of categories are often better presented as graphs or as statistical summaries (e.g. average age). Graphs are normally a better way of emphasizing the shape of a distribution, whereas a table is better suited to a report where the precise figures are important.

How to Read a Frequency Table

Table 28.1 illustrates the elements of a frequency table:

Table 28.1 *Three frequency tables*

(a) Left–right wing political position

Own left–right position	Frequency	%	Valid %	Cumulative %
0 Left	41	2.2	2.6	2.6
1	13	0.7	0.8	3.4
2	36	1.9	2.3	5.6
3	121	6.4	7.6	13.2
4	171	9.0	10.7	23.9
5	635	33.5	39.7	63.6
6	182	9.6	11.4	75.0
7	173	9.1	10.8	85.9
8	137	7.2	8.6	94.4
9	25	1.3	1.6	96.0
10 Right	64	3.4	4.0	100.0
Total	1598	84.2	100.0	
Missing	299	15.8		
Total	1897	100.0		

(b) Views about effect of taxation

High tax makes people less willing to work	Frequency	%	Valid %	Cumulative %
Strongly agree	701	37.0	38.2	38.2
Agree	701	37.0	38.2	76.3
Neither	251	13.2	13.7	90.0
Disagree	163	8.6	8.9	98.9
Strongly disagree	21	1.1	1.1	100.0
Total	1837	96.8	100.0	
Missing	60	3.2		
Total	1897	100.0		

(c) Age

Age	Frequency	%	Valid %	Cumulative %
18	26	1.4	1.5	1.5
19	19	1.0	1.1	2.5
20	19	1.0	1.1	3.6
21	22	1.2	1.2	4.9
22	25	1.3	1.4	6.3
23	15	0.8	0.8	7.1
24	22	1.2	1.2	8.4
25	25	1.3	1.4	9.8
26	23	1.2	1.3	11.1
27	24	1.3	1.4	12.4

(Continued)

Table 28.1 *(c) Age (Continued)*

Age	Frequency	%	Valid %	Cumulative %
28	25	1.3	1.4	13.9
29	23	1.2	1.3	15.2
30	32	1.7	1.8	17.0
31	39	2.1	2.2	19.2
32	25	1.3	1.4	20.6
33	31	1.6	1.8	22.3
34	41	2.2	2.3	24.7
35	32	1.7	1.8	26.5
36	35	1.8	2.0	28.5
37	24	1.3	1.4	29.8
38	42	2.2	2.4	32.2
39	48	2.5	2.7	34.9
40	40	2.1	2.3	37.2
41	49	2.6	2.8	39.9
42	51	2.7	2.9	42.8
43	42	2.2	2.4	45.2
44	42	2.2	2.4	47.6
45	39	2.1	2.2	49.8
46	44	2.3	2.5	52.3
47	26	1.4	1.5	53.7
48	27	1.4	1.5	55.3
49	38	2.0	2.1	57.4
50	41	2.2	2.3	59.7
51	44	2.3	2.5	62.2
52	32	1.7	1.8	64.0
53	37	2.0	2.1	66.1
54	31	1.6	1.8	67.9
55	28	1.5	1.6	69.5
56	24	1.3	1.4	70.8
57	27	1.4	1.5	72.3
58	31	1.6	1.8	74.1
59	33	1.7	1.9	76.0
60	25	1.3	1.4	77.4
61	24	1.3	1.4	78.7
62	25	1.3	1.4	80.1
63	24	1.3	1.4	81.5
64	29	1.5	1.6	83.1
65	23	1.2	1.3	84.4
66	23	1.2	1.3	85.7
67	15	0.8	0.8	86.6
68	20	1.1	1.1	87.7
69	17	0.9	1.0	88.7
70	21	1.1	1.2	89.9
71	18	0.9	1.0	90.9
72	23	1.2	1.3	92.2
73	21	1.1	1.2	93.4
74	13	0.7	0.7	94.1
75	18	0.9	1.0	95.1
76	13	0.7	0.7	95.9
77	7	0.4	0.4	96.3

(Continued)

Table 28.1 *(c) Age (Continued)*

Age	Frequency	%	Valid %	Cumulative %
78	11	0.6	0.6	96.9
79	10	0.5	0.6	97.5
80	6	0.3	0.3	97.8
81	4	0.2	0.2	98.0
82	6	0.3	0.3	98.4
83	10	0.5	0.6	98.9
84	5	0.3	0.3	99.2
85	5	0.3	0.3	99.5
86	4	0.2	0.2	99.7
89	2	0.1	0.1	99.8
90	1	0.1	0.1	99.9
91	1	0.1	0.1	99.9
92	1	0.1	0.1	100.0
Total	1768	93.2	100.0	
Missing	129	6.8		
Total	1897	100.0		

- The *first column* contains the values or categories of the variable (political position, level of agreement, age).
- The *frequency column* indicates the number of people in each category.
- The *percentage column* lists the percentage of the *whole sample* in each category. These percentages are based on the total sample size, including those who did not answer the question (see the bottom row of each table).
- The *valid percentage column* contains the percentage *of those who gave a valid response to the question* that belong to each category. This is the percentage that is normally used.
- The *cumulative percentage column* provides the *rolling addition* of percentages from the first category to the last valid category. For example, in Table 28.1b, 38.2 per cent *strongly* agree that high taxation is a disincentive to work. A further 38.2 per cent simply agree that high tax discourages work. The cumulative percentage column adds up the percentage who strongly agree with those who agree (38.2 + 38.2 = 76.3, the discrepancy being due to rounding). Thus 76.3 per cent *at least* agree (that is, agree or strongly agree) that high taxation discourages work. In Table 28.1c the cumulative percentage for the 40-year-old age group is 37.2 per cent. This means that 37.2 per cent (of those who gave their age) were 40 *or younger*. Cumulative percentages should usually only be used with ordinal or interval variables.
- The *third last row* lists the total number of respondents who gave *valid* answers to this question. This is the base for calculating the valid percentages (e.g. there are 635 who indicated a middle-of-the-road political position (score of 5). 1598 people answered the political position question. [635 ÷ 1598) x 100 = 39.7 per cent].

Table 28.2   *Basic elements of a frequency table*

Include	Do not include
Table number and title	Decimal points: round percentages to whole numbers
Labels for the categories of the variable	Number of cases in each category (can be recalculated by dividing the percentage by 100 and multiplying the result by the valid total number)
Column headings to indicate what the numbers in the column represent	Cumulative percentages
Valid percentages	Percentages (can be calculated from category numbers and total number)
The total number of valid cases	Sample size (can be calculated from valid total number plus missing cases)
The number of missing cases The source of the data Notes (e.g. actual question)	

- The *second last row* shows the number of cases that did *not* give a valid response for this variable. These are called 'missing' cases.
- The *bottom row* indicates the total sample size (including 'missing' cases).

What Information to Put in a Frequency Table

The first principle of presenting a table is to be accurate, the second principle is to *avoid clutter* and the third principle is to ensure that the table is informative. The precise information that should be included will partly depend on the use to which the table will be put. In most cases, however, the percentage column, the frequency column and the cumulative percentage column can be left out. However, when information is removed from the table you should ensure that sufficient information remains for the deleted information to be reconstructed should the need arise. Table 28.2 lists the type of information that should normally be included and excluded from a frequency table.

Table 28.3 reproduces the tables in Table 28.1 with only the required information. All the information that has been removed could be calculated from the information that remains. Without the clutter the tables are easier to read and are liable to lead to fewer misinterpretations. The simplicity of these tables (especially Tables 28.3a and 28.3b) also makes it easier to examine the shape of the distribution (see below).

The guidelines in Table 28.2 are not rules. They simply provide useful ways to minimize clutter. But common sense must prevail. I have not rounded off

Table 28.3 *Uncluttered versions of the frequency tables from Table 28.1*

(a) Left–right political position   **(b) Views about effect of taxation**

Left–right position	%	High tax makes people less willing to work	%
0 Left	3	Strongly agree	38
1	1	Agree	38
2	2	Neither	14
3	8	Disagree	9
4	11	Strongly disagree	1
5	40		
6	11	N = 1837	100
7	11	Missing = 60	
8	8		
9	2		
10 Right	4		
Total = 1598 Missing = 299			

(c) Age

Age	%	Age	%	Age	%
18	1.5	42	2.9	66	1.3
19	1.1	43	2.4	67	0.8
20	1.1	44	2.4	68	1.1
21	1.2	45	2.2	69	1.0
22	1.4	46	2.5	70	1.2
23	0.8	47	1.5	71	1.0
24	1.2	48	1.5	72	1.3
25	1.4	49	2.1	73	1.2
26	1.3	50	2.3	74	0.7
27	1.4	51	2.5	75	1.0
28	1.4	52	1.8	76	0.7
29	1.3	53	2.1	77	0.4
30	1.8	54	1.8	78	0.6
31	2.2	55	1.6	79	0.6
32	1.4	56	1.4	80	0.3
33	1.8	57	1.5	81	0.2
34	2.3	58	1.8	82	0.3
35	1.8	59	1.9	83	0.6
36	2.0	60	1.4	84	0.3
37	1.4	61	1.4	85	0.3
38	2.4	62	1.4	86	0.2
39	2.7	63	1.4	89	0.1
40	2.3	64	1.6	90	0.1
41	2.8	65	1.3	91	0.1
				92	0.1
				Total	100.0
				Missing	129
				Total	1768

the percentages in Table 28.3c, despite the guidelines. The reason for this is that it would have left too many categories with no percentages and it could have led to too much rounding error over the whole table.

What to Look for in a Frequency Table

The two main ways of reading a frequency table are by examining:

- particular figures (see above);
- the shape of the whole distribution.

There are at least three aspects of the shape of the distribution that can be gleaned from a frequency table.

Typically/Central Tendency

Do cases tend to belong to particular categories? To which category (or categories) do people typically belong? Examining the size of percentages in categories or adjacent categories can quickly give a general idea of the sorts of responses that are typical and those that are fairly rare. In Table 28.3a it is easy to see that the typical response clusters around the middle political position. In Table 28.3b the typical response is to agree or strongly agree. However, the typical age is much more difficult to judge in Table 28.3c. For this type of distribution a summary statistic such as the mean is a better way of describing typical values.

Variation

Variation refers to the degree of similarity among the cases. Examining the scatter of percentages across the categories gives an indication of whether the sample is fairly homogeneous (low variation) or heterogeneous (high variation). Where reasonable percentage figures occur across the different categories (as for age in Table 28.3c) then the sample is fairly heterogeneous. If just a few categories account for the bulk of the cases (as in Table 28.3b, where 76 per cent of cases fall into the top two categories) then the sample is fairly homogeneous.

Symmetry/Skewness

For variables where categories are rank-ordered from low to high the distribution can be described in terms of its symmetry. A symmetrical distribution is one where the shape of the distribution is much the same either side of the middle point. A non-symmetrical distribution is called a *skewed* distribution and can be identified by a clustering of cases towards one end or the other (pp. 224–6). A quick scan of the percentages in a frequency table can indicate whether the distribution is relatively symmetrical or whether it is skewed. Do the percentages tend to cluster towards the low or the high end, or do they cluster towards the middle of the variable? Table 28.3b indicates a skewed pattern. The middle point is the 'neither' category. Examining the percentages either side of the midpoint shows that most cases fall to one side (agree or strongly agree). Table 28.3a illustrates a more symmetrical distribution. The middle point (5) represents a 'middle-of-the-road' position. This category has the highest percentage of respondents (40 per cent). The percentages on each side of this point are similar to one another both in size and shape – the percentages progressively get smaller as we move towards the extremes and both show a small increase at the very extreme.

Using SPSS

The following menu selections produce frequency tables for the listed variables.

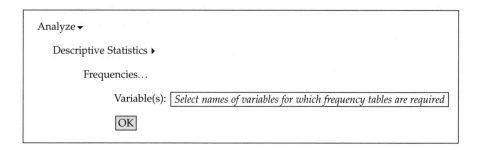

202

29

How to Use Graphs for Single Variables

Simple-to-use but powerful graphing software has increased the use of graphs in data analysis and reports, and these graphs can be an excellent way of displaying distributions. However, many graphs produced with such software are cluttered, confusing and downright misleading. Graphs must be selected appropriately and constructed correctly. Paying attention to three matters will assist in the appropriate use of simple univariate graphs:

- the information that a graph should contain;
- selecting the appropriate type of graph;
- identifying and avoiding distortions.

What are the Main Parts of a Graph?

As illustrated in Figure 29.1, there are four main elements of univariate graphs:

- the x axis;
- the y axis;
- data values and markers;
- labels.

The X Axis

Units. This axis represents the values of the variable being displayed. The x axis may be divided into discrete categories (dot chart, bar chart and pie chart) or into a range of continuous values (line graph or histogram). Which units are used depends on the level of measurement of the variable being graphed.

Placement. The x axis may be placed across the bottom of the graph (e.g. histogram and line chart), on the side (dot graph and box-and-whisker plot), or either the bottom or side (bar chart).

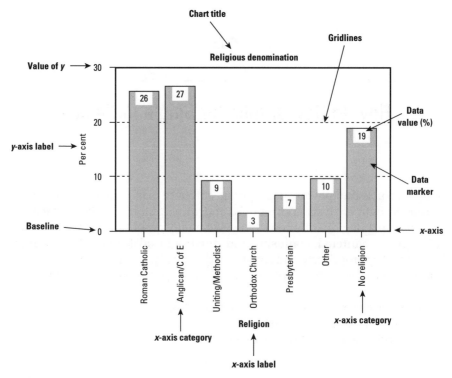

Figure 29.1   *Elements of a univariate graph*
Source: Australian Election Survey, 1998

The Y Axis

Scale. The *y* axis in univariate graphs can represent either percentages or frequencies. The histogram usually uses frequencies. For reasonably large samples percentages are usually preferable. Box-and-whisker plots do not have a *y* axis. Pie charts do not have a *y* axis, but the slices of the pie can be displayed as frequencies or percentages.

Placement. The *y* axis is placed perpendicular to the *x* axis. Whether it is on the side or bottom of the graph will depend on the placement of the *x* axis.

Data Values and Markers

Representation of categories. The categories of the variable are represented either by a line (line graph), bars (bar graph, histogram), dots (dot graph) or pie slices (pie chart).

Differentiating categories. Each of the bars in bar charts and histograms is represented by the same colour, pattern, line thickness, etc. Pie charts represent each category of the variable (pie slice) with a different colour or pattern. A line graph uses a single line to display all the values of a single variable.

Labels

A graph should include a number of different labels.

Graph title. This should include the figure number and a brief description of the graph (type and variable).

x axis. These labels will normally include an axis label that names the *x* variable (e.g. age, religious denomination) and labels for the categories or values of the variable.

y axis. These labels will indicate whether the variable is being displayed as raw numbers or as percentages. The *y* axis will also include numerical values indicating numbers or percentages.

Bars. Bars can contain data values indicating the precise percentage of cases in each category.

Footnotes. These may indicate the source of the data, the wording of the question or other information that may assist the correct interpretation of the graph.

Which Graph to Use

Several factors influence the type of graph that is used:

*   the level of measurement of the variable;
*   whether the variable's categories are discrete or continuous;
*   the number of categories or values of the variable;
*   whether fine detail of the distribution or the general shape of the distribution is more important;
*   the intended audience.

Bar Charts

Figure 29.2 illustrates the two types of bar chart: the vertical bar chart (sometimes called a column chart) and the horizontal bar chart (sometimes just called a bar chart).

Bar charts are appropriate for variables with a *small number of discrete categories*, which means that they are used mainly for nominal and ordinal variables. Since a separate bar is used for each category, variables with a large number of categories or values produce a large number of bars, which makes the graph difficult to interpret.

Each bar represents the relative frequency of the category. The bar may be displayed as a percentage or as the number of people in a category. The order in which the bars are presented depends on the nature of the variable.

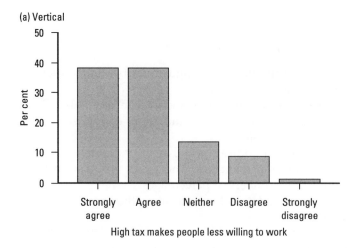

(a) Vertical

High tax makes people less willing to work

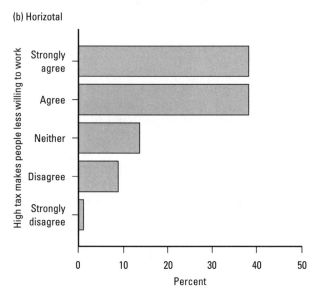

(b) Horizotal

Figure 29.2   *Vertical and horizontal bar charts*

Dot Chart

Dot charts (Figure 29.3) are a variation of horizontal bar charts and are only appropriate for variables with a relatively *small number of discrete categories*. Instead of using wide bars, a dot indicates the percentage of cases in any given category. To avoid misreading the graph an unobtrusive line links the dot to the relevant category label. The main advantage of the dot chart is that it is very simple, uncluttered, easy to read and takes less space than a bar chart.

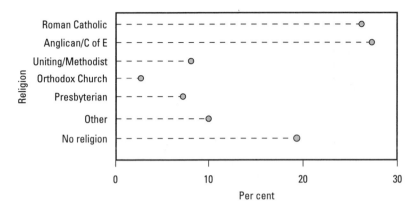

Figure 29.3   *Dot chart of religious preference*

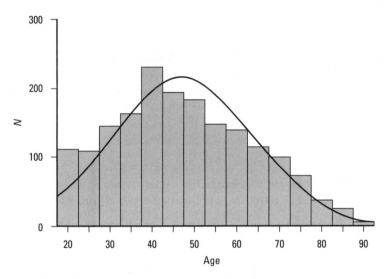

Figure 29.4   *Histogram of age with normal curve superimposed*

Histogram

Histograms are used to display the distribution of a single, *continuous interval-level variable* (Figure 29.4). Bars are used to represent a *range* of values on the variable (e.g. age groups). Unlike the bar chart, the bars are placed next to one another, with no space between them, to display the shape of the distribution.

The number of bars and the range of values covered by each bar can be set by users in most graphing programs. Decisions about the number and width of bars are important as they can affect the shape of the distribution.

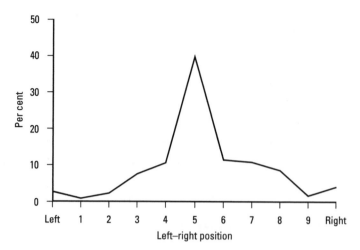

Figure 29.5   *Line graph of political position*

Histograms are particularly useful for obtaining a sense of the *shape* of the distribution and to examine the distribution's statistical properties. A *normal curve* can be superimposed on the graph to provide a visual idea of how far the distribution deviates from a normal distribution (Problem 11).

Line Graph

When used with a single variable, a line chart serves a similar function to a histogram. It should be used for *continuous interval-level variables* (Figure 29.5).

The main differences between a line graph and a histogram are that on a line graph:

- the frequency of any value on the *x* axis is represented by a point on a line rather than by a single column.
- the values of the continuous variable are not automatically grouped into a smaller number of groups as they are in histograms. As such the line graph reflects the frequency of *every* value of the *x* variable and thus avoids potential distortions due to the way in which values are grouped.
- the finer detail can make the graph appear more cluttered and complex. This can confuse rather than enlighten and, in turn, mask the main patterns of the graph (see Figure 29.6).

The choice between a histogram and a line graph will depend on the purpose of the graph and the extent to which the general shape is important or particular points of the graph are of special interest.

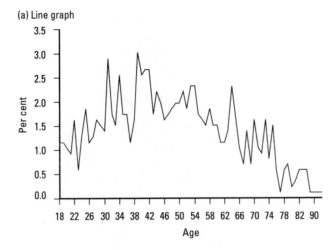

(a) Line graph

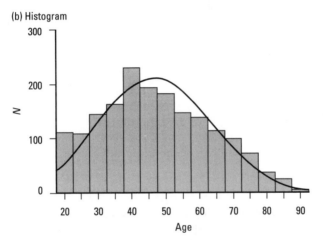

(b) Histogram

Figure 29.6 *Choice of graph type for continuous variable*

Pie Chart

Pie charts are used for *nominal or ordinal variables with relatively few discrete categories* (Figure 29.7). Rather than using bars to represent the frequency of a category, pie slices are used. The larger the slice, the greater the relative frequency of that category.

Pie charts can provide an attractive way of making a simple point. However, in general they are not the best way of graphing distributions. Where there are a large number of categories or a number of very small categories, pie charts can become difficult to read and label. In general, bar charts are suitable whenever pie charts can be used. Bar charts have the added advantage

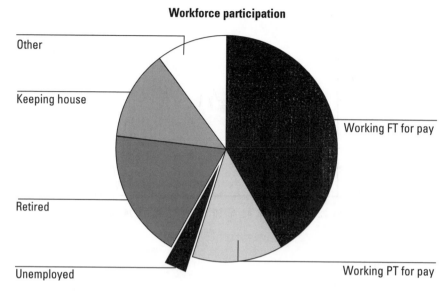

Figure 29.7   *Pie chart of workforce participation*
SOURCE: *Australian Election Survey, 1998*

that the relative length of the bars unambiguously indicates the relative size of categories.

Box-and-Whisker Plot

These plots differ from those described above in that they do not represent the distribution of the variable using frequencies or percentages. Instead they use various summary measures of a variable's distribution (Figure 29.8).

This graph indicates the spread of the variable. The box represents the middle 50 per cent of cases in an ordered distribution (i.e. on an ordinal or interval variable). The horizontal line in the box represents the median value – the value of the case in the middle of the distribution (p. 219). The top vertical line (whisker) represents the range of the top 25 per cent of cases, while the bottom whisker indicates the range of the bottom 25 per cent.

A comparison of the distance from the median to the top horizontal line (maximum value) with the distance below the median provides an indication of the skew and symmetry of the distribution. The shorter distance of the bottom half of the plot in Figure 29.8 indicates a clustering of incomes towards the bottom of the distribution with a tail of incomes in the higher income brackets (i.e. a positive skew).

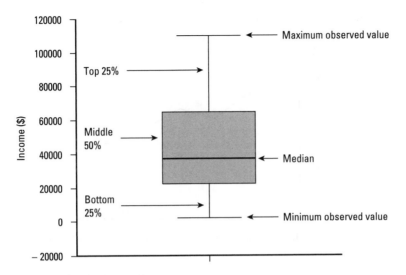

Figure 29.8   *Box-and-whisker plot*

Table 29.1   *Selection guide for graphs according to variable type*

	Number of categories	Discrete or continuous	Level of measurement of variable
Bar	Few	Discrete	Usually nominal or ordinal
Dot plot	Few	Discrete	Usually nominal or ordinal
Pie chart	Few	Discrete	Usually nominal or ordinal
Histogram	Many	Continuous	Interval
Line graph	Many	Continuous	Interval
Box-and-whisker plot	Many	Continuous	Ordinal or interval

Summary of Graph Selection by Type of Variable

Table 29.1 lists the various types of graph and summarizes the above guidelines on the appropriate choice depending on the type of variable being graphed.

Graphs to Watch Out for

While graphs can be an effective way of presenting data patterns, they can also misrepresent patterns. When presenting and reading graphs there are a

(a) Original graph: both axes approximately equal length; y-axis range 0–70

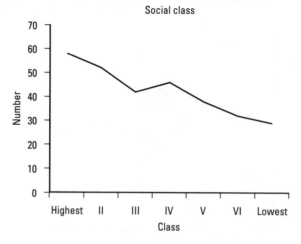

(b) Stretched y axis, shrunken x axis; y-axis range 0–70

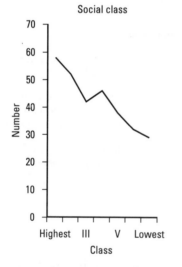

(c) Stretched y axis, shrunken x axis; y-axis range 25–60

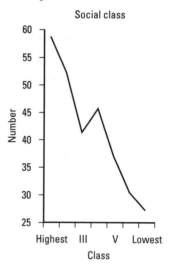

(d) Shrunken y axis, stretched x axis; y-axis range 0–100

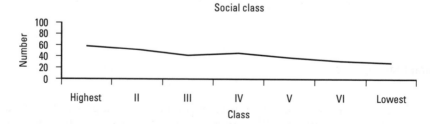

Figure 29.9   *Distorting graphs by changing scales on axes*

Table 29.2 *Unequal intervals on the x axis*

Year	1950	1960	1970	1980	1985	1990	1992	1994	1996	1997	1999	2000
%	10	11	12	13	14	15	16	17	18	19	20	21

number of factors to which special attention should be paid so that distortions are avoided.

Distorted Scales on the X and Y Axes

This problem is most easily explained with the help of an example. While all the graphs in Figure 29.9 have been produced with the same data, they give very different impressions. These graphs have been distorted using two methods:

- *Changing the 'aspect ratio' of the x and y axes.* By stretching one axis and not stretching the other, the trend line can be flattened or made much steeper.
- *Changing the value range of the y axis.* The original y axis began at 0 and extended to 70. The maximum value needed to accommodate the data was 58. By extending the top value to 100 the line is flattened. By only displaying the y axis from 25 to 60 the graph line is made to appear much steeper.

These distortions can be avoided by following two guidelines:

- Begin the y axis at zero and extend it to just a little beyond the maximum required value.
- Try to make the x and y axes approximately the same length.

Unequal Intervals

Where the intervals on the x axis are, in reality, an unequal distance apart but are presented as being equidistant, patterns in graphs can be easily and unintentionally distorted. Table 29.2 presents observations for 12 different years between 1950 and 2000. Between each observation the percentage increases uniformly by one percentage point.

Figure 29.10a treats the observations as though they are separated by periods of equal length. Since the percentage increases uniformly between each period this results in a straight-line graph indicating a uniform rate of increase. However, the observation points are *not* equidistant. Until 1980 observations were only available every ten years. From 1980 to 1990 they are every five years. Thereafter we have data at uneven intervals of one or two years. Figure 29.10b presents the data correctly. The x axis is divided into five-year divisions and the data have been plotted against the years correctly.

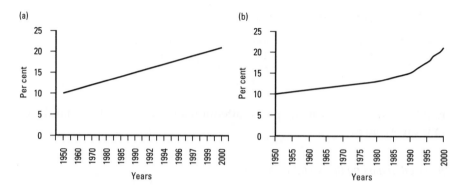

Figure 29.10   *The effect of ignoring unequal intervals on the X axis*
(a) Unequal intervals on the X axis treated as equal
(b) Adjustments to X axis for unequal intervals between observations

Table 29.3   *An example of extreme variation in scores*

Year	1950	1955	1960	1965	1970	1985	1990	1995	2000	2005
Rate	10	11	14	13	17	16	13	14	10	90

Extreme Variation

An extreme value that might be an outlier or a data error can distort graphs badly. Care needs to be taken to ensure that an odd or extreme value is not masking important patterns in the data. Table 29.3 provides hypothetical data on suicide rates per 100 000 population between 1950 and 2005. Figure 29.11 shows how an extreme value can hide patterns. In Figure 29.11a the extreme figure of 90 for the year 2005 is included. Since the extreme value of 90 means that the scale of the y axis has to be stretched to accommodate this value, its inclusion hides an important pattern in the earlier years. Figure 29.11b reproduces the graph without the extreme value, and quite a different picture appears. Removing the extreme value has the effect of giving us a close-up view of the actual variations in suicide rate. Of course, if the 2005 figure were correct it would represent an important pattern but it is far more likely that the 2005 figure is an error that should be 9 rather than 90.

Producing Charts With SPSS

SPSS has a large number of graphing options. For each graph there are several formatting and display options. It is not possible to cover all the formatting options in this book. Instead I will describe how to produce the basic graphs outlined in this section. Note that SPSS does not produce dot graphs.

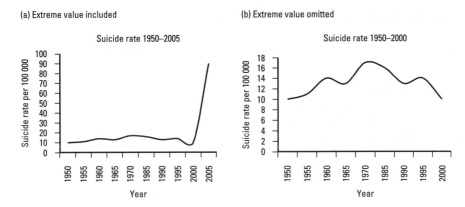

(a) Extreme value included

Suicide rate 1950–2005

(b) Extreme value omitted

Suicide rate 1950–2000

Figure 29.11 *The effect of extreme values on graphs*

Bar Chart

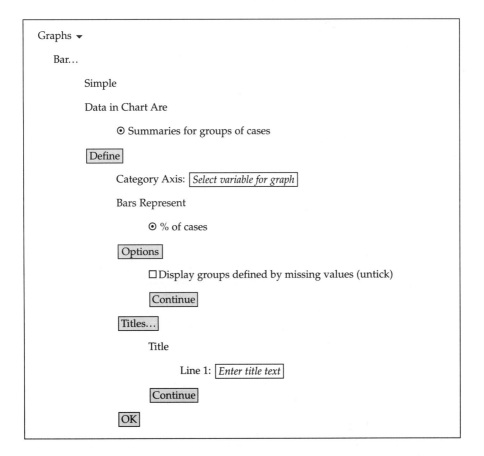

Graphs ▾

    Bar…

        Simple

        Data in Chart Are

            ⊙ Summaries for groups of cases

        Define

            Category Axis: *Select variable for graph*

            Bars Represent

                ⊙ % of cases

            Options

                ☐ Display groups defined by missing values (untick)

                Continue

        Titles…

            Title

                Line 1: *Enter title text*

            Continue

        OK

Histogram for Age (with Normal Curve Overlay)

Graphs ▾

   Histogram...

   Variable: Select variable for graph

   ☑ Display normal curve

     Titles...

        Title

           Line 1: Enter title text

       Continue

    OK

Line Graph of Left–Right Political Position

Graphs ▾

   Line...

      Simple

      Data in Chart Are

         ⊙ Summaries for groups of cases

        Define

        Category Axis: Select variable for graph

        Line Represents

          ⊙ % of cases

        Options...

          ☐ Display groups defined by missing values (untick)

          Continue

        Titles...

          Title

             Line 1: Enter title text

          Continue

        OK

Pie Chart of Workforce Participation

Graphs ▾

    Pie…

        Data in Chart Are

            ⊙ Summaries for groups of cases

        Define

            Define Slices by: Select variable for graph

            Slices Represent

                ⊙ % of cases

            Options…

                ☐ Display groups defined by missing values (untick)

                Continue

            Titles…

                Title

                    Line 1: Enter title text

                Continue

        OK

Box-and-Whisker Plot of Income

Graphs ▾

    Boxplot…

        Simple

        Data in Chart Are

            ⊙ Summaries for groups of cases

        Define

            Variable: Select variable for graph

            Category Axis: Select variable [Note that when using menus you must specify a second variable and a boxplot will be created for each category of the second variable.]

            Options…

                ☐ Display groups defined by missing values (untick)

                Continue

        OK

30

Which Summary Statistics to Use
to Describe a Single Variable

What is the Purpose of Summary Statistics?

Graphs and tables can provide a great deal of detail about distributions but they are associated with several problems:

- They can take a great deal of space and time to produce, read and absorb.
- The detail is often unnecessary and can result in very cluttered text and reports.
- They do not provide precise, quantitative measures of particular characteristics of a distribution.

Summary statistics provide a concise and precise way of summarizing characteristics of distributions. However, there are a large number of statistics from which to choose. Each statistic is designed for particular purposes and for specific circumstances. The problem is how to choose from among the confusing array of possibilities.

The selection of statistics is simplified if you can answer three questions:

- Do you want to describe the sample (descriptive statistic) or generalize to a wider population (an inferential test)?
- What is the level of measurement of the variable? Some statistics are only appropriate for interval variables.
- How many categories does the variable have? Some statistics are only appropriate for variables with two categories, while others require three or more categories.

This discussion focuses on how to select among the range of descriptive statistics when describing a single variable. Problem 31 shows how to select among the range of inferential statistics.

A distribution can be summarized in the following terms:

- *Typical responses.* Statistics that indicate typical or average characteristics in the distribution (e.g. average income) are called *measures of central tendency*.

Table 30.1 *Modal categories for two distributions*

(a) Marital status

	%
1 Never married	16
2 Now married/cohabiting	68
3 Widowed	6
4 Divorced/separated	10
Total = 1844	
Missing = 53	

Mode = 2 = Now married/cohabiting

(b) Religion

	%
1 Roman Catholic	27
2 Anglican/C of E	26
3 Uniting/Methodist	11
4 Orthodox Church	3
5 Presbyterian	6
6 Other	10
9 No religion	17
Total = 1835	
Missing = 62	

Mode = 1= Roman Catholic

- *Degree of variation.* Is the sample homogeneous or heterogeneous (p. 201)? Statistics that indicate the degree of variation are called *measures of dispersion.*
- *Shape.* The shape of a distribution can include characteristics such as symmetry, skewness, how 'flat' the distribution is and whether the distribution approximates certain theoretical distributions (e.g. the normal distribution).

How to Measure Typical Values

Measures of central tendency provide a single figure that indicates the typical value in a distribution. There are a number of such measures. The three most common measures are the *mode*, the *median* and the *mean*.

Mode

The mode is the value of the category with the single largest number of cases. The mode is not a particularly good way of measuring central tendency, since it is highly dependent on the way categories of a variable are combined. However, it is the only measure of central tendency that is appropriate for *nominal* variables.

The usefulness of the mode will depend on the particular distribution for which it is used. In Table 30.1a 'Married/cohabiting' (coded as 2) is the modal category since it has 68 per cent of cases. As such the mode is not a bad measure of the typical marital status. In Table 30.1b, the modal category is Catholic (coded 1). In this case the mode is an unsatisfactory way of describing the typical religion since only 27 per cent are Catholic. Since 73 per cent are *not* Catholic it is not very helpful to say that Catholic is the typical religious denomination in the sample.

Table 30.2   *Calculating the median from a frequency table*

	Self-stated level of political liberalism/ conservatism	%	Cumulative %	
	1 Extremely liberal	2.3	2.3	
	2 Liberal	12.5	14.8	
	3 Slightly liberal	13.4	28.2	
Median category	**4 Moderate**	36.3	**64.5**	*Middle person is in this category*
	5 Slightly conservative	15.7	80.2	
	6 Conservative	16.2	96.4	
	7 Extremely conservative	3.6	100.0	
	Total = 1427 Missing = 66			

Median

The median is the normal measure of central tendency used for *ordinal* variables. To calculate the median we must be able to rank cases from low to high on the variable being described. Suppose we have 1427 cases whose level of political conservatism or liberalism we know (see Table 30.2). We could line up these cases in groups, ordering these groups from extremely liberal (1) to extremely conservative (7). To calculate the median we would select the 714th person and see how liberal or conservative he or she is. The code associated with this person's liberalism/conservatism would be the median value of the variable. The 714th person is selected because he or she is the middle person in an ordered distribution.

The median can be obtained easily by examining the cumulative frequency column in a frequency table. Simply look down the cumulative percentage column until you see the cumulative percentage go beyond 50 per cent. The value associated with that row of the frequency table is the median of that variable. In Table 30.2 the cumulative percentage goes over 50 per cent in the 'Moderate' category. Since this category is coded 4 the median is 4.

Mean

The mean can only be calculated for interval data where the codes have a numerically meaningful interpretation. Calculating the mean involves adding the value of the variable for each case and dividing the sum by the number of cases. It makes sense to calculate a mean for numeric variables such as age since we can meaningfully add ages together and divide by the number of cases.

Table 30.3 *Two identical means for two very different distributions*

	Group A			Group B	
Age		N		Age	N
30		0		30	40
35		10		35	10
40		20		40	0
45		40		45	0
50		20		50	0
55		10		55	10
60		0		60	40
Total *N*		100		Total *N*	100
Mean		45 years		Mean	45 years

However, it makes no sense to add together the codes used in a nominal variable. For example, in Table 30.1a never marrieds were coded as 1, marrieds as 2, widowed as 3 and separated and divorced as 4. It does not make any sense to add together the codes of these variables to come up with a mean marital status.

The mean is a very useful statistic and is widely used in a great many of the more powerful and statistical techniques. However, it can also be misleading. When using the mean you should be aware of two particular dangers:

- The same mean can be obtained for very different distributions. As such, relying on the mean alone can lead to misleading conclusions.
- The mean can be distorted by extreme values and by skewed distributions.

SAME MEAN FOR DIFFERENT DISTRIBUTIONS In Table 30.3 the mean for both groups A and B is 45 years but the distributions are entirely different. If only the mean was used for both distributions we would say that the two groups were similar in terms of their age.

THE INFLUENCE OF EXTREME VALUES AND SKEWNESS When calculating the mean, the *size* of each person's value on the variable affects the final value of the mean. A very high or very low value therefore can inflate or deflate the average and provide a misleading summary of most of the cases in the distribution. In Table 30.4 the mean is $18 900. No individual earns exactly this amount, but it is the best summary of the range of incomes. However, if we added a person with an income of $1 000 000 the mean would be $108 091. The mean is now a less adequate reflection of the income of all members of the group.

When variables have extreme values or are skewed there are several options:

- the outlier might be excluded (Problem 13);
- the distribution might be transformed (p. 78);

Table 30.4   *Calculating the mean for ten cases*

Case	Income ($)
1	12 000
2	13 000
3	15 000
4	16 000
5	18 000
6	20 000
7	21 000
8	22 000
9	25 000
10	27 000
11	1 000 000
Total Income	$1 89 000
Total Cases	10
Mean	$18 900
Add Case II	$1000 000
Total income	$1 189 000
Total cases	11
Mean	= $1 189 000/11
	= $108 091

- an alternative measure of central tendency (e.g. the median) that is not affected by extreme values or skewness could be used.

How to Summarize Diversity

Measures of dispersion are useful for two main reasons:

- They provide a summary of a different aspect of a distribution than is provided by a measure of central tendency. Rather than measuring what is typical, measures of dispersion summarize how alike or unalike members of a group are.
- They provide a means of assessing how well the measure of central tendency summarizes the distribution. We have seen that on their own measures of central tendency can provide misleading summaries of a distribution. As a general rule, a measure of central tendency will be a better summary of a group in which there is a high degree of similarity, and less so in heterogeneous groups. Accordingly, it is highly desirable to use a measure of variation or dispersion in conjunction with measures of central tendency to provide a context within which to 'read' the measure of central tendency.

There are a variety of measures of dispersion. Each of these is a companion to a particular measure of central tendency. Table 30.5 indicates which measure of dispersion is used in conjunction with each measure of central tendency.

Table 30.5 *Summary statistics according to the level of measurement*

| Type of statistic | Level of measurement of variable | | |
	Nominal	Ordinal	Interval
Measure of central tendency	Mode	Median	Mean
Measure of dispersion	Variation ratio	Range, decile range, interquartile range	Variance, Standard deviation
Shape			Skewness Kurtosis

Note: Measures that are appropriate for variables at a lower level of measurement (e.g. nominal) can be used for higher-level variables (e.g. ordinal or interval). Normally this is not recommended. However, measures designed for higher levels of measurement (e.g. mean) cannot be used for lower-level variables (e.g. ordinal or nominal).

Variation Ratio

The *variation ratio* is the simplest measure of dispersion. It is used with *nominal* variables in conjunction with the mode. The variation ratio (v) is the proportion of cases that are *not* in the modal category. In Table 30.1a, 68 per cent are in the modal category. Expressed as a proportion this is 0.68, which means that the proportion not in the modal category is 0.32.

The variation ratio can be any figure between 0 and 1.0. The higher v is the *less* well the mode summarizes the whole distribution. In Table 30.1b, v is 0.73. Since this is a high figure it means that there is a high degree of variation in religious group membership and that the mode is not a very satisfactory reflection of the religious group membership of the sample as a whole.

Range

The *range* is used in conjunction with the median for *ordinal* variables. It is the difference between the highest and lowest value in a distribution (maximum – minimum). The wider the range, the more variation there is in a group.

The range can be unduly affected by extreme cases. To avoid such distortions, the range is often calculated by excluding the 10 per cent of cases with the lowest values and 10 per cent with the highest values. By excluding the bottom and top extremes the range of the more typical cases is calculated. This range is called the *decile range* since the top and bottom deciles (10 per cent of cases) have been excluded.

An alternative is to exclude the bottom quarter and top quarter of cases and calculate the range based on the middle 50 per cent of cases. This is called the *interquartile range*.

Table 30.6   *Mean and standard deviation of the two distributions in Table 30.3*

	Group A	Group B
$\bar{X}$ (mean)	45 years	45 years
s^2 (variance)	30	200
s (standard deviation)	5.5 years	14.1 years

Whichever version of the range is used, the same principle applies. The higher the range the more variation in the group and the less well the median summarizes the typical value of the group.

Variance and Standard Deviation

The *variance* and *standard deviation* are used in conjunction with the mean for *interval* variables. They are closely related statistics that reflect how well the mean captures the typical value in a distribution. The standard deviation is measured in the same units of measurement as the variable it is used to summarize. Essentially the variance and standard deviation reflect the average distance of cases from the mean. The larger the typical distance, the less well the mean reflects a set of cases. The procedures for calculating the variance and the standard deviation need not concern us here.

The mean, variance and standard deviation of groups A and B for Table 30.3 are summarized in Table 30.6. The standard deviation is much lower for group A than group B, which indicates the greater age similarity in group A. It also indicates that the mean is a better summary for group A than for group B. This is what we would expect from an examination of the actual distributions in Table 30.3.

How to Describe the Shape of a Distribution

There are two statistics that are used to summarize the shape of the distribution of an *interval* variable:

- skewness;
- kurtosis.

What is Skewness

The skewness statistic indicates the degree to which a distribution is asymmetrical. A positive value indicates a positive skew, a negative value

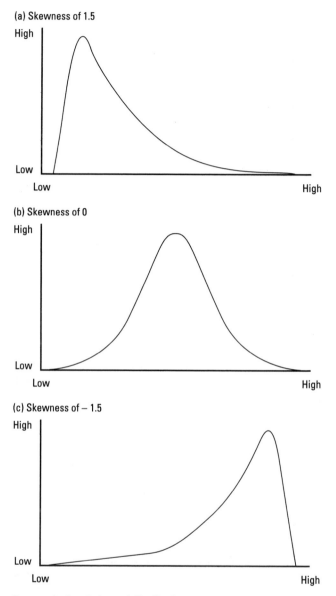

Figure 30.1   *Symmetrical and skewed distributions*

reflects a negative skew while a skewness of 0 indicates symmetry (Figure 30.1). A normal distribution will have a skewness of 0. A skewness of greater than 1 in absolute value normally indicates that the distribution is non-symmetrical.

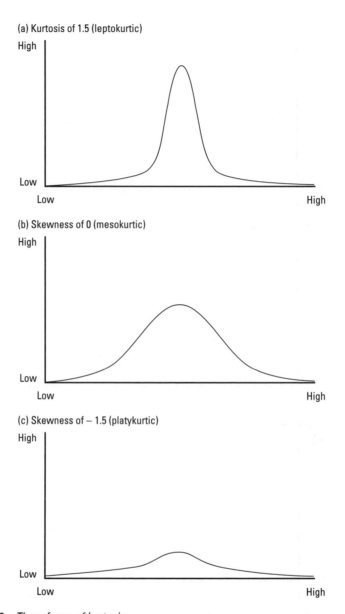

Figure 30.2   *Three forms of kurtosis*

[1]Strictly speaking a mesokurtic distribution has a value of 3 but in line with the practice used in packages such as SPSS the adjusted version is used here

What is Kurtosis?

Kurtosis indicates the degree of 'flatness' or 'peakedness' in a distribution relative to the shape of a normal distribution. A kurtosis of 0 indicates a peakedness that is the same as a normal distribution[1]. A negative kurtosis indicates a relatively flat distribution (platykurtic), while a positive figure indicates a 'peaked' (leptokurtic) distribution (Figure 30.2).

Using SPSS

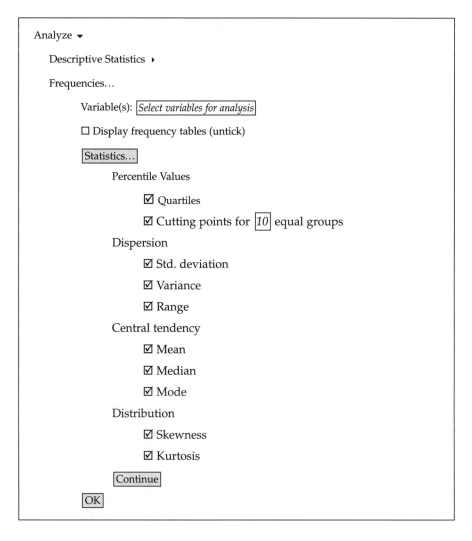

Analyze ▾

   Descriptive Statistics ▸

   Frequencies…

      Variable(s): Select variables for analysis

      ☐ Display frequency tables (untick)

      Statistics…

         Percentile Values

            ☑ Quartiles

            ☑ Cutting points for 10 equal groups

         Dispersion

            ☑ Std. deviation

            ☑ Variance

            ☑ Range

         Central tendency

            ☑ Mean

            ☑ Median

            ☑ Mode

         Distribution

            ☑ Skewness

            ☑ Kurtosis

         Continue

      OK

Notes

1. Strictly speaking kurtosis has a value of 3 when the distribution is normal. However packages such as SPSS adjust this figure so that a normal distribution has a value of 0.

31

Which Statistic to Use to Generalize
about a Single Variable

What is the Problem?

As with descriptive statistics, there is a wide and confusing range of *inferential* statistics that can be used with single variables. Again, the problem is to use inferential statistics appropriately and to select the correct one. The choice of inferential statistics is influenced by the:

- *type* of inferential test that is required;
- *number of categories* of the variable;
- *level of measurement* of the variable.

Both types of inferential statistic – confidence intervals and significance tests – can be used with single variables.

Using Confidence Intervals with Interval-level Variables

When using a random sample, confidence intervals can be calculated for the mean, skewness and kurtosis. The purpose of confidence intervals was discussed in detail in Problem 27, so you may need to refresh your memory of confidence intervals before reading further.

Table 31.1 provides the summary statistics and standard errors of these statistics for a sample of ages. We can use the standard error to estimate the range within which each summary statistic is likely to lie. We apply the rule that at the 95 per cent confidence level the population parameter will be within ± 2 standard errors of the sample estimate.

Using each statistic and its standard error, the confidence interval (last column) can be calculated easily. The first row of Table 31.1 indicates the confidence interval for the mean age – there is a 95 per cent probability that the average age in the population will be between 46.39 years and 47.95 years.

Table 31.1   *Age: mean, skewness, kurtosis and their standard errors and confidence intervals*

	Statistic	Standard error	2 standard errors	Confidence interval
Mean	47.17	0.39	0.78	46.39 to 47.95
Skewness	0.26	0.06	0.12	0.14 to 0.38
Kurtosis	−0.67	0.11	0.22	−0.45 to 0.89

Note: These kurtosis are the adjusted kurtosis figures calculated in SPSS where 0 indicates normal kurtosis.

Source: Australian Election Survey, 1998

The second row provides the confidence interval for skewness. Since this interval does not include zero within its range, we can be confident that the distribution in the population will also be skewed to the extent indicated by the range of the confidence interval – the skewness will be positive and modest.

The third row of Table 31.1 indicates that the kurtosis is negative (i.e flat relative to a normal curve), and the fact that its confidence interval does not include zero means that in the population the distribution is also likely to be similarly 'flat'.[1]

Which Test of Significance to Use

The logic and interpretation of tests of significance and of testing null hypotheses was outlined in Problem 23. You may want to refresh your memory of this matter before proceeding.

Tests of significance employ the logic of testing a 'null hypothesis'. This involves specifying or assuming a particular pattern and then comparing the *actual* pattern in the sample with the specified or *assumed* pattern. Since the sample pattern will not be identical to the specified pattern, the question is whether the difference between the sample pattern and the specified pattern is:

- small enough as to be attributable to sampling error;
- so large that the difference is most unlikely to be due to sampling error.

When working with a single variable the null hypothesis will assume a particular distribution and the tests of significance will compare the actual distribution of cases against the assumed distribution.

There are a range of tests of significance applicable to single variables. The choice between these tests largely depends on two factors:

Table 31.2   *The binomial test*

		Category	N	Observed prop.	Test prop.	Sig.
Own a	Group 1	No	1613	**0.88**	**0.85**	**0.001**
firearm?	Group 2	Yes	229	0.12		
	Total		1842	1.00		

- the number of categories of the variable;
- the level of measurement of the variable.

Binomial Test for Variables with Two Categories

The binomial test can be used for any variable with just two categories (or that has been collapsed to two categories). The test can be used *regardless of the level of measurement* of the variable. The use and interpretation of the test is best understood by examining a couple of examples.

Suppose we want to establish whether the sample is representative of its population or whether it is biased. We begin with the null hypothesis that the sample is an unbiased sample of the population – that any discrepancies are due simply to sampling error. The binomial test will indicate whether or not we can reject the null hypothesis.

For example, suppose that we know that in the population 85 per cent of people do *not* own guns. Our sample indicates that 88 per cent of the sample do not own guns. Is our sample biased, or can we continue to assume that the 88 per cent figure is due to sampling error? Table 31.2 provides the figures to evaluate the null hypothesis.

The first row shows a sample observation of 88 per cent of people who were not gun owners. The known population proportion of non-owners is 85 per cent. The significance figure of 0.001 means that there is an extremely low chance that the *difference* between 0.88 and 0.85 is due to sampling error – it reflects a real difference between the sample and the population. Since we know the correct figure in the population, the 0.88 figure must reflect sample bias. We can reject the null hypothesis that the sample is unbiased.

Suppose that we assumed that 50 per cent of a population are male and 50 per cent are female. We begin with a null hypothesis of a 50/50 distribution in the population. In a sample of the population we discover that 49 per cent are male and 51 per cent are female (Table 31.3). Could this be because the assumption of a 50/50 distribution was wrong or is the sample split of 49/51 likely to be due to sampling error?

In this case the significance test is well above the 0.05 level. This means that there is a high probability that the difference between the sample proportions and the population proportions is simply due to sampling error.

Table 31.3   *Binomial test with non-significant differences*

		Category	N	Observed prop.	Test prop.	Sig.
	Group 1	Female	944	0.51	0.50	0.610
Gender	Group 2	Male	921	0.49		
	Total		1865	1.00		

We would not reject the null hypothesis and we would continue to assume that the gender split in our population is 50–50 – there is nothing about our sample that would convince us otherwise.

Variables with More than Two Values

NOMINAL AND ORDINAL VARIABLES: THE ONE-SAMPLE CHI-SQUARE TEST   The one-sample chi-square test compares the distribution of cases across the categories of a variable with a hypothesized distribution.

Suppose we asked a group of 300 students to indicate which of three universities they most wanted to attend. The null hypothesis might be that preferences would be spread evenly between the three universities (see Table 31.4). However, these students gave a different set of responses to that anticipated in the null hypothesis (see the observed frequencies for example 1 in Table 31.4). Is the difference between the observed student choices and the assumption that each university will be equally desirable likely to be due to sampling error? Or is the discrepancy because our assumption was wrong – that in fact some universities are more desirable than others? The chi-square test results in a significance level of 0.37. This means that the sample preferences vary from the assumption of equality simply because of sampling error. We would not reject the null hypothesis of equal preference of university.

In example 2 in Table 31.4 we have a sample of 900 students. Again the stated preferences of students differ from the assumption of equality of preference. In this example, however, the chi-square test results in a significance level of 0.04, which means a relatively low chance that the stated preferences differ from the assumption of equality of preference, simply because of sampling error. We would reject the null hypothesis and argue that in the population university A is seen as more desirable than the others and that university C was seen as the least desirable.

Interval Variables: One-sample t Test

The one-sample *t* test compares the mean in a sample with an assumed or known population mean. For example, we may want to know whether our sample has an income bias. We may know that the mean income in the population is $40 500. In our sample of 1704 cases the mean income is

Table 31.4   *The one-sample chi-square test applied to two examples*

	N		A	B	C	Chi-square	Interpretation
			University				
Example 1	300	Expected	100	100	100	$\chi^2 = 2.0$	Assumption of equality of
		Observed	110	100	90	Sig = 0.37	preference is correct
Example 2	900	Expected	300	300	300	$\chi^2 = 6.0$	Assumption of equality of
		Observed	330	300	270	Sig = 0.04	preference is incorrect

Table 31.5   *One-sample t test*

	N	Mean
Income	1703	$42 044

One-Sample t Test

	Test Value = $40 500			
	t	df	Sig.	Mean Difference
Income	2.17	1703	0.03	$1544

Table 31.6   *One-sample Kolmogorov-Smirnov Z test*

One-Sample Kolmogorov-Smirnov Z Test		Income
	N	1703
	Mean	$42 044
Normal parameters	Std. Deviation	$29 426
	Absolute	0.118
Most extreme differences	Positive	0.118
	Negative	−0.090
Kolmogorov–Smirnov Z		4.86
	Sig.	0.000

$42 044. Is the difference between $42 044 and $40 500 likely to be due to sampling error or is our sample a biased representation of the population?

In Table 31.5 the difference between the sample and population means is $1544. The significance level of 0.03 indicates a low probability that a

Table 31.7   *Inferential statistics for single variables*

Level of measurement of variable

Number of categories	Nominal	Ordinal	Interval
2 only	Binomial test	Binomial test	• Binomial test • Confidence interval for mean, skewness and kurtosis
More than 2	One-sample chi-square test	One-sample chi-square test	• One-sample t test • One-sample Kolmogorov-Smirnov Z test • Confidence interval for mean, skewness and kurtosis

difference this large ($1544) would be due to sampling error. Since we know that the population mean is correct, we can reject the null hypothesis that the sample is unbiased.

Interval Variables: the Kolmogorov–Smirnov Z test

Some statistical methods (parametric statistics) assume that variables approximate a normal distribution. One way of establishing whether an actual distribution approximates a normal distribution is to compare it to the theoretical normal distribution. This is done with the one-sample Kolmogorov–Smirnov Z test.

This test evaluates the null hypothesis that the observed distribution approximates a normal distribution. Table 31.6 illustrates the output for the one-sample Kolmogorov–Smirnov Z test for income. It tests the null hypothesis that income is normally distributed.

The shaded section of the table indicates that the sample distribution is being compared against a normal distribution and that given the data a normal distribution would have a mean of $42 044 and a standard deviation of $29 426 (as well as other statistical properties).

The Kolmogorov–Smirnov value reflects the extent to which the sample distribution deviates from a theoretical normal distribution. The significance test indicates whether or not to reject the null hypothesis (of no difference between the sample and theoretical normal distribution). The low significance level indicates that the differences are unlikely to be due to sampling error – that the sample distribution does not approximate the normal distribution. If the significance level were above 0.05 we would not reject the null hypothesis and we would treat the distribution as though it were normal.

Summary of Inferential Statistics for Single Variables

Table 31.7 summarizes the inferential statistics available for single variables.

Using SPSS

Binomial Test

> Analyze ▾
>> Nonparametric Tests
>>> Binomial…
>>>> Test Variable List: [Insert variable name(s)]
>>>> Test Proportion: [Enter test value]
>>>> OK

One-Sample Chi-Square Test

> Analyze ▾
>> Nonparametric Tests
>>> Chi-Square…
>>>> Test Variable List: [Insert variable name(s)]
>>>> Expected Values
>>>>> ⦿ All categories equal: [if testing equal distribution hypothesis] OR
>>>>> ⦿ Values: ☐ [enter and Add expected values]
>>>> OK

One-Sample t Test

> Analyze ▾
>> Compare Means
>>> One-Sample T Test…
>>>> Test Variable(s): [Insert variable name]

Test Value: ☐ [*enter expected or known population mean*]

OK

One-sample Kolmogorov-Smirnov Z Test

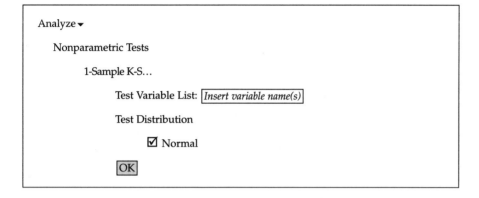

Analyze ▾

   Nonparametric Tests

      1-Sample K-S...

         Test Variable List: [*Insert variable name(s)*]

         Test Distribution

            ☑ Normal

         OK

Notes

1. This is based on using the adjusted version of the kurtosis statistic where 0 indicates a normal level of kurtosis.

Part Six How to Analyse Two Variables

32

How and When to Use Crosstabulations

Crosstabulations are one of a number of ways of showing whether two variables are linked to each other. They can provide a great deal of detail about a relationship between two variables and are widely used in research reporting. However, crosstabulations are only appropriate in certain types of situations and for particular types of variables. Even when crosstabulations are a suitable way of analyzing and presenting data, care must be taken to include the correct information and to present tables in such a way that relationships between the variables can be detected.

What is a Crosstabulation?

A crosstabulation provides a simple way of showing:

- the responses of subgroups in a sample;
- how two variables are related to each other.

The best way of thinking about crosstabulations is as a series of related frequency tables combined into one table. Table 32.1 contains three separate frequency tables. Table 32.1a shows the level of interest in politics for a sample of 2994 people. Table 32.1b reproduces the same table for the males only, and Table 32.1c shows the level of interest among females.

Table 32.2 presents a crosstabulation of two variables – gender and interest in politics. You will see that there are three columns in the table – a column for males, a column for females and a total column. The figures in each column are identical to those in the separate frequency tables in Table 32.1.

Had we used age group rather than gender, there would have been a separate column for each age group. In any crosstabulation there will be as many columns as there are categories of the variable placed on the top of the table. There will be as many rows as there are categories of the second variable.

Table 32.1   *Three frequency tables indicating interest in politics among males, females and the whole sample*

(a) Interest in politics (all)			(b) Males only			(c) Females only		
	N	%		N	%		N	%
A good deal	965	32.2	A good deal	577	39.7	A good deal	388	25.2
Some	1399	46.7	Some	636	43.8	Some	763	49.5
Not much	630	21.0	Not much	239	16.5	Not much	391	25.4
Total	2994	100.0	Total	1452	100.0	Total	1542	100.0

Table 32.2   *Crosstabulation of interest in politics by gender*

		Gender		Total
		Male	Female	
		(577)	(388)	(965)
	A good deal	39.7%	25.2%	32.2%
		(636)	(763)	(1399)
Interest in politics	Some	43.8%	49.5%	46.7%
		(239)	(391)	(630)
	Not much	16.5%	25.4%	21.0%
	Total	(1452)	(1542)	(2994)
		100.0%	100.0%	100.0%

What Information to Include in a Crosstabulation

A crosstabulation consists of a number of elements, illustrated in Figure 32.1.

Table Elements

Columns. There will be a column for each category of the column variable.
Rows. There will be a row for each category of the row variable.
Cells. A cell is the intersection of a row and column. It represents cases that have *both* that column characteristic *and* that row characteristic. The number of cells is in a table the number of rows multiplied by the number of columns.

Column Elements

Column variable name. A brief description of the column variable.
Column category (value) labels. A very brief description of the column category.
Column marginals. The column marginals (at the bottom of each column) indicate the number of people belonging to that column or subgroup.

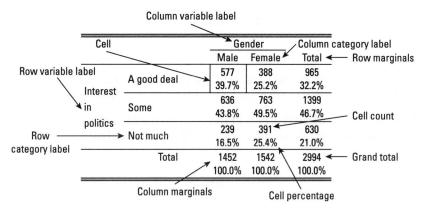

Figure 32.1   *Elements of a crosstabulation*

Row Elements

Row marginals. The row marginals (at the end of each row) indicate the number of people in that row (e.g. the number who have a great deal of interest in politics) and *the percentage of the whole sample who belong to that row.*
Row variable name. A brief description of the row variable.
Row category (value) labels. A very brief description of the row category.

Cell Elements

The cell elements are the cell count and cell percentages. The *cell count* is the number of cases that belong to the given cell. The cell can also contain one of three *percentages*, column, row or total, depending on whether the row total, column total or grand total is used to calculate it. Each of these percentages will be different and have a very different meaning.

Column percentages are calculated using the column total and indicate the percentage of those in that column that have the particular row attribute of the cell. In the case of males with a good deal of interest in politics this gives the following calculation:

$$\frac{577}{1452} \times \frac{100}{1} = 39.7\%$$

The column percentage has a very precise interpretation. It means 39.7 per cent *of that column (i.e. of males)* have a good deal of interest in politics.

Row percentages are based on the row total for that cell. In the case of males with a good deal of interest in politics this gives the following calculation:

$$\frac{577}{965} \times \frac{100}{1} = 55.7\%$$

The row percentage should be read as the percentage *of those in that row*. That is, 55.7 per cent *of those with a good deal of interest in politics* are male.

Total percentages are based on the grand total. In the case of males with a good deal of interest in politics this gives the following calculation:

$$\frac{577}{2994} \times \frac{100}{1} = 17.3\%$$

A total percentage is read as the percentage *of the total sample* that have both the column and the row characteristics. That is, 17.3 per cent of the sample are males with a good deal of interest in politics.

Which Percentages to Include

Selecting the correct percentage in a crosstabulation depends on two main considerations:

- the purpose of the crosstabulation;
- the way the table is structured – in particular, which variable is the column variable and which is the row variable.

PERCENTAGES FOR DESCRIPTIVE ANALYSIS If the purpose is purely descriptive, the selected percentage will depend on your particular focus. If you want to specify the percentage of a sample that has a particular mix of characteristics the total percentage would be used. For example, if we wanted to know what percentage of a sample were politically apathetic females, then the total percentage would be used.

If the interest is in the characteristics of a particular group, then the column or row percentage of that group would be used. If we are interested in the political interest of males then we would use the column percentages (i.e. percentage *of males* who are interested in politics). Alternatively, if we were interested in the characteristics of the politically apathetic we would select that row of the table and use the row percentages of that row.

PERCENTAGES WHEN DETECTING RELATIONSHIPS More often than not, the purpose of a crosstabulation is to test whether two variables are related. Often we will be looking at relationships in cause and effect terms and ask questions such as whether gender affects interest in politics (Figure 32.2).

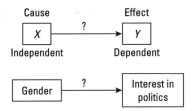

Figure 32.2   *Causal diagram of a two-variable relationship*

To use a crosstabulation to answer this type of question we must:

- identify which variable is presumed to be the cause and which is the presumed effect (i.e. which is X and which is Y?). The X variable, the presumed cause, is called the *independent variable*. The Y variable, the presumed effect, is called the *dependent variable* – it is presumed that the values of Y are dependent on the impact of X.
- decide on the placement of each variable in the crosstabulation.

Selecting the appropriate cell percentage is a function of the placement of the independent and dependent variables (X and Y) in the table:

- If the X variable is the *column* variable use *column* percentages.
- If the X variable is the *row* variable use *row* percentages.

Although there is no uniform practice regarding the placement of the X variable, my advice is always to place it at the *top of the table* and use the column percentage.

How to Produce Readable Crosstabulations

The crosstabulation we have used so far is relatively simple since it has only two columns and three rows. In addition, I have only included one of the three possible cell percentages. Crosstabulations can become extremely cluttered and very difficult to read. How can the presentation of a crosstabulation be simplified so that only the necessary information is included? Table 32.3 reproduces Table 32.2, but omits the unnecessary information.

When constructing a crosstabulation, ensure that the following information is included:

- *Table number and title.* The title should read: dependent variable by independent variable, (e.g. Table 32.3: Interest in politics by gender).

Table 32.3 *Crosstabulation with only the essential information included*

Interest in politics	Gender	
	Male	Female
A good deal	40%	25%
Some	44	50
Not much	16	25
N	1452	1542

- *Labels* that clearly identify the column and row variables and their categories.
- *Percentage signs* after the first percentage in each column. These indicate that the figures are percentages (see Table 32.2).
- *Footnotes* to provide necessary clarifying information.
- *Excluded cases* should be indicated in a footnote (e.g. 'don't know' and 'no answer' responses).
- *Column percentages* should be placed in each cell (assuming the independent variable is across the top of the table).
- *The total* number of cases in each *column* should be placed at the bottom of each column.

There is a rationale behind what has been included and excluded in Table 32.3. There is sufficient information in Table 32.3 to recompute all the information in the original table should that be necessary (except the decimal places).

The following information can be safely omitted:

- The *grand total* can be reconstructed by adding the two column totals.
- *Cell counts* can be recomputed by dividing the cell's column per cent by 100 and multiplying by the column total.
- *Row marginals* can be recomputed once cell counts have been reconstructed.
- *Row percentages and total percentages* can be recomputed once cell counts and row and grand totals have been recomputed.

How to Read a Crosstabulation to Detect Relationships

Two variables are related when people's characteristics on one variable are related to their characteristics on a second variable. To the extent that a person's characteristics on one variable help predict their characteristics on a second variable, the variables are related.

Table 32.4   *Two unrelated variables*

		Variable X				
		X_a		X_b		X_c
Variable Y	Y_a	25%	↔	25%	↔	25%
	Y_b	40	↔	40	↔	40
	Y_c	35	↔	35	↔	35
	N	200	↔	250	↔	300

Table 32.5   *Crosstabulation with both small and inconsistent column differences*

		Age		
		18–33	34–49	50 and older
Frequency of attendance at religious services	Never	17%	18%	16%
	Rarely	41	33	29
	Monthly	22	24	21
	Weekly	19	26	34
	Total	420	500	540

How you read a crosstabulation depends on the way it is constructed. Being the independent variable, X is at the top of the table. If X makes any difference to Y then the category of X to which a person belongs should make a difference to their responses on the Y variable. To see whether X affects Y, compare the column percentages *across* the columns *within* a row. If the percentages are much the same across the columns within the rows then the two variables are not related – they are independent of each other. In the example in Table 32.4, being in category X_a, X_b or X_c makes no difference to responses on the Y variable – the same percentage (25 per cent) of each category of X gave Y_a as response, and 40 per cent gave response Y_b regardless of whether they belonged to X_a, X_b or X_c.

Differences between column percentages (within rows) indicate that the two variables are related. The greater the percentage differences the more strongly the variables are related. In Table 32.3 there are percentage differences across the columns within rows. For example, 40 per cent of males compared to 25 per cent of females indicated a good deal of interest in politics. Similarly, only 16 per cent of males compared to 25 per cent of females had little interest in politics. These differences between males and females mean that gender is related to the level of interest in politics – being male or female is linked to the level of interest.

When reading crosstabulations in this way an immediate question arises. What if the percentage difference is tiny – say, 1 per cent (Table 32.5) – or there

Table 32.6 *Example of a very weak relationship*

		Gender	
		Male	Female
Approve of abortion	Yes	45%	47%
	No	55	53
	Total	427	541

is a percentage difference in some rows and not others? This matter will be discussed more fully in Problem 35. However, the quick answer is as follows:

- If there are clear percentage differences in some rows but not others the variables are related. Thus in Table 32.5, since there are clear age differences in weekly and rare religious attendance we would say that age and religious attendance are related.
- Tiny percentage differences do indicate a relationship between the variables *in the sample* but where these differences are very small (as in Table 32.6) they are of so little importance and are likely to be due to sampling error that we would, for all intents and purposes, treat the two variables as being unrelated.

When to use Crosstabulations

While crosstabulations can be an effective way of presenting information, they are not appropriate in all circumstances. They are likely to be inappropriate when:

- space is limited, since crosstabulations can take up a great deal of space.
- variables have a large number of categories.
- the sample is small – especially if the variables have quite a few categories. Subdividing a small sample into a large number of cells can result in unstable and misleading percentages.
- the detail may make it difficult for readers to see the patterns in the data – this is especially true in larger tables.

These problems can be reduced by collapsing categories of variables (pp. 34–8), and producing uncluttered tables using the guidelines outlined above. But in other situations it will be more helpful to provide a clear graph (Problem 33) or to use a statistic to summarize all the detail contained in a complex crosstabulation (Problems 35–37).

Using SPSS

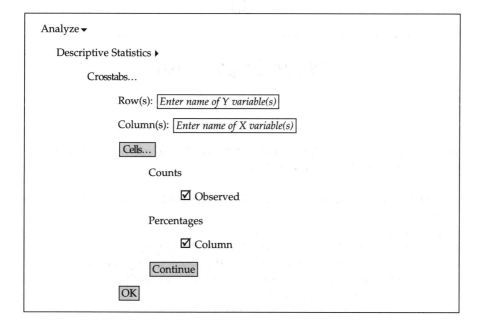

Analyze ▾

   Descriptive Statistics ▶

      Crosstabs...

         Row(s): [Enter name of Y variable(s)]

         Column(s): [Enter name of X variable(s)]

         [Cells...]

            Counts

               ☑ Observed

            Percentages

               ☑ Column

            [Continue]

         [OK]

33

Which Graph to Use

There is a wide range of choices and decisions when graphing the relationship between two variables. These include:

- which types of graph can be used to display relationships between two variables;
- which variable goes on which axis;
- how to choose between the types of bivariate graph;
- how the level of measurement of variables affects graphing decisions;
- the number of categories of the variables to be graphed;
- ensuring that a graph is easy to read;
- varying the scale on the Y axis to present data in new ways.

The key to successful graphing is to select the right graph for the right set of variables and to structure the graph so that it is uncluttered and the key features of the graph stand out.

Which Bivariate Graph?

Many bivariate graphs are extensions of the univariate graphs that have already been discussed (Problem 29). Rather than repeat that discussion, we focus here on two matters:

- how to represent two variables in the one graph;
- ways of constructing the scale of the Y axis.

When constructing a graph it is helpful to revisit the way in which crosstabulations are constructed and read. Crosstabulations consist of dividing the sample according to the category of the X variable to which cases belong and comparing the groups in relation to the Y variable (Problem 32).

Clustered Bar Chart

Graphs are constructed using much the same logic. Table 33.1 illustrates the relationship between age group and attitude to people having children

Table 33.1   *Attitude to ex-nuptial children by age group*

| | | Age group | | | | |
		18–34		35–55		55+
Attitude to	OK	61%	↔	42%	↔	17%
ex-nuptial children	Ambivalent	8		7		6
	Not OK	31	↔	52	↔	77
	Total	606		851		572

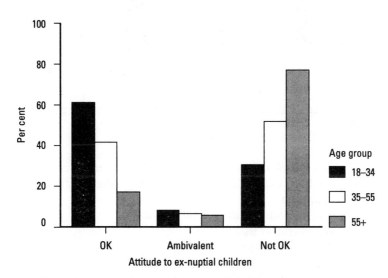

Figure 33.1   *Vertical barchart of attitude to ex-nuptial children by age group (percentages)*

outside marriage. A quick scan of the 'OK' row and the 'Not OK' row shows that the older the age group, the less approving people are of unmarried people having children.

Figure 33.1 translates this table into a bar chart. This bar chart is similar to the bar chart for a single variable, except that instead of three bars – one for each category of attitude to ex-nuptial children – there are three *clusters* of bars. Each cluster relates to a category of the Y variable ('OK', Ambivalent', 'not OK'). Each cluster has a separate bar for each category of the X variable. Reading each cluster is the same as reading a row in a crosstabulation – simply compare the bars within the cluster. By doing so we can observe the age group differences.

STEPS IN CONSTRUCTING A CLUSTERED BAR CHART   The steps in constructing a clustered bar chart are as follows:

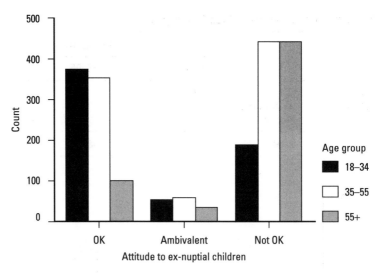

Figure 33.2 *Clustered bar chart of attitude to ex-nuptial children by age group (frequencies)*

1. Decide which variable is the *X* variable (the presumed cause, the independent variable) and which is the *Y* variable (the effect, outcome, the dependent variable).
2. Select the type of scale for the *Y* axis (vertical).
3. Construct the graph so that:
   (a) a cluster is constructed for each category of the *Y* variable. The categories of the *Y* variable will appear on the *X* axis (bottom).
   (b) each cluster is subdivided into bars with a separate bar for each category of the *X* variable. The categories of the *X* variable will appear in the legend.

TYPES OF VARIABLES APPROPRIATE FOR A CLUSTERED BAR CHART   The more categories these variables have the more clusters and bars are produced, so only use variables with a small number of categories. This normally restricts bar charts to nominal and ordinal variables.

SHOULD PERCENTAGES OR FREQUENCIES BE USED FOR THE *y* AXIS?   The *Y* axis can be scaled in a number of different ways (see below). When producing bar charts for two variables, avoid using simple frequencies for the *Y* axis – use percentages instead, as in Figure 33.1.

If the same set of responses is displayed as the *number* of people rather than as the *percentage* of people, a somewhat different picture emerges. In Figure 33.2 it appears that there is no difference between the 35-55-year-olds and the 55+year-olds. This is correct in that about the same *number* of 35–55-year-olds and 55+year-olds think that being unmarried and having children is OK or not OK. But (as Table 33.1 shows) there are more

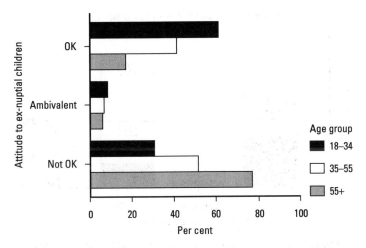

Figure 33.3   *Horizontal clustered bar chart of attitude to ex-nuptial children by age group (percentages)*

35–55-year-olds in the sample. That there is the same number in the two age groups approving or disapproving is meaningless. Using percentages standardizes for the different numbers in each category of the independent variable and enables comparisons across the categories.

Horizontal Clustered Bar Chart

The clustered bar chart can be have vertical bars (above) or horizontal bars (Figure 33.3).

Stacked Bar Chart

Another way of displaying the same information is to used a stacked bar for each cluster (Figure 33.4). Instead of placing the bars in each cluster side by side, we place them on top of one another. This chart is read by comparing the size of the segments *within* each bar. Thus in the 'OK' bar the 61 per cent figure for the young age group is compared with 42 per cent and 17 per cent for the middle and older groups, respectively.

Dot Graph

The dot graph can be easily adapted to display two variables at once. Rather than producing separate lines for each category of the Y variable, separate dots are placed on the same line (Figure 33.5). The categories of the

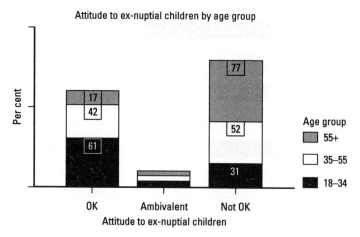

Figure 33.4 *Stacked bar chart of attitude to ex-nuptial children by age group (percentages)*

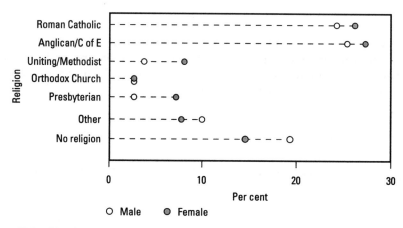

Figure 33.5 *Bivariate dot graph of religious preference by gender*

independent variable are indicated by distinctly different dots (e.g. hollow and solid). These dot charts are most effective when the independent variable has only two categories.

Line Graph

The appearance of a line chart is affected by several factors:

- *The level of measurement of the Y variable.* The Y variable should be ordinal or interval.
- *The number of categories/values of the Y variable.* Line graphs are more suitable for Y variables that have more than five or six categories.

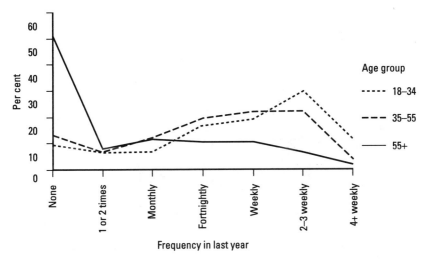

Figure 33.6 *Line chart of frequency of sexual intercourse in last year by age group (percentages)*

However, they are often not suited to variables with a very large number of values as this can produce a very jagged and confusing graph (see Figure 33.10a).

- *The number of categories of the X variable.* Since a separate line is produced for each category of the X variable, only X variables with a small number of categories should be used. This will normally mean that the X variable is a nominal or ordinal variable.
- *The scale on the Y axis.* The Y axis on a line chart should have a percentage scale rather than a frequency scale. Like the bar chart, the appearance of the lines in a line graph will be misrepresented if frequencies are used.

Figure 33.6 illustrates a line chart of frequency of sexual intercourse in the last year by age group. A separate line is used for each age group and the Y axis has a percentage scale.

Box-and-Whisker Plot

Box-and-whisker plots are (see Figure 33.7) appropriate when the:

- Y variable is interval,
- Y variable has quite a few categories or values,
- X variable has a small number of categories (a separate plot is produced for each category of X).

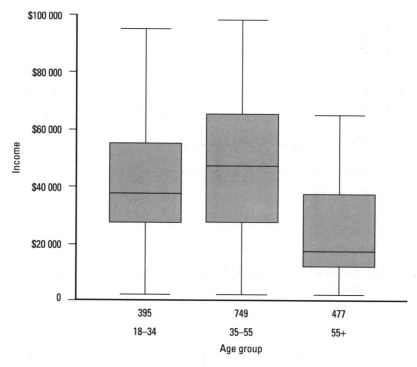

Figure 33.7   *Box-and-whister plot of income by age group*

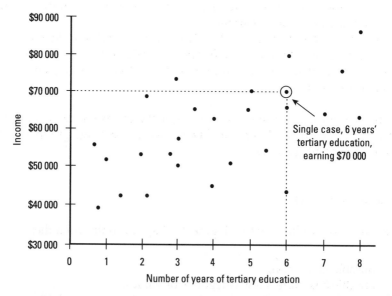

Figure 33.8   *Scatterplot of income by years of tertiary education*

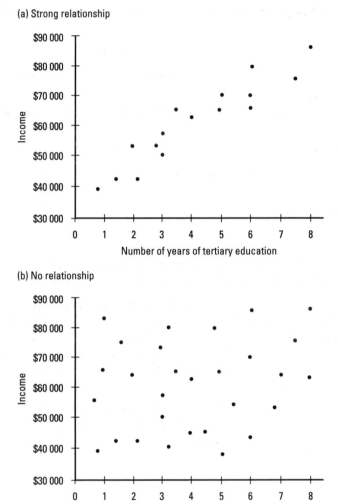

Figure 33.9   *Scatterplots indicating a strong and a non-existent relationship*

Scatterplot

The scatterplot (sometimes called an X–Y graph) is appropriate when both the X and Y variables:

- are interval;
- have quite a few categories.

In a scatterplot the X axis (horizontal) contains the values of the X variable and the Y axis (vertical) contains the values of the Y variable. Rather than

Table 33.2 *Matching graph type to level of measurement and number of categories of variables*

Level		No. of categories	Nominal	Ordinal			Interval		
			Few	Few	Medium	Many	Few	Medium	Many
X variable	Nominal, Ordinal, Interval	Few	Bar	Bar	Line	✘	Bar	Line	Box & Whisker
	Interval	Many	✘	✘	✘	✘	✘	✘	Scatter-plot

✘ = graph not suitable

using lines or bars each case is plotted on the scatterplot according to its value on the two variables. An example is shown in Figure 33.8.

To 'read' a scatterplot look for a pattern in the way the data points are scattered. In Figure 33.9a the data points fall more or less in a straight line and indicate that as the number of years of tertiary education increases so does the income. In contrast, in Figure 33.9b the data points are scattered over the graph and present no discernible pattern thus illustrating that the two variables are unrelated.

Scatterplots can be an effective way of examining relationships between two interval variables for a small number of cases. However, in large samples scatterplots can become extremely cluttered and very difficult to read (see Figure 33.10d).

Selecting the Type of Graph

Table 33.2 summarizes the discussion of this section in terms of the characteristics of the X and Y variables.

How should the *Y* axis be scaled?

I have already discussed the choice between using a percentage scale and a frequency scale on the Y axis and argued against the use of frequencies. However, we are not limited to percentage scales. Table 33.3 indicates a variety of ways in which the Y axis may be scaled and illustrates graphs using a variety of different ways of scaling the Y axis.

Table 33.3 *Matching methods of scaling Y with the level of measurement of Y*

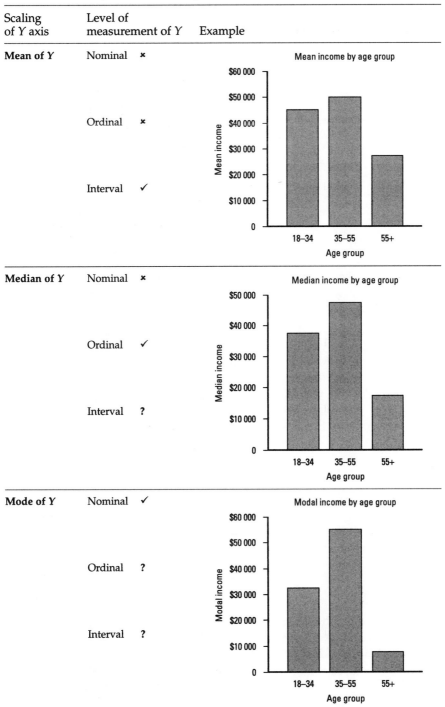

Scaling of Y axis	Level of measurement of Y	Example
Mean of Y	Nominal ✗	
	Ordinal ✗	
	Interval ✓	
Median of Y	Nominal ✗	
	Ordinal ✓	
	Interval ?	
Mode of Y	Nominal ✓	
	Ordinal ?	
	Interval ?	

(Continued)

Table 33.3 *Continued*

Scaling of Y axis	Level of measurement of Y	Example
Std deviation of Y	Nominal ✗	
	Ordinal ✗	
	Interval ✓	
Percentage above a given value of Y	Nominal ✗	
	Ordinal ✓	
	Interval ✓	
Percentage below a given value of Y	Nominal ✗	
	Ordinal ✓	
	Interval ✓	

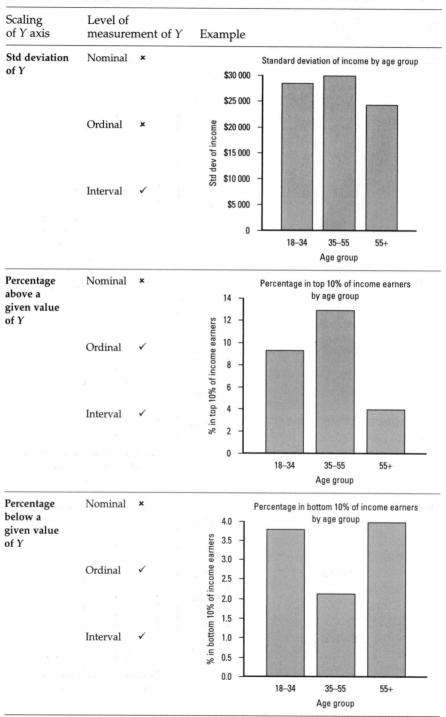

(Continued)

Table 33.3   *Continued*

Scaling of Y axis	Level of measurement of Y	Example
Percentage in a given category of Y	Nominal ✓	
	Ordinal ?	
	Interval ?	
Full range of values	Nominal ✗	
	Ordinal ✗	
	Interval ✓	

Legend: ✓ = appropriate; ? = sometimes appropriate; ✗ = inappropriate

Using alternative methods of scaling the Y axis has two important advantages:

- It can help focus on particular features of a distribution (mean, variance, etc.) and thus highlight particular characteristics of the distribution that would not be so evident if simple percentages were used.
- Using a different Y-axis scale can greatly simplify complex graphs. In Figure 33.10 some of the alternatives to the unreadable graphs use means on the Y axis to overcome the complexity of the unreadable graphs.

Since not all methods of scaling are appropriate to all levels of measurement, Table 33.3 also indicates the level of measurement of the Y variable for which the particular scaling method is most appropriate.

Graphs to Avoid (and how to Avoid them)

It is easy to make a simple graph into an unreadable mess. Simply select variables with the wrong number of categories, ignore the level of measurement of the variable and keep to the same scale for the Y axis regardless of the graph. Figure 33.10 presents difficult-to-read versions of the types of graph that have already been discussed. In the right-hand column I have provided alternative ways of graphing the same variables by using a different way of scaling the Y variable.

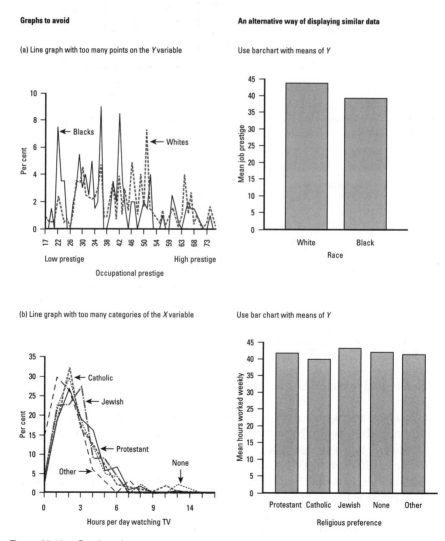

Graphs to avoid

(a) Line graph with too many points on the Y variable

An alternative way of displaying similar data

Use barchart with means of Y

(b) Line graph with too many categories of the X variable

Use bar chart with means of Y

Figure 33.10   *Continued*

Continued

Graphs to avoid

(c) Scatterplot with interval *X* variable with limited number of values

An alternative way of displaying similar data

Reduce categories of *X* and use mean of *Y*

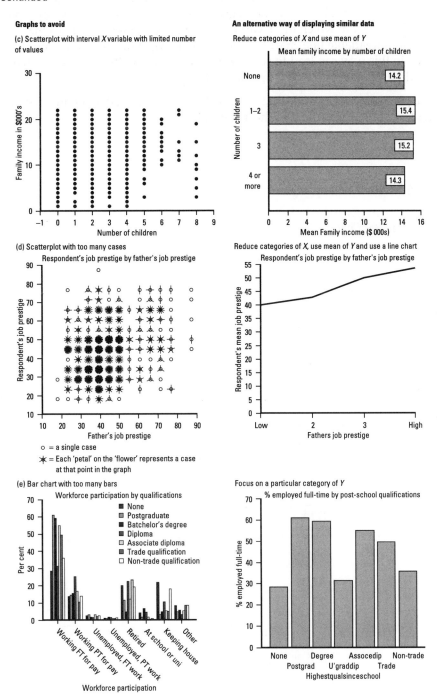

(d) Scatterplot with too many cases

o = a single case

✳ = Each 'petal' on the 'flower' represents a case at that point in the graph

Reduce categories of *X*, use mean of *Y* and use a line chart

(e) Bar chart with too many bars

Focus on a particular category of *Y*

Figure 33.10 *Graphs to avoid and some alternatives*

Using a different scaling method for the Y axis can be a good solution to the problem of Y variables with too many categories for a readable bar graph or for a line chart in which the Y variable has a large number of values that creates an unreadable line chart (see Figure 33.10(a)) While re-expressing the Y scale in this way can lead to some loss of information, this is exactly what is required to make difficult graphs readable.

The particular way in which the vertical axis is scaled will depend partly on the level of measurement of the Y variable.

Using SPSS

Clustered Bar Chart

Graphs ▾

    Bar...

        ☐ Clustered (click picture)

        Data in Chart Are

            ⦿ Summaries for groups of cases

        |Define|

            Bars Represent

                ⦿ % of cases

            Category Axis: | Insert Y variable |

            Define Clusters by: | Insert name of X variable |

            |Options...|

                ☐ Display groups defined by missing values (untick)

            |Continue|

        |Titles...|

            Title

                Line 1: | Graph title Y variable name by X variable name |

            |Continue|

        |OK|

Scaling the Y Axis to Frequencies or Percentages

Proceed as above, except that the selection

Bars represent

⊙ % of cases

---

is replaced by

Bars represent

⊙ N of cases

Stacked Bar Chart

Same as for clustered bar chart except for underlined sections:

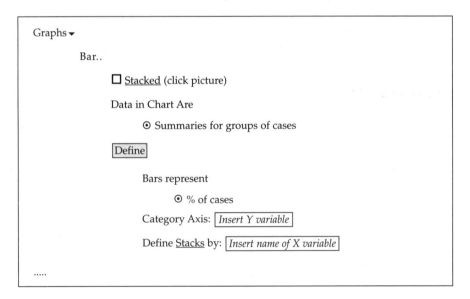

Graphs ▾

     Bar..

          ☐ Stacked (click picture)

          Data in Chart Are

               ⊙ Summaries for groups of cases

          Define

               Bars represent

                    ⊙ % of cases

               Category Axis: *Insert Y variable*

               Define Stacks by: *Insert name of X variable*

   .....

Line Graph

Graphs ▾

    Line…

         ☐ Multiple (click picture)

         Data in Chart Are:

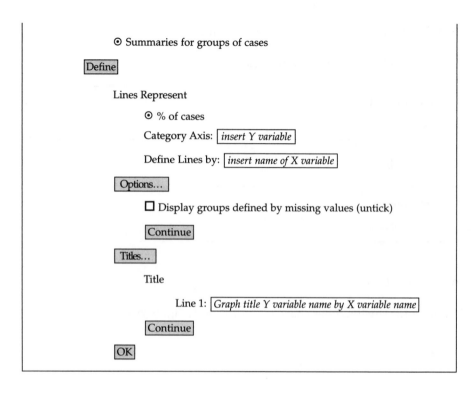

⊙ Summaries for groups of cases

Define

Lines Represent

⊙ % of cases

Category Axis: insert Y variable

Define Lines by: insert name of X variable

Options...

☐ Display groups defined by missing values (untick)

Continue

Titles...

Title

Line 1: Graph title Y variable name by X variable name

Continue

OK

Box-and-whisker Plot

Graphs ▾

Boxplot...

☐ Simple (click picture)

Data in Chart Are:

⊙ Summaries for groups of cases

Define

Variable: Insert Y variable

Category Axis: Insert name of X variable

Options...

☐ Display groups defined by missing values (untick)

Continue

OK

Scatterplot

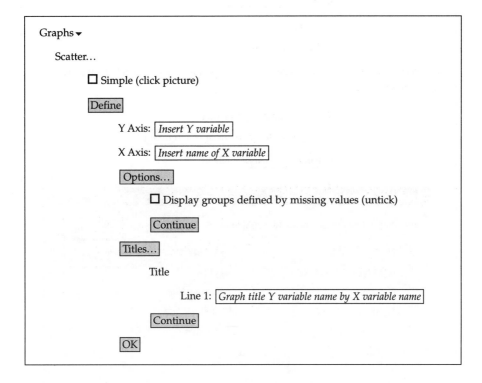

Changing the Y Axis for Bar Charts and Line Graphs

Select the graph type (Bar or Line) and then select the Simple option. Then within the Define window select 'Other summary function' and within the window that follows select the scaling method required.

Graphs ▾

   Line... [or Bars...]

      ☐ Simple (click picture)

      Data in Chart Are:

         ⊙ Summaries for groups of cases

      Define

         Bars [or Lines] represent

            ⊙ N of cases

            ⊙ Cum. n of cases

⊙ Other summary function

⊙ % of cases

⊙ Cum. % of cases

To select Count or % of cases select the appropriate options. To select other ways of scaling the Y axis select

⊙ Other summary function

Variable: [Enter name of Y variable]

[Change Summary...] [click]

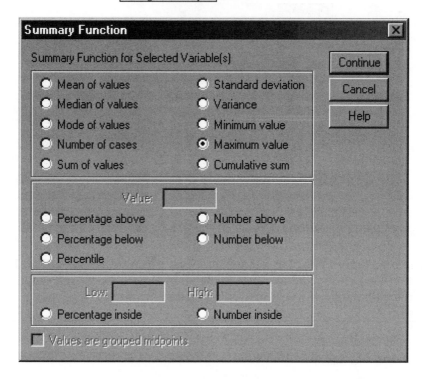

Select the required scaling method for the Y axis

[Continue]

[OK]

34

How to Narrow Down the Choice when
Selecting Summary Statistics

What is the Problem?

There is a vast and confusing choice of statistics that can be used for analyzing and summarizing relationships between two variables. To find one's way through this maze of alternatives it is helpful to have some signposts to help narrow down the range from which to select. This section provides a framework to help narrow down the choice. Problems 35–40 use these signposts to focus on the selection of statistical methods for bivariate analysis.

The first question to ask is whether a descriptive or inferential statistic is required. Descriptive statistics summarize patterns in a sample. Inferential statistics are used for generalizing from the sample to its population. Both types of statistics may be required, but you will still need to select particular statistics from among these two broad types.

Table 34.1 lists a number of questions that help identify the particular statistics that will be appropriate to your data. This section does not list the *particular* statistics from which you might select – that is the function of Problems 35–40.

Table 34.1 *Guidelines to help select bivariate statistics*

Descriptive	Inferential
Which Type of Descriptive Statistics do you need?	**What Type of Sample do you Have?**
Descriptive statistics for bivariate analysis fall into several types of statistics. These are: • Correlation statistics; • Regression statistics; • Statistics used for comparing groups.	• Probability? • Non-probability (inferential statistics assume a probability sample)?
What is the Level of Measurement of the X Variable • Nominal? • Ordinal? • Interval?	**Which Type of Inferential Statistics do you want?** • Point or interval estimate. • Test of significance.
How many Categories does the X Variable have? Are the categories: • Discrete? • Continuous? If discrete, how many categories does the variable have? • Two. • More than two.	**What are the Characteristics of the X Variable** Is the level of measurement • Nominal? • Ordinal? • Interval?
What is the Level of Measurement of the Y Variable • Nominal? • Ordinal? • Interval?	**How many Categories does the X Variable Have?** Are the categories • Discrete? • Continuous? If discrete, how many categories does the variable have? • Two. • More than two.
How many Categories does the Y variable have? Are the categories: • Discrete? • Continuous? If discrete, how many categories does the variable have? • Two. • More than two.	**What is the Level of Measurement of the Y Variable** • Nominal? • Ordinal? • Interval?
What type of Relationship are you Expecting between the X and Y Variables? • Linear. • Nonlinear.	**How many categories does the Y Variable Have?** • Discrete? • Continuous? If discrete, how many categories does the variable have? • Two? • More than two? **What is the Distribution of the Y Variable** • It can be assumed to be normally distributed in the population. (Use parametric statistics.) • It cannot be assumed that it is normally distributed in the population. (Use nonparametric statistics if sample is small. Can use either type of statistics in the larger sample.)

35

How to Interpret a Correlation Coefficient

Correlation coefficients provide an efficient means of detecting and summarizing relationships between variables. New researchers face two main problems when using correlation coefficients. The first is knowing how to 'read' them. The second is knowing which of the many different correlation coefficients to use with any given pair of variables. This section provides help with reading these coefficients, and Problem 36 helps work out which correlation coefficient to select in particular circumstances.

What is a Correlation Coefficient?

Correlation coefficients are a class of statistics designed to measure the extent to which variables are related. There are a large number of different correlation coefficients designed to take account of matters such as the level of measurement of and the number of categories in the variables.

These coefficients measure the relationship between two variables using an index that ranges from 0 (no relationship) to 1.0 (perfect relationship). While correlations close to 0 are quite common in the social sciences, correlations of 1 or near 1 are rare. The exception to this is when testing for the reliability of measures where similar measurement items are correlated. In such cases very high correlations can be achieved.

What Information does a Correlation Summarize?

All correlation coefficients detect whether the values on two variables co-vary. That is, they indicate if different values on one variable tend to be associated with different values on the other variable. For example, do people with different amounts of education also tend to have predictably different incomes? If so, the two variables co-vary.

Table 35.1 *Crosstabulations illustrating a weak and a strong relationship*

(a) Weak relationship   *(b) Strong relationship*

Agree with statement A	Gender		Agree with statement B	Gender	
	Male	Female		Male	Female
Yes	60%	65%	Yes	20%	70%
No	40	35	No	80	30
N	300	300	N	300	300

Establishing that two variables are correlated does *not* mean that one variable is caused by the other. While correlation is necessary for establishing causal relationships, it is not sufficient to demonstrate a causal relationship. A correlation *may* indicate a causal relationship, but it does not demonstrate it.

In addition to indicating co-variation, correlation coefficients can provide up to three types of information about a relationship.

Strength

The strength of a relationship is indicated by the size of the correlation coefficient: the larger the correlation, the stronger the relationship (Figure 35.3). A strong relationship exists where cases in one category of the X variable usually have a particular value on the Y variable while those in a different value of X have a different value on Y. For example, if people who exercise regularly nearly always have better health than those who do not exercise, then exercise and health are strongly correlated. If those who exercise regularly are just a little more likely to be healthy than the non-exercisers then the two variables are only weakly related.

The idea of weak and strong relationships can be illustrated with two simple crosstabulations (Table 35.1). In Table 35.1a the relationship between gender and attitude is weak since being male or female makes very little difference to whether a 'yes' answer is given. In Table 35.1b the relationship is much stronger – the differences between the answers of males and females are much greater.

Direction

When working with *ordinal* and *interval* variables we can talk about the direction of a relationship. A relationship can be either positive or negative.

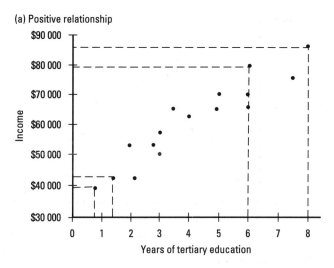

(a) Positive relationship

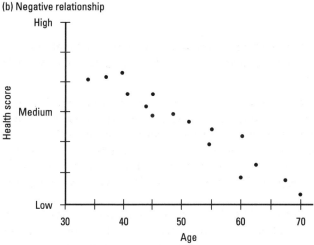

(b) Negative relationship

Figure 35.1   *Illustration of positive and negative relationships*

A positive relationship is one in which cases with *high* values on one variable are linked to *high* values on the other variable. Low values on one variable are related to low values on the other variable. In Figure 35.1a the dots represent cases. Notice that cases with high values on X (years of education) tend to also have high values on Y (income). Similarly, cases with low values on X tend to have low values on Y.

A negative relationship is one in which cases with *high* values on one variable are linked to *low* values on the other variable. In Figure 35.1b notice that cases with high values on X (age) tend to have low values on Y (health score) and vice versa.

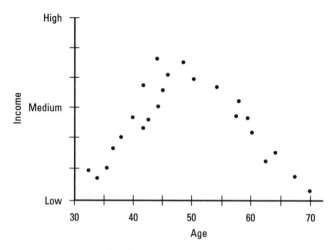

Figure 35.2   *A nonlinear relationship*

Negative relationships are denoted by negative correlations – a minus sign placed before the coefficient (e.g. –0.35) while positive relationships have no sign (e.g. 0.35).

Note that, since the notions of low and high are integral to the concepts of positive and negative relationships, it only makes sense to think of positive and negative relationships for variables where the notions of low and high make sense – ordinal and interval level variables. Correlation coefficients designed for ordinal and interval variables can take negative values, while coefficients designed for nominal variables never have a negative value.

DIRECTION AND STRENGTH   The direction of a relationship has no bearing on the strength of a relationship. A negative sign in front of a coefficient does not mean that the correlation is weaker than one without a negative sign. Thus a correlation of –0.35 is equally as strong as a correlation of 0.35.

Linearity

Relationships between variables measured at either the ordinal or interval level can also be linear or nonlinear. A linear relationship is one where the distribution of cases tends to form a straight line. Both negative and positive relationships can be linear (see Figure 35.1). A nonlinear relationship is one where the variables are related but not in such a straightforward way as a simple straight line. In a nonlinear relationship the value of a case on X makes a difference to the value that cases have on Y but not in a consistent direction (Figure 35.2).

Since linearity relies on the concepts of low and high values on variables, it is only appropriate to use the concept of linear relationships with ordinal

Table 35.2 *Information provided by coefficients designed for different levels of measurement*

Correlations designed for variables that are	Strength	Direction	Linearity
Nominal	✓	✗	✗[a]
Ordinal	✓	✓	✓
Interval	✓	✓	✓

[a]Coefficients for nominal variables identify nonlinear relationships and can therefore detect nonlinear relationships in relationships between ordinal and interval variables.

and interval variables. Any relationship that includes a nominal variable cannot sensibly be described as linear.

STRENGTH AND LINEARITY   Most correlation coefficients designed specifically for ordinal and interval variables are only sensitive to linear relationships. If there is a strong nonlinear relationship these particular correlations will still have a very low correlation coefficient (close to 0). A high coefficient therefore means that there is a strong *linear* relationship between the two variables. A low coefficient indicates the absence of a linear relationship but there may well be a nonlinear relationship that remains undetected by the linear measure.

Overview

- Correlation coefficients can contain up to three sets of information about a relationship: strength, direction and linearity.
- Directional and linear relationships only apply when using ordinal and interval variables.
- Different correlation coefficients are available, and their selection depends substantially on the level of measurement of the variables being correlated, (see Problem 36).

Does it Matter which Variable is the *X* Variable?

Sometimes. Most correlation coefficients are *symmetric*, which means that it does not matter which variable is treated as the *X* variable. The same size of coefficient will be obtained regardless. However a few of the coefficients are calculated in such a way that a different coefficient is obtained depending on which variable is treated as the *X* variable. These coefficients are called *asymmetric* coefficients. When using these coefficients, make sure that you correctly specify which variable is the *X* variable.

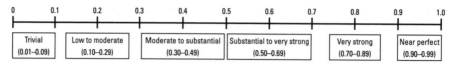

Figure 35.3   *Descriptors of various sized correlation coefficients*

More on Strength, Direction and Linearity of Relationships

How Strong is a Strong Relationship?

How high does a correlation coefficient have to be to be called strong? How small is a weak correlation? Although the answer to these questions varies to some extent with the particular correlation being used and the size of the sample (p. 176), it is nevertheless useful to provide some rules of thumb for different-sized correlation coefficients. The descriptors in Figure 35.3 are similar to those provided by Davis (1971) and Cohen (1988). (The website *http://www.sportsci.org/resource/stats/effectmag.html* provides a fuller discussion of what constitutes a strong relationship.)

Does Coding Affect the Direction of Relationships?

To make sense of the sign associated with a correlation coefficient, we also need to know about the *direction of coding of the variables*. The computation of a correlation coefficient is based on the numeric codes associated with each category of the variables – not the meaning of the labels attached to the categories.

We therefore need to pay careful attention to the way in which variables are numerically coded when interpreting what a negative or positive relationship actually means. Problem 8 discussed the problem of variables being coded in an inconsistent direction (Table 8.4) and proposed ways of avoiding this problem. Any correlation between the variables in Table 8.4 would be negative. This would mean that the higher a person's *code* was on the qualifications variable, the lower the income *code*. It would not mean that the higher the qualification was, the lower the income.

To avoid this awkwardness when interpreting correlation coefficients it is highly desirable to first code the variables so that low numeric codes are used to indicate a low 'quantity' of the variable and high codes are used to indicate a high 'quantity' (pp. 55–6). When the value of the code corresponds to the 'quantity' of the variable we can more easily discuss the correlation in substantive terms such as 'the higher the education, the higher the income'.

Interpretion of correlations involving a dichotomous variable must take the direction of coding of the dichotomous variable into account. Suppose, for example, that we find a negative correlation of –0.25 between gender and income. The negative sign means that the lower the gender *code* is, the more the income. But what does this mean? It depends on how gender is coded. If gender is coded so that male = 0 and female = 1 then the statement 'the lower the gender code' refers to males. Therefore the negative correlation indicates that males earn more than females. Had gender been coded in the opposite way, the correlations would have had a positive sign.

How to Check if the Relationship is Nonlinear

Since most correlation coefficients for ordinal and interval variables are only sensitive to linear relationships, how can we check for nonlinear relationships? There are a number of ways.

* *Use eta.* When the *Y* variable is interval level and the *X* variable has a limited number of categories, eta is an excellent coefficient that is sensitive to nonlinear relationships.
* *Use a nominal-level coefficient.* If a coefficient designed for ordinal or interval variables indicates no linear relationship then a coefficient for nominal variables (e.g. Cramér's *V*, Goodman and Kruskall's tau) can be used to check for nonlinear relationships. If these coefficients are higher than the linear measure there is a good chance that the relationship is nonlinear.
* *Examine graphs or tables.* Graphs and tables provide more detail than a single coefficient. An inspection of tables and graphs can show whether there is a nonlinear relationship.

36

Which Correlation?

The choice between correlation coefficients is largely a function of the:

- level of measurement of each of the variables;
- number of categories of the variables.

This section provides guidance for selecting among the large number of different correlation coefficients.

Two Nominal Variables

Table 36.1 *Correlation coefficients for two nominal variables*

	No. of categories		X Nominal	
			2	2+
Y Nominal	2		• Phi[a] • Yule's Q • Lambda[b] • Goodman and Kruskall's tau[c]	• Cramér's V • Lambda[b] • Goodman and Kruskall's tau[c]
	2+		• Cramér's V • Lambda[b] • Goodman and Kruskall's tau[c]	• Cramér's V • Lambda[b] • Goodman and Kruskall's tau[c]

[a]Phi is the 2 x 2 version of Cramér's V.
[b]Comes in both a symmetric and asymmetric version.
[c]Asymmetric coefficient will have different values depending on which coefficient is treated as X.

Two Ordinal Variables

Table 36.2   *Correlation coefficients for two ordinal variables*

		No. of categories	**X** **Ordinal**		
			2	2+	Many
		2	• Gamma[a] • Somers'd^c • Kendall's tau-b[d]	• Gamma[b] • Somers'd^c • Kendall's tau-c[e]	• No obvious choice[a]
Y	**Ordinal**	2+	• Gamma[a] • Somers' d^c • Kendall's tau-c[e]	• Gamma[a] • Kendall's tau-b[d]	• Kendall's rank-order tau[f]
		Many	• No obvious choice[a]	• Kendall's rank-order tau[f]	• Spearman's rho • Kendall's rank-order tau[f]

[a]If the variable with many values can be treated as interval, Pearson's *r* could be used.
[b]Gives higher correlations than other coefficients.
[c]Comes in a symmetric and asymmetric version.
[d]Used when the *X* and *Y* variables have the same number of categories.
[e]Used when the *X* and *Y* variables have a different number of categories.
[f]More appropriate than Spearman's rho where there are many tied ranks – a situation that occurs when one variable has relatively few categories.

Two Interval Variables

Table 36.3   *Correlation coefficients for two interval variables*

		No. of categories	**X** **Interval**	
			2	2+
		2	• Pearson's *r* • Phi[a] • Biserial r[a]	• Pearson's *r*
Y	**Interval**	2+	• Pearson's *r* • Eta[b]	• Pearson's *r* • Eta[b]

Notes
[a]Reduces to Pearson's *r* in the 2 x 2 case.
[b]Asymmetric and sensitive to nonlinear relationships.

One Nominal and One Interval Variable

Table 36.4   Correlation coefficients for one nominal and one interval variable

(a) When the X variable is nominal		
	X **Nominal**	
No. of categories	2	2+
Y **Interval** 2	• Pearson's r • Phi[a] • Biserial r[a]	• Cramér's V[c] • Lambda[c] • Goodman and Kruskall's tau[b,c]
2+	• Pearson's r • Eta[b] • Biserial r	• Theta • Eta[b]

[a]The same as Pearson's r in the 2 × 2 case.
[b]Asymmetric and sensitive to nonlinear relationships.
[c]Used in the absence of better coefficients.

(b) When the X variable is interval		
	X **Interval**	
No. of categories	2	2+
Y Nominal 2	• Pearson's r • Phi[a] • Biserial r[a]	• Pearson's r
2+	• Cramér's V[c] • Lambda[b,c] • Goodman and Kruskall's tau[b,c]	• Cramér's V[c] • Lambda[b,c] • Goodman and Kruskall's tau[b,c]

[a]The same as Pearson's r in the 2 × 2 case.
[b]Asymmetric.
[c]Used in the absence of better coefficients.

One Interval and One Ordinal Variable

Table 36.5   *Correlataion coefficients for one ordinal and one interval variable*

	Interval	
No. of categories	2	2+
Ordinal 2	• Pearson's r • Phi[a] • Biserial r[a]	• Pearson's r
2+	• Pearson's r • Biserial r[a]	• Jasper's multiserial correlation

[a]The same as Pearson's r in the 2 × 2 case

Using SPSS

Correlations for Variables in Crosstabulations

Analyze ▾

  Descriptive Statistics ▶

    Crosstabs...

      Row(s): [*Insert Y variable*]

      Column(s): [*Insert X variable*]

      ☑ Suppress tables

      [Statistics...]

          ☑ Chi-square

        Nominal

              ☑ Phi and Cramér's V

              ☑ Lambda [also computes Goodman and Kruskall's Tau]

        Ordinal

              ☑ Gamma

              ☑ Somers'*d*

              ☑ Kendall's tau-b

              ☑ Kendall's tau-c

        Nominal by Interval

              ☑ Eta

        ☑ Correlations

        [Continue]

      [OK]

Pearson's correlation, Spearman's rho and Kendall's tau-b

Analyze ▾

  Correlate ▶

      Bivariate...

Variables: [*Select variables to correlate*]

Correlation Coefficients

      ☑ Pearson

      ☑ Kendall's tau-b

      ☑ Spearman

Test of Significance

      ☑ Two-tailed

☐ Flag significant correlations (untick)

[Options...]

Missing values

      ⊙ Exclude cases pairwise

[Continue]

[OK]

37

How much Impact does a Variable have?

Correlation coefficients indicate the extent to which two variables are related – how *consistently* differences in one variable are associated with differences in the other variable. If gender and income were strongly related (men earning more than women) then most women would earn less than most men. If education were strongly related to income then most people with the highest education would earn more than the rest. However, knowing that gender makes a consistent and predictable difference to income tells us nothing about *how much* difference it makes. It is one thing to say that males will predictably earn more than females, but quite a different thing to say how much more they will predictably earn. Regression is a method of analyzing data that provides this information. This section focuses on simple bivariate regression where one independent and one dependent variable are analysed. Problems 46 to 49 discuss multiple regression which is used when the influence of a set of independent variables is to be assesed.

What is Regression Used for?

Regression analysis is used for two related purposes:

- to estimate *how much impact* one variable has on another variable;
- to make *specific predictions* about how particular types of people will 'score' on the Y variable.

What are the Features of Regression Coefficients?

Regression coefficients express the amount of impact of the X variable on the Y variable. These coefficients:

- are expressed in the units of measurement of the Y variable (e.g. dollars);
- have a lower limit of 0 (indicating no impact) but have no upper limit;[1]
- are asymmetric – they have a different value depending on which variable is treated as the X variable;
- can be either negative or positive.

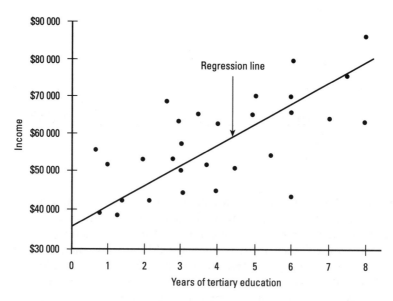

Figure 37.1 *Scatterplot with regression line*

When can Regression be used?

Regression can be used when:

- the *Y* variable is an interval variable;
- the *X* variable is either dichotomous or interval level.

How to use Regression to Estimate Impact and Make Predictions

Using the Regression Line

The best way to understand regression is to use scatterplots. Figure 37.1 provides a scatterplot indicating the relationship between years of tertiary education and income. In this plot the cases are represented by dots. A *regression line* has been added to the plot to summarize the data points. This line is placed in such a way that it gives the best estimate of the position of each case. If the actual cases formed a perfectly straight line a regression line could be fitted that perfectly represented all the cases. However, since the cases do not form a perfect line we must settle for the best approximation of all the cases.

One way of thinking about the regression line is to think of the mean in univariate analysis. The mean is a single value that summarizes the typical

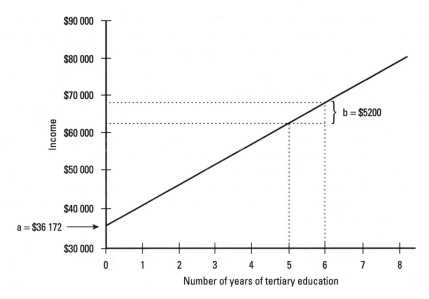

Figure 37.2   *The regression line*

value of an interval variable. A regression line is a single *line* that summarizes the typical value on the Y variable according to the corresponding value on the X variable.

Making Predictions

A regression line can be used to predict values on the Y variable for hypothetical people based on values of the X variable. Figure 37.2 reproduces Figure 37.1 but omits the actual cases. Using the regression line, we can predict the income for a hypothetical person with 6 years of tertiary education. By moving vertically from the 6-year point on the X axis until we meet the regression line and then moving horizontally to the Y axis we can locate a value on the Y axis – it is $67 372 (you will see shortly how I can get such precise dollar values). This income estimate is our best approximation of the income of a typical person with 6 years of tertiary education.

Estimating Impact

If we want to know how much difference education makes to income we need a *regression coefficient*. A regression coefficient is an estimate of the amount of change in Y for each unit change in X. In this example the regression coefficient is the extra income earned for each extra year of tertiary education.

The regression coefficient can be calculated from the scatterplot. Using Figure 37.2, the income level of a person with 6 years of tertiary education is $67 372, and that of a person with 5 years of tertiary education, is $62 172.

How much extra income does an extra year of education produce, on average? It is the difference between the predicted income of a person with 5 years and a person with 6 years of tertiary education (or between any two values that are a year apart). This gives an income difference of $5200 – for an extra year of tertiary education we anticipate an annual 'pay-off' of $5200. One 'unit of education' has an impact of '5200 units of Y'. This impact is the regression coefficient and is symbolized as b. In this case the coefficient is measured in dollars and is positive. A regression coefficient can be negative. If it were negative it would mean that for an extra year of education income declines by $5200.

A regression coefficient is sometimes called a *slope*. Figure 37.2 shows why. The gradient of the line is $1 : 5200$. The steeper the gradient the greater the impact of X on Y.

How to Use the Equation for a Straight Line

Using a scatterplot with a regression line can be a cumbersome way of working. A more efficient method is to use a simple algebraic equation. This is one equation that is well worth remembering. It is an equation for expressing a straight line in an X–Y plot:

$$Y = a + bX,^3$$

where Y is the predicted value on the dependent variable, a is the constant (the point where the straight line crosses the Y axis in the graph), b is the regression coefficient and X is a person's score on the independent variable.

Using the information in Figure 37.2, we can use this equation to predict values for any person. We have $a = \$36\,172$ – this represents the average income of a person with no units of the X variable – and $b = \$5200$. Thus our regression equation is

$$Y = 36\,172 + 5200X.$$

If a person has 2 years of tertiary education, we predict that they will earn:

$$Y = 36\,172 + 5200 \times 2 = 36\,172 + 10\,400 = \$46\,572.$$

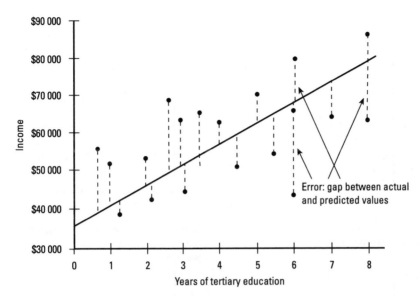

Figure 37.3 *Error when predicting from the regression line*

How does Regression Relate to Correlation?

Regression and Pearson's correlation are closely related, but they provide different information. The simplest way of expressing this is with scatterplots.

Figure 37.1 provides a set of data points and a regression line. Using the regression line, we would make predictions of the income of people with various amounts of tertiary education. If we then take *actual* cases and compare the income *prediction* for a person with their level of education with their *actual* income there will often be a gap. This gap represents an error of prediction. If we calculated the gap (error) between predicted and actual values of each case (Figure 37.3) and added the error for each case we would have a measure of the total error. That is, we would have a measure of how much error we make in predicting income by using just the regression line.

If all the cases were very close to the regression line the amount of error would be small since the vertical distance between each case and the line would be small. If the cases were more scattered the vertical distance of cases from the line would be much greater and the total error would be greater. Where cases are scattered the regression line would not be a very good basis for accurately predicting actual incomes.

Pearson's correlation provides a basis for assessing the accuracy of the predictions based on the regression line. When Pearson's correlation is squared

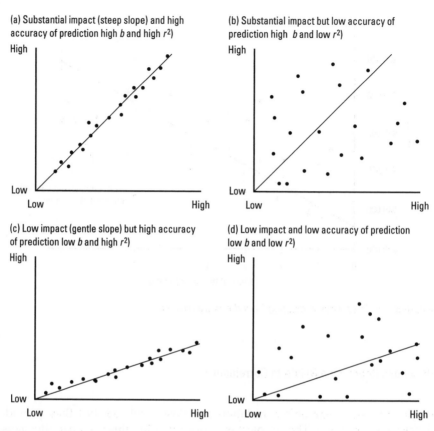

Figure 37.4   *The relationship between regression and correlation*

(r^2) it provides an index of how accurate any regression predictions will be. Where the data points are widely scattered there is a lot of prediction error. This is reflected by a low r^2. Where the data points are clustered around a regression line there will be little prediction error and r^2 will be high.

There is no necessary relation between the size of r^2 and the size of a regression coefficient or slope. A regression line with a high regression coefficient (steep slope) might have a strong correlation coefficient associated with it. This will occur when the data points are clustered closely to the line. Where this clustering occurs the regression line is a good summary of the data points and provides a good basis for prediction (Figure 37.4 a). However, a high steep slope can have a low associated r^2. This will occur where the data points are widely scattered and the regression line cannot provide very accurate predictions of actual cases (Figure 37.4b).

Similarly, a low regression coefficient (gentle slope) does not mean that the associated r^2 will also be low. Where the data points are closely clustered around a relatively flat line, the predictions of Y from that line can be quite

Table 37.1   *Model summary of the regression of education on income*

Model	R	R Square	Adjusted R Square	Std. Error of the Estimate
1	0.26	0.07	0.07	28 408

a Predictors: (Constant), No. years tertiary education

Table 37.2   *F statistic and significance level for regression model*

Model		Sum of Squares	df	Mean Square	F	Sig.
1	Regression	100016812085	1	100016812085	124	0.00
	Residual	1336494180073	1656	807061702		
	Total	1436510992159	1657			

a Predictors: (Constant), No. years tertiary education
b Dependent Variable: Income

accurate. Thus a low regression coefficient can have a high r^2 (Figure 37.4c). Finally, a low regression coefficient can have a low r^2 (Figure 37.4d) – it all depends on the scatter of the data points in relation to the slope of the line. The two dimensions of a relationship – slope and clustering – can operate quite independently of each other.

It makes sense to use both the regression coefficient (*b*) and the correlation (r^2) together. The regression coefficient provides very useful information on how much impact *X* has on *Y* and enables us to make outcome predictions for individuals. However, since any such information and predictions will be subject to inaccuracy, the r^2 helps assess how accurate any regression-based estimates will be.

Reading Regression Output

The output displayed in this section was generated with SPSS, but similar output will be generated by most reasonable statistics packages. The output reports the results for the analysis of income by years of tertiary education. There are three parts to the output.

The first part reports the *model summary*. The important statistics are R and R^2. These indicate *how well* the number of years of tertiary education predicts income. The value of r^2 is low, which means that tertiary education is not a very good predictor of income. In fact, only 7 per cent of the variation in incomes in the sample is due to differences in levels of tertiary education (Table 37.1).

The second part of the output reports the F statistic and significance level (Table 37.2). This statistic indicates the statistical significance of the r^2 and of

Table 37.3   *Regression statistics for the regression of income on education*

Model		Unstandardized Coefficients B	Std. Error	Standardized Coefficients Beta	T Sig.
1	(Constant)	**$36 609**	874		0.00
	No. years tertiary education	**$3364**	302	0.26	**0.00**

a Dependent Variable: Income

the regression coefficient. The very low significance level means that, although r^2 is low, it nevertheless is greater than zero – it is not simply due to sampling error (see Problem 39).

The third part of the output provides the regression coefficient (for the present we will ignore the other figures). In this data set the coefficient is $33645. That is, for each year of tertiary education a person's income is predicted to increase by $33645. However, because of the low r^2 we know that although this is our best prediction we will often be wide of the mark in real cases. The constant of $36 609 is the *a* coefficient in the regression equation. The significance level in this table indicates that our estimate of impact is unlikely to be due to sampling error (Table 37.3).

USING SPSS

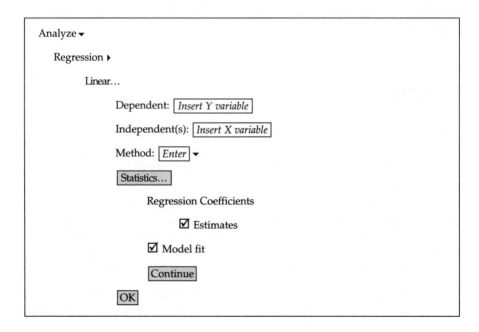

Analyze ▾

    Regression ▸

        Linear...

            Dependent: | *Insert Y variable* |

            Independent(s): | *Insert X variable* |

            Method: | *Enter* | ▾

            | Statistics... |

                Regression Coefficients

                      ☑ Estimates

                ☑ Model fit

            | Continue |

        | OK |

NOTES

1 Regression coefficients can be standardized or unstandardized. Standardized regression coefficients are generally only used in multiple regression and will be discussed in Problem 49. The discussion in this section relates only to unstandardized regression coefficients.

2 Any prediction based on a set of coefficients will be subject to error. The complete equation includes an 'error' term so that

$$y = a + b\,X + e$$

For the sake of simplicity I have not included this in equations in this book. Since we do not know what the figure for e is we cannot use it to arrive at more accurate predictions.

38

How to Tell if Groups are Different

Correlation and regression represent two common ways of statistically representing the relationship between two variables. Both approaches focus on analyzing the relationship between two variables. However, these methods are designed for interval-level X and Y variables.[1] A widely used way of analyzing relationships between interval-level Y variables and categorical X variables is to think about bivariate analysis in terms of comparing groups. In experimental contexts these groups will be differentiated in terms of their exposure to experimental interventions. In cross-sectional research such as a survey, groups are defined in terms of the presence or absence of a particular characteristic (e.g. being male or female; living in an urban or rural location; stage in the life cycle). In these contexts the grouping variable is the X variable and the groups are compared in relation to an outcome variable (e.g. income, attitude, performance, behaviour).

Groups can be compared on many different dimensions. However, the general model is to use a univariate summary statistic (e.g. mean, median, variance, skewness) to summarize a particular aspect of the Y variable. This summary statistic is obtained for each group and then the summaries for each group are compared. In other words, groups are compared using their 'score' on summary measures of the Y variable.

The most common method of comparing groups is in terms of the mean of each group on the Y variable. This will be the focus of this chapter, but other summary measures, including other measures of central tendency, variation or shape, can be used instead.

What can a Comparison of the Group Means Reveal?

The approach itself is simple: obtain a mean for each group and observe the differences in means between the groups. The mean is given in the units of measurement of the Y variable. Thus in Table 38.1, which indicates the mean income for a group of males and females, the means (44 639 and 39 340) are expressed in dollars. These two means readily indicate that males, on average, earn $5299 more than females.

Table 38.1 *Mean income by gender*

Gender	Mean ($)	N	Std. deviation
Male	44 640	860	30 285
Female	39 341	838	28 248
Total	42 024	1698	29 409

Examining mean differences between groups can indicate a number of important aspects of the relationship between X and Y.

Strength

The difference between the group means indicates something about the strength of the relationship between X and Y. Large differences indicate a stronger relationship than small differences. While a rough sense of the strength of the relationship can be captured by examining the differences between the means of each group, there is a more systematic way of examining the strength. We can calculate a correlation coefficient to capture the strength of the relationship between the two variables. A common correlation used when comparing means across groups is *eta*, since this is sensitive to nonlinear relationships.

Direction

When the X variable is ordinal, examining the pattern of change in the means across groups can indicate whether the relationship between X and Y is positive or negative. If the means increase as the group value increases, the relationship is positive (Figure 38.1a). If the means decline then the relationship is negative.

Linearity

Mean comparisons can also indicate whether the relationship is linear or nonlinear. If the means change in a consistent direction across a set of ordered groups the relationship is probably linear – especially if the gaps between the means are consistent (Figure 38.1a). If a comparison of the means has an up-and-down pattern or a consistently and marked reducing gap, then the relationship is probably nonlinear (Figure 38.1b).

As well as indicating the strength of the relationship, eta can also indicate whether or not the relationship is linear or nonlinear. Earlier I suggested that one way of detecting nonlinear relationships is to compare a correlation that measures only linear relationships with one that is also sensitive to nonlinear

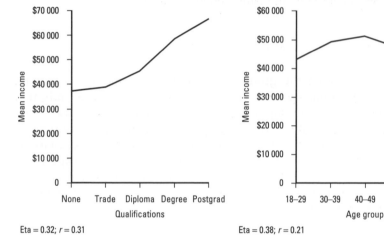

(a) Positive linear relationship

Mean income by qualifications

Qualifications	Mean ($)	N	Std. deviation
None	**37 365**	521	27 685
Trade	**38 890**	723	26 481
Diploma	**45 507**	64	28 172
Degree	**58 750**	180	30 568
Postgrad	**66 777**	128	32 919
Total	43 081	1616	29 504

(b) Curvilinear relationship

Mean income by age group

Age group	Mean ($)	N	Std. deviation
18–29	**43 154**	237	28 477
30–39	**49 186**	332	28 757
40–49	**51 246**	381	29 006
50–59	**47 179**	296	31 011
60+	**22 473**	375	19 217
Total	42 242	1621	29 476

Eta = 0.32; r = 0.31

Eta = 0.38; r = 0.21

Figure 38.1   *Linear and nonlinear relationships based on means*

relationships (Problem 12). In this context comparing eta with Pearson's r will indicate whether the difference between the group means is linear or nonlinear. If eta and r are similar the relationship is linear (as in Figure 38.1a). If eta is substantially higher than r the relationship is nonlinear (as in Figure 38.1b).

Another way of displaying mean differences between groups is to use a tree diagram (Figure 38.2).

Analysis of Variance

Analysis of variance (ANOVA) is a way of examining differences between the means of groups and of evaluating whether the mean differences found in the sample would hold in the population. One-way ANOVA is used for analysis when there is just one X variable, as in the cases described above. The analysis produces an F ratio which is used to indicate whether the differences between the group means are attributable to sampling error. *Post hoc*

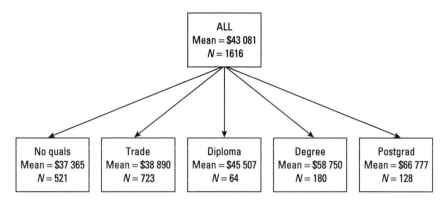

Figure 38.2   *Tree diagram of means: Income by qualifications*

comparisons are frequently used in conjunction with one-way ANOVA to identify *which* pairs of groups show statistically significant mean differences. These methods of analysis are discussed further in Problem 39.

Using SPSS

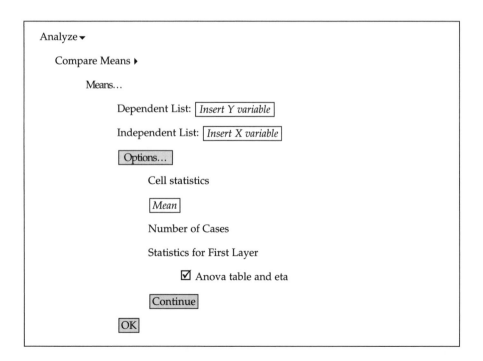

Notes

1 These methods can be used with dichotomous X variables, and dummy regression provides a way of dealing with categorical X variables.

39

Which Test of Significance?

There is an abundant and confusing array of bivariate tests of statistical significance. This section provides guidelines to help select the correct one.

When to Use Significance Tests

When you have a Probability Sample

Statistical inference only makes sense when data come from a probability sample. The tests assess the likelihood that correlations, differences between groups, etc. are due to sampling error or whether they reflect patterns in the population. This inference is only possible with probability samples.

With Measures of Effect Size

Tests of significance should be used together with descriptive measures that indicate the way in which variables are related. The term *effect* size refers to any type of statistic that describes the way two variables are related. Typically this class of statistic (see Problems 23–27) indicates the strength, direction and sometimes the nature (linearity) of the relationship or group differences.

Different tests of significance are used in conjunction with different measures of relationships. We have seen that different correlation coefficients are used depending on the level of measurement of the X and Y variables and the number of categories of the variables. The same applies to tests of significance.

The following discussion is divided into two parts. The first lists tests that are used with different correlation coefficients, while the second section outlines tests when the research design is based on comparing groups on a dependent variable.

Table 39.1 *Tests of significance for measures of association*

Measure of association[a]	Test of significance	References
Biserial r	Compute critical ratio and compare to unit normal curve	McNemar (1969)
Cramér's V	Pearson's chi-square	Reynolds (1977)
Eta	F test	Sheskin (1984)
Gamma	Test designed for gamma	Kendall (1970)
Goodman and Kruskall's tau	Pearson's chi-square	Reynolds (1977)
Kendall's tau-b or tau-c	Test designed for tau	Kendall (1970)
Lambda	Test designed for lambda or Pearson's chi-square	Reynolds (1977)
Pearson's r	F test or Fisher's transformation of r to z-score for comparison with unit normal curve	Hayes (1973)
Phi	Fisher's exact test or Pearson's chi-square	Peatman (1947)
Somers'd	Test designed for d	Kendall (1970)
Spearman's rho	Test designed for rho	Siegel (1956)

[a] See Problem 36 for situations where each measure is appropriate.

Tests of Significance with Correlation Coefficients

Problem 36 describes criteria for selecting particular correlation coefficients. The selection of tests of significance to be used in conjunction with these correlations is fairly unproblematic when using modern statistical analysis packages. On requesting a particular correlation, most packages automatically compute a test of significance for it. The combinations are listed in Table 39.1, and references are provided for those who might like to read about the particular ways in which these tests are calculated.

Selecting Tests of Significance when Comparing Groups

Selecting between tests for comparing groups depends on:

- the nature of the distribution (parametric or nonparametric);
- the number of groups or variables to be compared (2 samples or 2+ samples);
- the nature of groups or samples (related or independent);
- the level of measurement of variables (nominal, ordinal or interval);
- the number of categories of variables (dichotomous or 3+).

Tables 39.2–39.5 indicate which tests are used depending on the mix of these characteristics.

Should a Parametric or a Nonparametric Test be Used?

Tests of significance come in two 'flavours': parametric and nonparametric. Parametric tests assume that the data for the variable are drawn from a population in which that variable forms a normal distribution. Nonparametric statistics do not assume normality and are based on the *ranks* of categories rather than the distribution of scores. As such they treat variables as ordinal and the statistics are not as powerful as parametric statistics.

Where both a parametric and nonparametric test are available, which should be selected? The following guidelines can help with the decision:

- If possible use the parametric test since these are more powerful statistics that take the *amount* of difference between cases into account rather than just the *order* of cases.
- If the data are not from a normal distribution you might transform them so that parametric tests can be used (see Problem 11).
- *For larger samples* (100 or more) you can safely use parametric statistics. The central limit theorem (see Problem 11) ensures that parametric tests will work well even for non-normal distributions.
- *For small samples* it is important to use nonparametric tests for non-normal distributions. Parametric tests will be unreliable.

What is the Difference Between Independent Samples and Related Samples?

The distinction between *independent samples* and *related samples* is an important one in selecting and interpreting tests of significance. However, the distinction is more confusing than it needs to be because of the variety of terms used and because of the way in which the term 'sample' is used.

INDEPENDENT SAMPLES   A number of other terms are used to describe independent samples, including *unrelated samples*, *unmatched samples* and *samples based on random selection*. Independent samples are those in which the selection of one sample has no implications for the membership of the other sample(s). Members of one sample are not part of the other sample(s) and members are either recruited randomly or allocated randomly among the samples. In experimental designs cases are randomly allocated to each group (sample) in the experiment. In cross-sectional survey designs the 'samples' are derived from dividing cases into groups based on their characteristic on the X variable (e.g. gender, age group).

Conducting analysis with independent samples usually involves a single data set. A grouping variable (the X variable) is selected. If the grouping variable has two categories (or is collapsed into two categories) the analysis will require a *two-sample* statistic. If the grouping variable has three or more categories a *k-sample* statistic (i.e. a statistic for three or more subgroups) will be used. Responses on the *Y* variable are analysed and compared across the samples (or subgroups defined by the grouping variable).

RELATED SAMPLES   Other terms used to describe related samples are *paired samples*, *matched samples* and *repeated measures samples*. Related samples are those in which membership of one sample either defines or influences selection into the other samples. In many contexts the related 'samples' consist of the same cases. For example, in a panel study or a before-and-after design the same cases are tracked over time and measurements are taken on two or more occasions. 'Before' measures are compared with 'after' measures to evaluate the impact of events or interventions occurring between the two measures.

In cross-sectional designs the same people respond to a set of *related questions*. For example, each person may answer three separate questions asking them to indicate on a 0–100 scale how warmly they felt about three different political leaders. In related samples designs the three questions, answered by the *same* sample, are treated as three related samples. The pattern of responses across these three variables (or three 'samples') is examined to see if there are differences in the pattern of responses across the three 'samples'.

Related samples designs differ from independent samples designs in that:

- related samples designs do not specify a grouping variable;
- related samples designs compare the same (or matched) cases on related variables (i.e. variables that have the same form – values, content, level of measurement categories, etc.).

What is the Difference Between Two Samples and K Samples?

When the grouping variable has two values a two-sample test is required. If the grouping variable has three or more categories we require a *k*-sample test (i.e. a test for more than two samples).

When the analysis involves comparing responses of the same (or matched cases) on two or more related variables or the same characteristic at two time points a two-sample test is used. If three or more variables or the same characteristic is examined at three or more time points a *k*-sample test is required.

Tests for Two Independent Samples

These tests compare two independent groups for differences on the *Y* variable. Different tests are available depending on the level of measurement and the number of categories of the *Y* variable (Table 39.2).

Table 39.2 *Significance tests for two independent samples (groups)*

Characteristics of Y

Number of values	Level of measurement	Test	Comments
Two	Nominal	Chi-square Fisher's exact test	• Better than chi-square for two dichotomous variables
	Ordinal	Chi-square Fisher's exact test	See above
	Interval	Chi-square Fisher's exact test	See above
More than two	Nominal	Chi-square	
	Ordinal	Mann–Whitney U	• Popular test based on difference in rank positions of cases from the two samples
		Kolmogorov–Smirnov z	• Compares the distributions of the two groups
		Wald–Wolfowitz runs	• The least powerful of these tests for ordinal Y variables
		two-sample medians test	• Compares medians of two groups
	Interval	Mann–Whitney U	See above
		Kolmogorov–Smirnov z	See above
		Wald–Wolfowitz runs two-sample medians test	See above See above
		two-sample z test	• Compares means of two groups • Same as F test in one-way ANOVA when only two groups • Parametric • OK for larger samples
		t test (independent samples)	• Parametric • Normal distribution of Y • For small samples (less than 100)

In all these tests a low significance level indicates that the differences between the groups are unlikely to be due to sampling. Whatever distinguishes the two groups (e.g. gender, experimental intervention) is related to the Y variable.

Table 39.3 *Significance tests for k independent samples (groups)*

Characteristics of Y

Number of values	Level of measurement	Test	Comments
Two	Nominal	Chi-square	• Tests whether the distributions of the groups are independent of each other.
	Ordinal	Chi-square	See above
	Interval	Chi-square	See above
More than two	Nominal	Chi-square	See above
	Ordinal	Kruskall–Walis H	• Extension of the Mann–Whitney U test • The nonparametric equivalent of one-way analysis of variance and the F test • Does not indicate *which* groups differ
			• Compares medians of three or more groups • An extension of the two-sample median test, interpreted in the same way
		k-sample medians test	• Does not indicate *which* groups differ
	Interval	Kruskall–Walis H	See above
		k-sample medians test	See above
		F test	• Parametric • Normal distribution of Y • Does not indicate *which* groups differ

Tests for Three or More Independent Samples

These tests are conceptually similar to the two independent samples tests, except that they can test for differences between three or more groups. This means that in cross-sectional survey designs the X variable can have three or more categories and in experimental designs there can be additional experimental conditions. Different tests are available for nominal, ordinal and interval Y variables (Table 39.3).

An example of a k independent samples design in an experimental setting would be where workers in a factory are randomly allocated to one of four bonus systems: (a) individual bonuses based on individual work performance; (b) bonuses calculated on the performance of a small work group; (c) factory-wide bonuses based on factory-wide performance; (d) automatic bonuses at a set level for everyone. The research question is whether the type

Table 39.4 *Significance tests for two related samples (variables)*

Characteristics of *Y*

Number of values	Level of measurement	Test	Comments
Two	Nominal	McNemar	• Typically used for repeated measures tests with the same cases (before and after) • Only suitable for just two categories of the *Y* variable (pass, fail)
	Ordinal	McNemar	See above
	Interval	McNemar	See above
More than two	Nominal	Marginal homogeneity test	• An extension of the McNemar test. • Useful in before-and-after tests where there are three or more possible responses
	Ordinal	Sign test	• Compares the responses of the same cases on both variables and classifies each person's responses on the second variable as being higher, lower or the same as the first variable
		Wilcoxon signed ranks	• Similar to sign test except that it also takes into account the *amount* and not just the direction of difference between a person's rank on the two variables
	Interval	Sign test	See above
		Wilcoxon signed ranks	See above
		t test (paired samples)	• Parametric • Normal distribution of *Y* • For small samples (less than 100)

of bonus system affects individual work productivity. The statistical test would evaluate whether any group differences in productivity could be attributed to the bonus system or whether any productivity differences were simply random fluctuations.

A low significance level in these tests indicates that there are differences between the groups that are not simply random. However, a low significance level does not indicate whether all the groups differ from one another or whether just particular groups differ. To determine which groups differ a *post hoc* test would be required.

Table 39.5   *Significance tests for k related samples (variables)*

Number of values	Level of measurement	Test	Comments
Two	Nominal	Cochran's Q	• Y variable should be coded as 0 or 1 • Same as McNemar's test except that it compares three or more variables (samples)
	Ordinal	Cochran's Q	See above
	Interval	Cochran's Q	See above
More than two	Nominal		
	Ordinal	Friedman's test	• Extends Cochran's test to variables with more than two categories
	Interval	Friedman's test	See above

Characteristics of *Y* (heading above the table columns "Number of values / Level of measurement")

Tests for Two Related Samples

The language describing tests for related samples can be somewhat confusing. Normally you will have a single data set and your actual analysis involves selecting *two variables* from a single data set (sample). The key point is to note the term *related* samples. In many situations the *same* sample is examined *twice*. That is, the responses from the sample on one variable are examined and then the responses of the sample on another related variable are examined. This might be the same characteristic (e.g. depression) measured on two occasions. Related samples tests are frequently used to analyse experiments in which data are collected from the sample before an intervention and again afterwards. The before measure is treated as the measure from sample 1, and the after measure is treated as the measure from sample 2 (see the SPSS section below for the method of specifying the analysis).

Since this approach to analysis involves comparing two variables it is a little more difficult to think in terms of an *X* and a *Y* variable. The easiest way to frame this approach in *X* and *Y* variable terms is to think of the *X* variable as being whatever differentiates the two measures. In a before-and-after context the *X* variable is whatever distinguishes before from after the intervention.

Tests for Three or More Related Samples (Variables)

In practice, when we talk about three or more related samples we mean comparing the distributions of three or more related *variables* from the same sample (see above). An example of a study in which these statistics would be appropriate is an experiment in which the same group was tested on three or more occasions. Each test constitutes a separate 'sample'. In a cross-sectional design these tests might be used when three or more similar measures are obtained from the same sample. For example, a sample of final-year high school students might be asked to rate the four local universities on a scale of 1 (low rating) to 10 (high rating). This design would produce four similar variables: university A rating, university B rating, university C rating and university D rating. The test would examine whether there is any difference in the way the four universities are rated.

Using SPSS

Since SPSS automatically computes tests of significance for the correlation coefficients listed in Table 39.1, there is no need to indicate how to obtain these tests beyond indicating how to obtain the correlations. This was covered in Problem 36.

Two Independent Samples Tests

CHI-SQUARE AND FISHER'S EXACT TEST   See Problem 32, where instructions are given for obtaining crosstabulations. One of the Statistics options when producing crosstabulations is Chi-square. When both variables in a crosstabulation are dichotomous and chi-square is requested, Fisher's exact test is also produced.

MANN–WHITNEY U TEST, KOLMOGOROV–SMIRNOV Z TEST AND WALD–WOLFOWITZ TEST

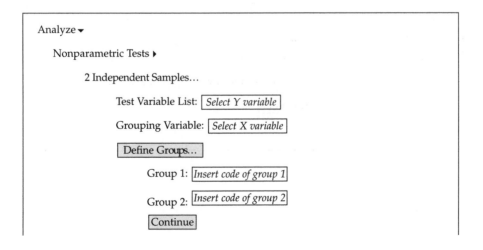

Test type

☑ Mann-Whitney *U*

☑ Kolmogorov-Smirnov *Z*

☑ Wald-Wolfowitz runs

Options...

Missing Values

⊙ Exclude cases test-by-test

Continue

OK

T TEST

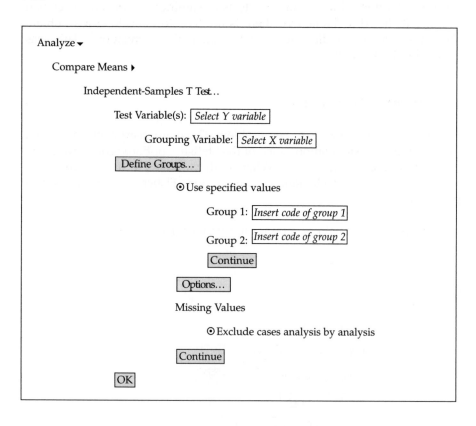

Analyze ▾

Compare Means ▸

Independent-Samples T Test...

Test Variable(s): *Select Y variable*

Grouping Variable: *Select X variable*

Define Groups...

⊙ Use specified values

Group 1: *Insert code of group 1*

Group 2: *Insert code of group 2*

Continue

Options...

Missing Values

⊙ Exclude cases analysis by analysis

Continue

OK

TWO-SAMPLES Z TEST

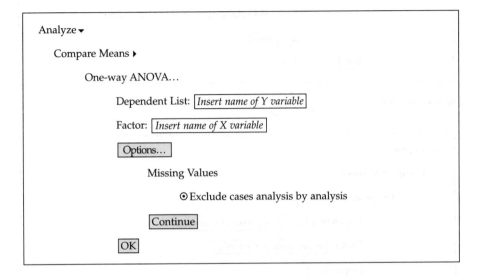

Analyze ▾

   Compare Means ▸

      One-way ANOVA…

         Dependent List: | *Insert name of Y variable* |

         Factor: | *Insert name of X variable* |

         | Options… |

            Missing Values

               ⊙ Exclude cases analysis by analysis

            | Continue |

         | OK |

K Independent Samples Tests

KRUSKAL–WALLIS *H* AND MEDIANS

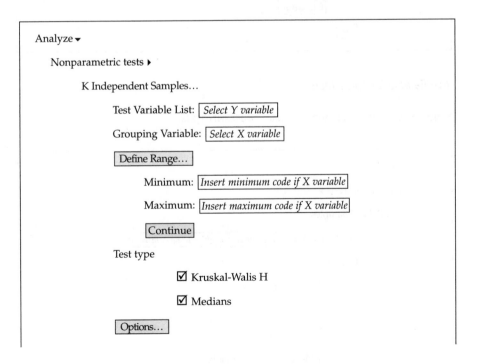

Analyze ▾

   Nonparametric tests ▸

      K Independent Samples…

         Test Variable List: | *Select Y variable* |

         Grouping Variable: | *Select X variable* |

         | Define Range… |

            Minimum: | *Insert minimum code if X variable* |

            Maximum: | *Insert maximum code if X variable* |

         | Continue |

         Test type

            ☑ Kruskal-Walis H

            ☑ Medians

         | Options… |

Missing Values

⊙ Exclude cases analysis by analysis

Continue

OK

ANOVA AND *F* TEST

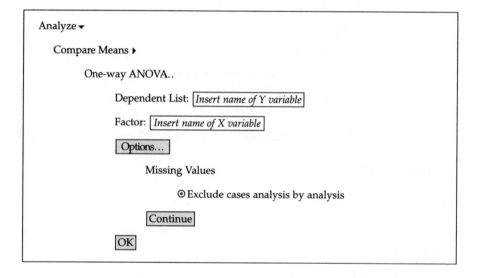

Analyze ▾

Compare Means ▸

One-way ANOVA..

Dependent List: *Insert name of Y variable*

Factor: *Insert name of X variable*

Options...

Missing Values

⊙ Exclude cases analysis by analysis

Continue

OK

Two Related Samples Tests

MCNEMAR, WILCOXON, SIGNS AND MARGINAL HOMOGENEITY TESTS

Analyze ▾

Nonparametric Tests ▸

2 Related Samples...

Test Pair(s) List: *Select both variables to be compared*

Test type

☑ Wilcoxon

☑ Signs

☑ McNemar

☑ Marginal Homogeneity

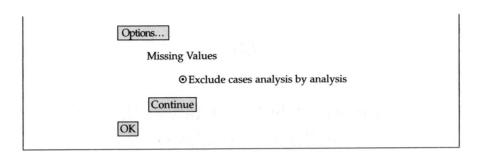

PAIRED SAMPLES *t* TEST

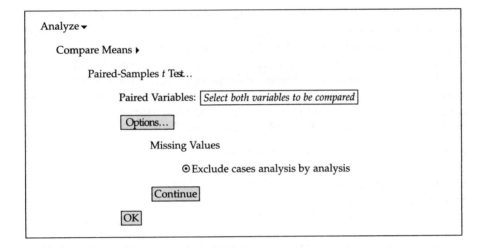

k Related Samples Tests

FRIEDMAN AND COCHRAN'S Q

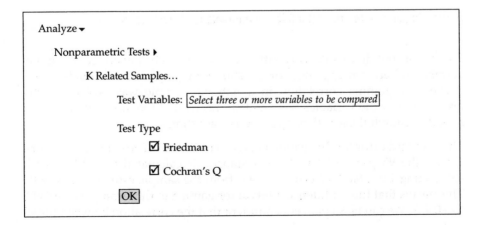

40

How are Confidence Intervals Used
in Bivariate Analysis?

The reliance on tests of statistical significance as the sole means of statistical inference has been widely criticized (p. 171, 173). A suggested alternative is to use confidence intervals rather than significance tests. Confidence intervals avoid the black-and-white accept–reject decisions required with tests of significance and provide an estimate of the margin of error for any population estimates. We have already discussed the concept and interpretation of confidence intervals in Problem 27, so the following discussion focuses on the use of confidence intervals in bivariate analysis.

A confidence interval can be calculated for:

- a correlation between two variables;
- a regression estimate;
- the difference between the means of groups.

Confidence intervals are based on standard errors. Each statistic has a different standard error. Therefore different confidence intervals are calculated for different statistics.

How to Obtain and Interpret Confidence Intervals for Correlations

The use of confidence intervals with correlations can be illustrated using the correlation between approval for abortion and frequency of church attendance. The gamma correlation in a national sample was –0.458 which, given the way the variables were coded, means that the more often people attended church the less they approved of abortion.

The standard error for this gamma coefficient is 0.025. The confidence interval (at the 95 per cent level) for a statistic is calculated by adding and subtracting 1.96 standard errors (0.049) from the sample estimate of –0.458. This means that the confidence interval for gamma in this example is –0.507 to –0.409. We can be 95 per cent confident that the correlation between these two variables in the population is somewhere within this range. Since the range does not include zero we can be very confident that there is a real relationship in the population.

A confidence interval can be calculated for most correlations. Table 40.1 reports the output from SPSS for the relationship between church attendance and approval of abortion. Although a number of these correlations are not appropriate for these variables, I have provided the results for illustrative purposes.

SPSS presents the correlations in two parts – those for asymmetric (directional) correlation coefficients (Table 40.1a) and those for symmetric (non–directional) measures (Table 40.1b). These tables have a number of columns of direct importance to the current discussion.

- The first column indicates the type of correlation coefficient (lambda, gamma, etc.).
- The figures in the 'Value' column are the correlation coefficients.
- The figures in the 'Asymp. Std. Error' column are the standard error figures for the correlations. Two points should be noted about these figures. First, given the way they are calculated, caution should be used when using them on small samples. Second, these figures are for one standard error.
- The 'Approx. Sig.' column indicates whether the correlation coefficient differs significantly from zero.

Using the information in the table, the confidence intervals can be calculated for any of the correlations. Problem 27 discusses more fully exactly how to interpret the confidence interval of a correlation coefficient (pp. 190–1).

How to Interpret Confidence Intervals for Regression Coefficients

Confidence intervals can also be calculated for regression coefficients. These can be very useful since regression coefficients are used to predict outcomes. When predicting outcomes, it is useful to know within what range of the estimate the real outcome is likely to lie.

Table 40.2 reproduces some of the regression output reported in Problem 37. The data report the regression coefficient for the impact of years of tertiary education on income. In the last two columns of Table 40.2 the upper and lower limits of the 95 per cent confidence interval are provided. This means that the sample estimate that each additional year of tertiary education has a 'pay-off' of $3365 is translated to a range from $2772 to $3957. That is, our best estimate of the actual effect of an extra year of tertiary education in the population is that the impact will most likely be somewhere between $2772 and $3957.

Table 40.1 *Correlations, standard errors and significance levels for the relationship between approval of abortion and frequency of church attendance*

(a) *Asymmetric correlations, standard errors and significance levels*

		Value (correlation)	Asymp. Std. Error	Approx. T	Approx. Sig.
Lambda	Abortion dependent	0.16	0.02	8.87	0.00
	Religious attendance dependent	0.04	0.01	6.34	0.00
Goodman and Kruskal tau	Abortion dependent	0.09	0.01		0.00
	Religious attendance dependent	0.06	0.01		0.00
Somers' d	Abortion dependent	−0.28	0.02	−16.68	0.00
	Religious attendance dependent	−0.36	0.02	−16.68	0.00
Eta	Abortion dependent	0.36			
	Religious attendance dependent	0.42			

(b) *Symmetric correlations, standard errors and significance levels*

	Value	Asymp. Std. Error	Approx. T	Approx. Sig.
Phi	0.47			0.00
Cramér's V	0.27			0.00
Kendall's tau-b	−0.32	0.02	−16.68	0.00
Kendall's tau-c	−0.28	0.02	−16.68	0.00
Gamma	−0.46	0.03	−16.68	0.00
Spearman correlation	−0.37	0.02	−16.64	0.00
Pearson's r	−0.35	0.02	−15.87	0.00
No. of valid cases	1797			

Table 40.2 *Regression coefficients and confidence intervals: income by qualifications*

	Unstandardized coefficients		Standardized coefficients			95% confidence interval for B	
	B	Std. Error	Beta	t	Sig.	Lower Bound	Upper Bound
(Constant)	$36 609	874		41.89	0.00	$34 895	$38 324
No. of years' tertiary education	$3 365	302	0.26	11.13	0.00	$2 772	$3 957

a Dependent Variable: Income

Using Confidence Intervals when Comparing Means

When comparing the mean of two groups, the next question is what is the likely difference between the means in the population. The first part of

Table 40.3 *Independent samples t test with confidence intervals: income by gender*

	Gender	N	Mean	Std. Deviation	Std. Error Mean
Income	Male	860	$44 640	30 288	1033
	Female	838	$39 341	28 248	976

Independent Samples Test

t-Test for Equality of Means						95% Confidence Interval of the Difference	
	t	df	Sig. (2-tailed)	Mean Difference	Std. Error Difference	Lower	Upper
Income	3.73	1696	0.00	$5299	1422	$2509	$8088

Table 40.4 *Number of unique group comparisons with a five-category variable*

	Qualifications				
	No qual	Trade	Diploma	Degree	Postgrad
Qualifications					
No qual					
Trade		1	2	3	4
Diploma			5	6	7
Degree				8	9
Postgrad					10

Table 40.3 reports the mean incomes for males and females. The second part of the table reports the difference between these two means ($5299) and then indicates the confidence interval for this difference. The confidence interval means that the difference in average male–female income levels in the population is most probably between $2509 and $8088.

When the X variable has more than two categories the comparison of means and the calculation of confidence intervals is a little more complicated. Since the focus is on *differences* between the means of groups, we can only compare two groups at a time. But if the X variable has, say, five categories there will be ten unique pairs of groups for comparison (see Table 40.4).

The analysis strategy in this type of situation is as follows:

1. Examine each *unique pair*.
2. Calculate the mean difference within each pair.
3. Test for statistical significance of the difference.
4. Examine the confidence interval for the mean difference within each pair.

These tasks are accomplished by using a *post hoc comparison* test. Many such tests are available, but I will illustrate the process with just one such test, the Scheffé test. Table 40.5 reports the output from a Scheffé test of qualifications by income.

Table 40.5 *Multiple comparisons (Scheffé): income by qualifications*

(I) QUALS (J) QUALS		Mean Difference (I–J)	Std. Error	Sig.	95% Confidence Interval	
					Lower Bound	Upper Bound
None	Trade	−1524	1607	0.92	−6 480	3 431
	Diploma	−8142	3704	0.31	−19 564	3 280
	Degree	−21 384	2418	0.00	−28 840	−13 929
	Postgrad	−29 412	2759	0.00	−37 919	−20 905
Trade	Diploma	−6618	3647	0.51	−17 864	4629
	Degree	−19 860	2329	0.00	−27 043	−12 677
	Postgrad	−27 887	2682	0.00	−36 157	−19 618
Diploma	Degree	−13 242	4070	0.03	−25 792	−692
	Postgrad	−21 270	4281	0.00	−34 472	−8068
Degree	Postgrad	−8027	3233	0.19	−17 998	1943

*The mean difference is significant at the 0.05 level.
Dependent Variable: Income

The first two columns define the possible comparisons between groups. The third column reports the difference between the average income of each group constituting the comparison. Thus the first figure in column three means that on average those with no qualifications earn $1524 less than those with trade qualifications. The fourth figure in column three means that those with no qualifications earn an average of $29 412 less than those with postgraduate qualifications.

The fifth column indicates the statistical significance of the difference between the means of the two groups being compared. The significance for the none–trade comparison is 0.92. This means that there is a very high probability that the income difference between these two groups is due to sampling error and that there will be no real difference in the population. Similarly, the significance level for the none–diploma income comparison is 0.31, which also means that this difference could be due to sampling error and that we should assume no difference in the population. However, the income difference between those with no qualifications and those with a degree is $21 384. This difference is unlikely to be due to sampling error, since the significance level is given as 0.000.

The final two columns indicate the upper and lower bounds of the confidence interval for the pair of groups in each row. For the first pair, none–trade, the confidence interval is −$6480 to $3431. For the next pairing the confidence interval is −$19 564 to $3280. This means that the real population figure will lie somewhere within this range. Notice that both these confidence intervals include zero (no difference) in the range. This means that we cannot be confident that the difference is not zero. This is the same conclusion we came to with the significance level.

The next row indicates a confidence interval of –\$28 840 to –\$13 929 for the none–degree comparison. This range does not include zero. This means that it is almost certain that the true population difference in the population is greater than zero. The significance level associated with this same pairing indicates the same thing. The advantage of the confidence interval over the significance level alone is that it gives us an idea of what the difference in incomes of these two groups is likely to be.

Using SPSS

Correlation Coefficients

The standard errors are automatically computed for all the correlations available through crosstabulations (except for eta, phi and Cramér's *V* for which they are not available); see Problem 36.

Regression

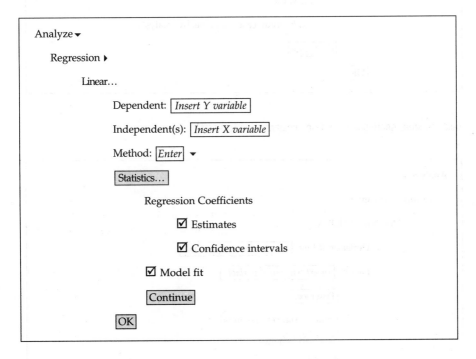

Comparing Means

TWO GROUPS: t-TESTS

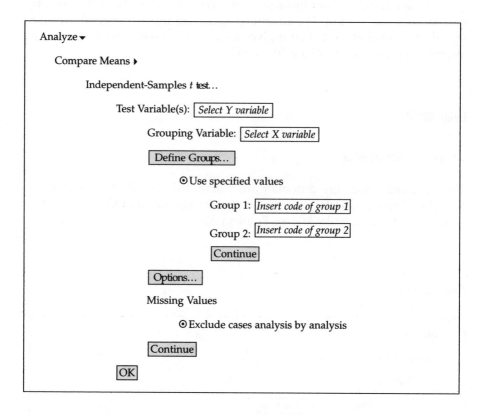

Analyze ▾

  Compare Means ▸

    Independent-Samples *t* test…

      Test Variable(s): | *Select Y variable* |

        Grouping Variable: | *Select X variable* |

        | Define Groups… |

          ⊙ Use specified values

            Group 1: | *Insert code of group 1* |

            Group 2: | *Insert code of group 2* |

            | Continue |

        | Options… |

        Missing Values

          ⊙ Exclude cases analysis by analysis

        | Continue |

      | OK |

THREE OR MORE GROUPS AND POST HOC COMPARISONS (SCHEFFÉ)

Analyze ▾

  Compare means ▸

    One-way ANOVA…

      Dependent List: | *Insert name of Y variable* |

      Factor: | *Insert name of X variable* |

      | Post Hoc… |

        Equal Variances Assumed

          ☑ Scheffe

      Continue

Options...

Missing Values

⊙ Exclude cases analysis by analysis

Continue

OK

41

Understanding Bivariate Relationships:
The Logic of Elaboration Analysis

What is the Problem?

Establishing that a relationship exists between two variables is an important part of analysis. However, it raises many questions.

In a good experimental design, establishing that the X variable is correlated with the Y variable should be strong evidence of a causal relationship. However, a weakness of the experimental design is that it is not good at establishing *how* or *why* X has the effect that it does (de Vaus, 2001b). If we establish that exposure to violent films produces aggression it is reasonable to try to understand the means by which this relationship operates.

When using a cross-sectional design in which we simply establish that two variables co-vary, we face an even bigger problem. We have to work out how to unpack the bivariate relationship we have established by asking questions such as:

- What is the nature of this relationship? Is it causal or non-causal?
- If the relationship is causal, is it direct or indirect (i.e. X affects Y via another variable)?
- If the relationship is indirect, what are the mechanisms by which X affects Y?
- If the relationship between X and Y is not causal, then what is it due to?

The Elaboration Approach

The elaboration technique developed by Kendall and Lazarsfeld (1950) is designed to address these questions. The technique 'elaborates' an initial bivariate relationship to see to what extent it is 'due to' the influence of other variables. For example, bivariate analysis may have indicated a relationship between gender and income – males typically have higher incomes than females. Elaboration analysis will explore the reasons for this relationship. It could be due to different education levels, different types of training, more women than men working part-time, gender discrimination and so on.

Elaboration analysis involves introducing a third variable into the analysis and assessing its impact on the other two. Depending on the nature of the third variable and its impact, conclusions can be drawn that provide further understanding of the initial relationship.

There are several ways of conducting elaboration analysis. I will distinguish between two broad approaches:

- using *conditional* tables and correlations;
- using *partial* tables and correlations.

These approaches will be outlined in problems 42–45. Before discussing the approaches, it is helpful to outline the different ways in which we might explain an initial bivariate relationship by introducing a third variable into the model.

At this point it is worth introducing two new terms. So far I have used the phrase 'initial bivariate relationship'. When using the elaboration approach this relationship is referred to as a *zero-order* relationship. It is the relationship between X and Y before a third variable is introduced into the model. When a third variable is added to the analysis the resulting relationship between X and Y (this will make sense shortly) is called a *first-order relationship*. The variable that is introduced into the model to try to elaborate on the zero-order relationship is called a *test variable*. It is symbolized as Z.

Ways in Which a Test Variable can Affect a Zero-order Relationship

The purpose of elaboration analysis is to elaborate on the initial zero-order relationship (Figure 41.1a) – to explore how and to what extent this relationship might be due to the influence of a third variable. There are a variety of ways in which Z might impact on the X–Y relationship. These are discussed below and presented diagrammatically in Figure 41.1.

- *Z has no influence*. Figure 41.1b illustrates the scenario where Z has no influence on the X–Y relationship.
- *Z is an intervening variable*. In this scenario the relationship between X–Y is an indirect causal relationship that is completely due to the intervening role of Z (Figure 41.1c). That is, the influence of X on Y is *via* Z. An example is the model that argues that the relationship between gender and income is via hours of work – women work fewer paid hours which in turn affects their income. If it were not for gender differences in hours of work, there would be no gender differences in income.

- *Direct and indirect influence.* Figure 41.1d illustrates a model in which X partly influences Y indirectly via the mediating role of Z but also has a direct impact. For example, gender might be said to affect income partly via the impact of gender on hours of paid work; however, there may remain an impact of X on Y that is above and beyond this influence.
- *Spurious relationship of X and Y.* A spurious relationship between X and Y is one where a relationship that appeared to be causal is not causal. Typically, a spurious relationship is where the correlation between X and Y is simply because they are both the outcome of a common cause. (Figure 41.1e). An example is the relationship between attending private fee-charging schools (X) and academic performance (Y). This relationship is assumed by many people to be causal – that is, private fee-paying schools produce better performance through one means or another. However, the better performance of students in private schools might simply be due to selective factors – student ability (Z). Students with greater ability are sent to private schools, and such students perform better academically.
- *Spurious and direct.* An X–Y relationship can have both a causal component and a non-causal (spurious) component (Figure 41.1f). For example, *part* of the reason why students in private schools perform better may be the selective (spurious) factor. However, the school may still enhance the performance of these students by better teaching, more support, better resources and so on (direct causal).
- *Spurious and indirect.* The initial relationship between X and Y may have no direct causal component. Instead, it may be a mixture of spurious and indirect effects (Figure 41.1g). For example, we may find that students attending religious schools are more religious than students attending non-religious schools. Is this because the religious schools directly cause students to become more religious? The link between religious schooling and student religiousness may be at least partly spurious. Religious parents are more likely than non-religious parents to send their children to religious schools. Religious parents are also more likely to bring their children up to be religious. The reason why religious schools have religious students may be because of the common causal factor – the religiousness of parents (Z). However, the schools themselves may reinforce parental religiousness and in this way also indirectly affect the religiousness of their students.
- *Spurious, direct and indirect.* This model allows for all three types of influence. Take our example of the link between attendance at a religious school and student religiousness, and add the factor of schools having a direct impact on their students' religiousness through teaching, example and the like (Figure 41.1h).
- *Conditional effects.* A final scenario is one where the direct relationship between X and Y operates under some conditions of Z but not under others (Figure 41.1i). For example, a new curriculum (X) may be introduced into a school and have an overall effect on student performance (Y). However, closer inspection shows that the new curriculum had a substantial impact on the performance of girls but none at all on that of boys. Thus the

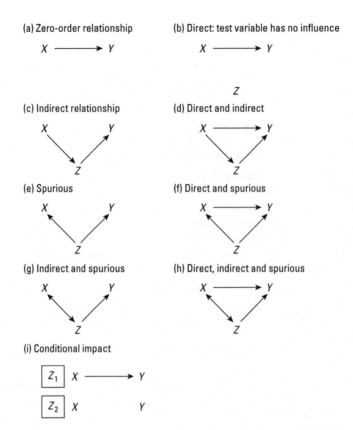

Figure 41.1 *Ways in which a test variable can influence the relationship between X and Y*

impact of X on Y is conditional on another attribute also being present – being a girl. When the two attributes (new curriculum and being female) are combined they somehow interact to produce better performance. On its own the curriculum has no impact on performance, as is evident from its lack of impact on boys.

The main point of the discussion of different ways of understanding a simple X–Y relationship is that we need to be aware of the possible ways of unpacking and testing the nature of the relationship. With this awareness of different possibilities, we can introduce test variables and evaluate whether the results support any particular model.

The Logic of Elaboration Analysis

To illustrate the logic of elaboration analysis I will concentrate on testing a model that proposes that the zero-order relationship is in fact an indirect

(a) Bivariate relationship

(b) Testing to see if bivariate relationship is 'due to' causal link between gender and hours

Figure 41.2 *Testing a bivariate relationship for the effect of an intervening variable*

causal relationship (see Figure 41.1c). An example of this is the relationship between gender (X) and income (Y). I will test the model that states that the reason for the lower income of women is that they work fewer paid hours (Z). This model is presented in Figure 41.2.

Elaboration analysis proceeds by asking what would happen to the relationship between gender and income if men and women worked the same number of hours. If the link between gender and income is *due to* the different number of paid hours, then it would follow logically that if men and women worked the same hours there should be no income differences.

Clearly we cannot undertake an exercise in social engineering and intervene so that men and women work the same number of paid hours. Fortunately, we can take advantage of diversity within the population to undertake 'statistical engineering' or a 'statistical intervention'.

Since there do exist men and women who work the same number of hours, why not compare these men and women and see if they have the same income? (This is called *controlling* for the test variable.) By just looking at men and women with equal hours of work we can remove any effect of hours from any relationship between gender and income. If men and women who work an equal number of paid hours earn the same amount as each other we have a fairly compelling argument that the zero-order difference was due to the role of hours of work.

To implement this 'statistical intervention' we simply examine the zero-order relationship within each category of the test variable (Figure 41.3).

Testing the Models

There are different approaches to using the logic of elaboration analysis – to doing the statistical experiment on which the logic is based. The following

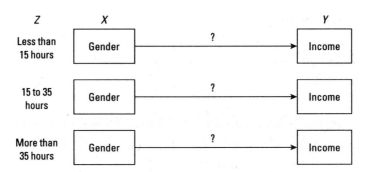

Figure 41.3   *Gender by income for each of three groupings of hours of work*

four sections outline four different approaches to applying this logic: examining *conditional* relationships using conditional tables (problem 42) or conditional correlation coefficients (problem 43), and examining *partial* relationships using partial tables (problem 44) or partial correlation coefficients (problem 45).

42

Using Conditional Tables as
a Method of Elaboration Analysis

This is the first of four chapters that provide a way of conducting elaboration analysis. Here we discuss how to use conditional tables and point to some of the problems with this approach.

The example below illustrates the statistical experiment or statistical intervention described in Problem 41. In this example I will use conditional tables and test the proposition that the zero-order X–Y relationship is an indirect causal relationship operating via hours of work.

How to Conduct a Statistical Experiment

This statistical experiment is conducted in a number of discrete steps.

1. Look at the relationship between gender and income without controlling for a third variable (the zero-order relationship). Table 42.1 indicates a strong relationship between gender and income. Only 25 per cent of males are low income earners, compared to 52 per cent of females. In contrast, 36 per cent of men are high income earners compared to only 14 per cent of women. This relationship is indicated by a gamma of 0.49.

Table 42.1 *Zero-order crosstabulation of annual income by gender*

Annual income	Gender	
	Male	Female
Low	25%	52%
Medium	39	34
High	36	14
Total	600	400

2. Examine the same relationship (between gender and income) separately within each category of the test variable. In this case the test variable is

Table 42.2   *Conditional crosstabulations of annual income by gender by weekly hours of work*

			Gender	
Hours per week (average)			Male	Female
Less than 15 hour	Annual income	Low	69%	72%
N=300		Medium	24	22
		High	7	6
		Total	100%	100%
15–35 hours	Annual income	Low	26%	29%
N=200		Medium	56	52
		High	18	19
		Total	100%	100%
More than 35 hours	Annual income	Low	17%	21%
N=500		Medium	29	28
		High	54	51
		Total	100%	100%

hours of work, grouped into three bands – less than 15 hours, 15 to 35 hours and 35+ hours. Thus the relationship between gender and income is examined three times – once for each band. The relationships between gender and income for each category of hours of work are called *conditional relationships*. (The SPSS section below indicates how to generate these three conditional tables.)

3. Compare the initial zero-order relationship with the conditional relationships.
4. Interpret the difference between the zero-order relationship and the conditional relationships.

In our example, if we examine the initial gender–income relationship *within* each of the hours bands the initial relationship has disappeared. Among those who work less than 15 hours the percentage of females in each category matches the percentage of males. Among those working 15–35 hours we find that males and females have the same income distributions. The same gender similarity is evident among those working more than 35 hours a week.

Since the initial relationship between gender and income disappears when we remove the influence of hours of work (by controlling hours) the gender–income relationship must somehow have been due to the influence of hours of work.

How to Interpret Differences Between Zero-order and Conditional Tables

This example provides a clear pattern. The relationship in *each* conditional table is much weaker than the zero-order relationship. We can conclude that

Table 42.3   *Interpreting conditional relationships*

Patterns of conditionals	Interpretation	Diagram
Conditional relationships are all weaker than the zero-order relationship but are still statistically significant	Relationship between X and Y is partly spurious or partly indirect. Remaining part of initial relationship is either direct or to be explained by some other variable	Spurious and direct ? $X \longrightarrow Y$ Z Indirect and direct ? $X \longrightarrow Y$ Z
Conditional relationships are all weaker than the zero-order relationship and are not statistically significant	Relationship between X and Y is completely spurious or indirect.	Spurious X Y Z Indirect X Y Z
Relationship between X and Y varies according to category of Z	Relationship is specific to certain subgroups. Interaction effects.	Z_1 $X \longrightarrow Y$ Z_2 X Y
Conditional relationships are all similar to the zero-order relationship	Replication. The zero order relationship is *not* due to the control variable.	$X \longrightarrow Y$ Z

when hours were held constant there was no remaining relationship between gender and income to explain.

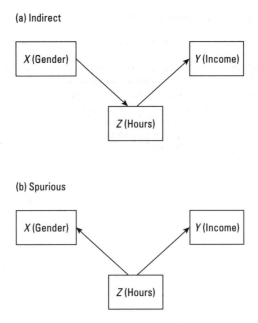

(a) Indirect

(b) Spurious

Figure 42.1   *Direct and spurious relationships compared*

This is the neatest and most straightforward pattern to interpret. However, a variety of different patterns that are not so straightforward can also occur (see Figure 41.1). What is required is a way of reading zero-order and conditional relationships to evaluate which of the models outlined in Problem 41 makes most sense empirically.

The elaboration model enables us to do this to some extent. The elaboration method involves comparing the conditional relationships with the zero-order relationship. The differences between these two sets of relationships provide a means of evaluating which of the various ways of elaborating a simple X–Y relationship (Figure 41.1) fits the data best.

Table 42.3 summarizes the patterns that are consistent with each of the models.

How to Tell the Difference Between Indirect and Spurious Relationships

One problem with the above approach is that the same pattern of zero-order and conditional relationships can indicate indirect causal relationships and spurious relationships. Since these two interpretations are radically different, how can we establish whether the indirect causal or the spurious interpretation makes most sense?

1. Draw a diagram of the three variables, name the variables and draw arrows in the causal direction implied by the two different interpretations. Often it will become clear from the diagram which of the two models is plausible.
2. Look at the nature of the X and Z variables. The indirect causal model argues that $X{\rightarrow}Z{\rightarrow}Y$, while the spurious model argues that $X{\leftarrow}Z{\rightarrow}Y$. If X is a relatively fixed variable (e.g. gender, age, race) then the spurious model will not make sense. How can Z cause gender, age or race? If Z is a fixed variable then the indirect causal model will not make sense since Z must be capable of change by X.
3. Examine the time sequence of the variables. If the indirect causal model is to make sense then Z must normally follow X in time. For the spurious model Z must normally precede X.
4. If these tests do not resolve the problem, explore which causal direction between the X and Z variables receives the strongest support from previous research and established theory.

If these tests are applied to the gender–income example it becomes clear which model makes most sense (Figure 42.1). The spurious model requires that Z (hours worked) affects gender (X). This makes no sense, so this spurious model can be put to one side. The indirect model argues that gender (X) can affect hours of work (Z) and that hours of work can affect income (Y). Both these propositions make sense: the dependent variable in each proposition (hours and income) are capable of being changed by the prior variables in the model. The results and common sense then support the indirect causal interpretation of the figures in Table 42.2.

What Problems Might be Encountered with Conditional Tables?

Apart from the question of interpreting patterns, a number of other problems confront anyone who uses conditional tables to elaborate bivariate relationships.

*   *Sample size.* The sample has to be divided into subgroups – one for each category of the test variable. Where the Z variable has more than a small number of categories, this can mean splitting the sample into quite small groups that can then create problems for obtaining stable and reliable analysis within the subgroups. One 'solution' to this problem is to collapse the categories of the Z variable. However, this can defeat the purpose of elaboration analysis. Collapsing categories of Z means that we combine people who are *dissimilar* on the Z variable, whereas the logic of elaboration analysis is to only look at people who are similar on the Z variable.
*   *Complexity.* Many people will find it difficult to correctly interpret a set of conditional tables. It requires a good understanding of the logic of elaboration and a good ability to read tables. As tables become more complex

and the number of tables grows, the complexity can confuse even experienced analysts. The complexity is compounded when the patterns are not as clear-cut as in the examples above.

- *Space.* Reporting sets of conditional tables requires substantial space. Frequently this is not available and a much more efficient way of providing the same basic information is required.

These problems are alleviated somewhat by some of the alternative ways of conducting elaboration analysis that are discussed in the following chapters.

Using SPSS

Conditional tables are obtained in a two-step procedure using crosstabulations. The first step generates the zero-order table and the second step generates the conditional tables.

Zero-order Table

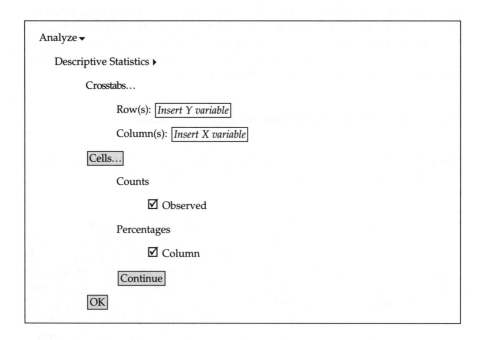

Conditional Tables

```
Analyze ▾
    Descriptive Statistics ▸
        Crosstabs...
            Row(s): [Insert Y variable]
            Column(s): [Insert X variable]
            Layer 1 of 1 [Insert test variable]
        [Cells...]
            Counts
                ☑ Observed
            Percentages
                ☑ Column
            [Continue]
        [OK]
```

43

Using Conditional Correlations for Elaboration Analysis

Conditional correlations are used for the same purposes as conditional tables – to elaborate the nature of zero-order bivariate relationships (see Problems 41 and 42). We have seen that a problem with using conditional *tables* is the complexity of reading, interpreting and presenting a set of conditional tables. Using conditional *correlations* is one solution to these problems.

What are Conditional Correlations?

Problems 35 and 36 outlined how correlation coefficients are an efficient way of summarizing relationships in crosstabulations. Conditional correlations are simply a set of correlations used to summarize the relationship in each of the conditional crosstabulations. Using coefficients rather than tables certainly saves space and can simplify the interpretation.

To use conditional correlations rather than conditional tables take the following steps:

1. Obtain the zero-order correlation between X and Y.
2. Obtain correlations of X and Y for each category of the test variable.
3. Compare the zero-order correlation with the set of conditional correlations.

Table 43.1 provides a set of gamma correlations that illustrate the use of conditional coefficients. These gammas are based on Tables 42.1 and 42.2. The set of conditional gamma coefficients all indicate the absence of a relationship between gender and income once the influence of hours of work is removed by controlling. The presence of a strong zero-order correlation and the absence of conditional correlations is clear and strong evidence that gender differences in hours of work were largely responsible for the initial relationship.

Table 43.1 *Zero-order and conditional gamma correlations of income by gender*

Zero order	gamma = −0.49 sig. <. 001

Conditional gammas	
Work less than 15 hours:	gamma = − 0.07; sig. = ns
Work 15–35 hours:	gamma = − 0.03; sig. = ns
Work 35 + hours:	gamma = − 0.07; sig. = ns

How to Interpret Conditional Correlations

The logic of using conditional correlations is exactly the same as that of using conditional tables. Accordingly the interpretation of patterns in the conditional correlations is the same as for the tables. Table 42.3 outlines the various interpretations of patterns of zero-order and conditional correlations.

What do Conditional Coefficients that are not Near Zero Mean?

The conditional correlations in Table 43.1 have behaved very well. They have all declined to statistically non-significant levels. We can treat them all as though they are effectively zero.

Unfortunately, a more common result is for conditional correlations to be just a little lower than the zero-order correlation. When the conditional relationships are just a little weaker than the zero-order relationships, the test variable *partly* explains the initial relationship. For example, in Table 43.2 the zero order correlation is − 0.45. When hours of work is introduced as a control variable the conditional correlations range from −0.33 to −0.37. These conditional correlations are weaker than the initial correlation of −0.45. This means that *some* of the initial correlation was due to the influence of the control variable. However since the conditional correlations are still substantially greater than zero there remains a good deal of the initial correlation that is not due to the influence of hours of work. In this case hours of work partly explains the relationship between gender and income. The question is *how much* difference there needs to be between the zero-order and conditional relationships before we say that the zero-order relationship is partly explained. Perhaps the drop in the correlations is so small that we should regard the conditionals as being the same as the zero-order. In this case we would treat the Z variable as being irrelevant to the zero-order relationship. In other words, when the conditional relationships just drop a little, how do we distinguish between the models in Figures 41.1b, 41.1d and 41.1f?

Table 43.2   *Zero-order and conditional correlations with confidence intervals*

	Correlation	Standard error	95% confidence interval
Zero order (Gender–income)	−0.45	0.04	−0.53 to −0.37
Conditionals			
(0–15 hours)	−0.35	0.07	−0.21 to −0.49
(16–35 hours)	−0.37	0.05	−0.27 to −0.47
(35+ hours)	−0.33	0.06	−0.21 to −0.45

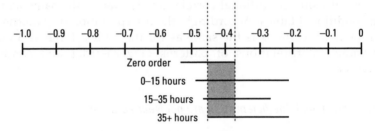

Figure 43.1   Confidence intervals of conditional correlations overlapping that of the zero order correlation

One solution is to examine the confidence intervals of the conditional correlations in relation to the confidence interval for the zero-order correlation. If the confidence intervals of the conditional correlations and the zero-order correlation *overlap*, then we would argue that there is no difference between the zero-order and conditionals.

Suppose we obtained the set of correlations and standard errors listed in Table 43.2. While the conditional correlations are all lower than the zero-order correlation, the confidence intervals of the conditionals overlap with that of the zero-order correlation (Figure 43.1). Given this overlap, we cannot be confident that the conditionals really are different from the zero-order correlation. Accordingly, we should treat the test variable, in this context, as not contributing to nor partly explaining the zero-order relationship.

Using SPSS

Undertaking elaboration analysis with conditional tables is achieved with SPSS using the Crosstabs procedure. Two steps are required. The first step generates the zero-order correlation and the second step generates the conditional correlations. There is no need to produce the tables.

Zero-order Correlation

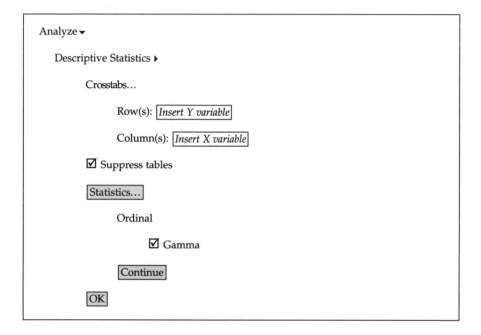

Analyze ▾

    Descriptive Statistics ▸

        Crosstabs...

            Row(s): [*Insert Y variable*]

            Column(s): [*Insert X variable*]

        ☑ Suppress tables

        [Statistics...]

           Ordinal

               ☑ Gamma

           [Continue]

      [OK]

Conditional Correlations

Analyze ▾

    Descriptive Statistics ▸

        Crosstabs...

            Row(s): [*Insert Y variable*]

            Column(s): [*Insert X variable*]

            Layer 1 of 1: [*Insert test variable*]

        ☑ Suppress tables

        [Statistics...]

Ordinal

☑ Gamma

Continue

OK

44

Using Partial Tables as a Method
of Elaboration Analysis

When we want to explore the nature of a bivariate relationship, elaboration analysis provides a useful technique. Conditional tables (Problem 42) present one approach but can result in a large number of tables that are difficult to interpret. Conditional correlations (Problem 43) address that problem, but have the disadvantage that the type of information provided by a table is unavailable. An approach that uses tables but avoids a large number of confusing conditional tables is to use *standardized partial tables*.

What are Standardized Partial Tables?

The standardized partial table involves some simple hand calculations, but the resulting simplicity is worth the effort. Instead of having a separate crosstabulation of the initial two variables for each category of the test variable, the standardized partial table approach produces just one simple table. This single table is then compared with the zero-order crosstabulation.

What Steps are Required to Produce a Standardized Partial Table?

1. Produce the normal zero-order table (see Table 42.1) and conditional tables (as in Table 42.2).
2. Produce *weighted conditional tables*. This is accomplished as follows:

    (a) Produce a set of blank conditional tables (i.e. no percentages).
    (b) Calculate a weight factor for *each* conditional table by dividing the total number of cases in each conditional table by the total number of cases across all the conditional tables (see Table 44.1).
    (c) Apply the weights by multiplying the percentages in the *unweighted conditional tables* with the weight factor and placing these percentages in the blank conditional tables you have produced (see Tables 44.2 and 44.3).

Table 44.1   *Calculating weights for conditional tables*

Condition	N		Weight
Less than 15 hours	300	300/1000	0.3
15–35 hours	200	200/1000	0.2
More than 35 hours	500	500/1000	0.5
Total	1000		

Table 44.2   *Applying weights to percentages for each cell for those working less than 15 hours per week*

Annual income	Male	Female
Low	69% × 0.3 = **20.7%**	72% × 0.3 = **21.6%**
Medium	24% × 0.3 = **7.2%**	22% × 0.3 = **6.6%**
High	7% × 0.3 = **2.1%**	6% × 0.3 = **1.8%**

3. Produce the standardized partial table (see Table 44.4). This is achieved as follows:

   (a) Produce a blank version of the zero–order table (no percentages).
   (b) Add together the percentages in the equivalent cells in each weighted conditional table and place the total in the corresponding cell in the standardized partial table.

4. Compare the patterns in the standardized partial table with that in the zero-order table.

How to Calculate Table Weights

Table 44.1 illustrates the calculation of weights for each of the conditional tables. For the 300 cases who work less than 15 hours the weight is calculated by working out the proportion of the whole sample that these cases represent. Since the whole sample consists of 1000 cases they constitute a proportion of 300/1000 = 0.3. The same calculations are done for those working 15–35 hours and more than 35 hours.

What is the Procedure for Applying Weights?

In Table 44.2 the percentages in bold for the first condition (less than 15 hours) were calculated by multiplying the unweighted percentage for each cell (see Table 42.2) by the weight factor (0.3). When the weights are applied to each of the conditional tables in Table 42.2 we obtain the three weighted conditional tables shown in Table 44.3.

Table 44.3   *Annual income by gender by weekly hours of work (weighted conditional tables)*

Hours per week (average)	Annual income	Gender Male	Female
Less than 15 hours	Low	20.7%	21.6%
	Medium	7.2	6.6
	High	2.1	1.8
	Total	100%	100%
15–35 hours	Low	5.2%	5.8%
	Medium	11.2	10.4
	High	3.6	3.8
	Total	100%	100%
More than 35 hours	Low	8.5%	10.5%
	Medium	14.5	14.0
	High	27.0	25.5
	Total	100%	100%

Table 44.4   *Annual income by Gender (standardized partial table)*

Annual income	Gender Male		Female	
Low	34.4%		37.9%	
		(207)		(152)
Medium	32.9		31.0	
		(197)		(124)
High	32.7		31.1	
		(196)		(124)
Total	100%	(600)	100%	(400)

Producing the Standardized Partial Table

Once the weighted conditional tables have been produced these can be combined into a single table. To do this:

1. Produce a copy of the zero-order table with empty cells.
2. Sum the weighted percentages in the corresponding cells across the three conditional tables.
3. Place the sum of these weighted cells in the corresponding cell in the empty table you have produced.

For example, the cell for male low income earners in Table 44.4 is computed by summing the cells for male low income earners in each of the three conditional tables in Table 44.3 (20.7 + 5.2 + 8.5 = 34.4). The equivalent procedure is used for each cell in the standardized partial table.

The standardized partial table can then be compared to the zero-order table (Table 42.1). Since there is only one table to compare with the zero-order table the comparison is simple. In the zero-order table a strong relationship exists, but in the standardized partial table, after gender differences in hours worked are removed, any relationship between gender and income has all but disappeared. This means that if it were not for gender differences in hours worked there would be no gender differences in income. In other words, the gender differences in income were due to gender differences in hours worked.

Using SPSS

You will need to generate a zero-order table and a set of conditional tables (see problem 42). To weight the tables and compute the standardized partial table you will either need to perform hand calculations or use a spreadsheet to compute and apply the weightings.

45

Using Partial Correlations for Elaboration Analysis

Using partial correlations for elaboration analysis is a response to the problem of the complexity of multiple tables and multiple coefficients. Partial correlations provide the most efficient way of elaborating zero-order relationships. No tables are produced, and only one partial correlation coefficient (rather than a series of conditional coefficients) needs to be compared with the zero-order correlation.

Can Partial Correlations be Used with Nominal and Ordinal Variables?

In the same way that a set of conditional tables can be reduced to a single table (the standardized partial table) a series of conditional correlations can be reduced to a single correlation coefficient that reflects the extent to which the zero-order relationship remains after removing the influence of the test variable. This single correlation is called a *partial correlation*. This approach will be illustrated initially using standardized partial tables. I will then point to some alternative ways of obtaining partial correlations.

There are four steps to an analysis using this approach:

1. Obtain the appropriate correlation for the variables in the zero-order table.
2. Produce a standardized partial table.
3. Calculate the correlation for the standardized partial table. This will yield a partial correlation coefficient.
4. Compare the partial correlation with the zero-order correlation.

Beyond creating the standardized partial table, the only additional work required for this method is computing the correlation from the standardized partial table. This is easily accomplished using a web-based calculator. There are a number of these calculators for different statistics. A useful calculator for gamma, Kendall's τ_b and Somers' d is located at *http://members.aol.com/johnp71/ordinal.html*. This program simply requires that you input the numbers used in the standardized partial table.

How to Obtain a Partial Gamma

To compute and use partial gamma correlations for the gender–income example, proceed as follows:

1. Obtain the zero-order gamma. This is obtained from SPSS or other programs when obtaining the zero-order crosstabulation.
2. Produce the standardized partial table for income by gender (Table 44.4).
3. Compute gamma for the standardized partial table. Figure 45.1 illustrates the computation of gamma with the calculator located at the web address given in the previous paragraph. Using this calculator produces a partial gamma of –0.05 with a significance level of 0.326.
4. Compare the partial gamma with the zero-order gamma.

Since the partial gamma is much lower than the zero-order gamma and is effectively zero, we can say that the initial relationship is completely explained by hours of work.

Alternative Ways of Obtaining Partial Correlations for Ordinal Variables

Partial gamma: SPSS computes partial gamma coefficients, but only through syntax commands. These commands are provided at the end of this section.

Partial Kendall's τ_b: A simple calculator is available for calculating a partial version of Kendall's τ_b. This can be very useful for ordinal variables that have more categories than can comfortably be handled in a crosstabulation. This calculator is available within a cheap program available for evaluation by going to the web page *http://members.aol.com/statware/pubpage.htm*. (When you have the program select menu options 6, 6, enter 4 to find the partial Kendall's test). This calculator computes a partial Kendall's τ_b from three zero-order correlations: the correlation of X with Y, of Z with X, and of Z with Y.

Partial Correlations for Interval Variables

If the initial bivariate relationship involved two interval variables or a dichotomous X variable and an interval Y variable, Pearson's correlation would be used to summarize this relationship. Pearson's correlation is readily available as a partial correlation that can be used in the same manner as described above.

*	Col 1	Col 2	Col 3	Col 4	Col 5
Row 1	207	152	0	0	0
Row 2	197	124	0	0	0
Row 3	196	124	0	0	0
Row 4	0	0	0	0	0
Row 5	0	0	0	0	0

Reset   Compute

Concordance = 75764 , Discordance = 84040

S.E.(Con-Dis) = 8427.989

z = -0.982 , p = 0.326

Other Statistics...

Gamma = -0.052

Somers'd = -0.025

Tied on X = 166661 , Tied on Y = 259500

Kendall Tau-b = -0.029

Figure 45.1   *Calculating partial gamma with a web calculator*
To use the calculator simply insert the frequencies from the standard partial
table (Table 44.4). The calculator does the rest.

Partial correlations can be obtained in one of two main ways. The first is to use a statistical analysis program in which the raw data for all cases are provided on the three variables (X, Y and Z). The program will calculate the correlation of X with Y with the influence of Z removed.

An alternative method is to use a partial correlation calculator. These are available online at no cost. Alternatively, very affordable programs are

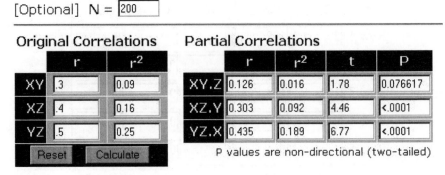

Figure 45.2   *Calculator for computing partial Pearson's r*

Table 45.1   *Interpreting partial correlations*

How do the zero-order and partial correlations compare on:

Size of the correlations	Statistical significance	Confidence intervals	Interpretation
Similar	Both significant	Overlap	Replication. Z has no impact on X and Y
Partial lower than zero-order	Zero order = significant Partial = non-significant	Do not overlap	Completely spurious or completely indirect or combination
Partial lower than zero-order	Both significant	Do not overlap	Partly spurious or partly indirect, but still some of the direct relationship remains

available that contain partial correlation calculators. All that is required to calculate the partial correlation using these calculators are the three bivariate correlations of X with Y, Z with X, and Z with Y.

Figure 45.2 illustrates one calculator available at *http://faculty.Vassar.edu/ lowry/VassarStats.html*. To use this calculator, enter zero-order correlations in the first column headed 'r'. I have also entered the sample size. In this example the zero-order correlation of 0.3 is reduced to a partial correlation of 0.126 between X and Y controlling for Z. This partial correlation has a significance level of 0.0766 which means that the original zero-order correlation is reduced to a statistically non-significant level by removing the influence of Z.

How to Interpret Partial Correlations

Like sets of conditional correlations, partial correlations should be compared with the zero-order correlation between X and Y. The difference between the zero-order and partial correlation provides the clue as to the interpretation (Table 45.1).

Using SPSS

Partial Gamma

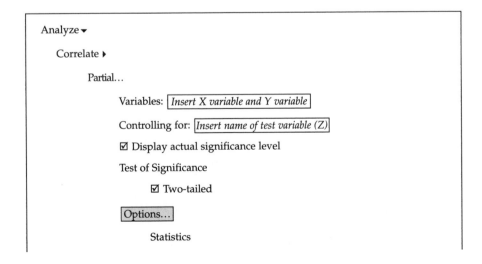

```
CROSSTABS
   VARIABLES = Y variable (minvalue, maxvalue), X variable (minvalue, maxvalue),
   test variable, (minvalue, maxvalue)
      /TABLES = Y variable BY X variable test variable
      /STATISTICS = GAMMA
      /FORMAT = NOTABLES
```

Partial Pearson's r

```
Analyze ▾
   Correlate ▸
      Partial...
         Variables: Insert X variable and Y variable
         Controlling for: Insert name of test variable (Z)
         ☑ Display actual significance level
         Test of Significance
            ☑ Two-tailed
      Options...
         Statistics
```

☑ Zero-order correlations

Missing Values

⊙ Exclude cases listwise

Continue

OK

46

What Type of Data are Needed for Multiple Regression?

Multiple regression is a powerful and flexible method of analyzing the relationship between a *set* of independent variables and a single dependent variable. The way in which this multivariate analysis is performed will differ according to the purpose of the analysis (see Problem 47).

However, before multiple regression can be used the data must be suited to this form of analysis. There are a number of assumptions that should be met before the results of a multiple regression analysis can be taken seriously. The problem for the data analyst is to evaluate:

- whether these assumptions are met;
- how serious any violations are;
- what to do about any violations.

What are the Assumptions of Multiple Regression Analysis?

There are seven main assumptions of ordinary regression analysis.

1. The Y variable is measured at the *interval* level.
2. The X variables are predominantly measured at the *interval* level. If an independent variable is not an interval variable it must be dichotomous.
3. Independent variables should not be highly intercorrelated (the assumption of the *absence of multicollinearity*). Multicollinearity leads to an unstable correlation matrix which is the core on which the main regression statistics are based. Consequently, multicollinearity can produce unreliable and unstable regression estimates, significance levels and confidence intervals.
4. There will not be outliers that could distort results. Outliers need to be avoided because they can artificially inflate or deflate estimates (see Problem 13).

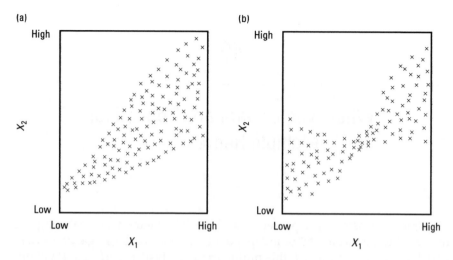

Figure 46.1 *Bivariate relationships illustrating heteroscedasticity*

5. The variables are related in a *linear* fashion. This includes relationships
    between pairs of individual variables, between individual variables and
    combinations of the other variables, and between combinations of vari-
    ables. Since multiple regression is based on Pearson's *r*, which is only
    sensitive to linear relationships, gross departures from linearity will
    mean that important relationships will remain undetected.
6. The variables are normally distributed. Failure of normality can lead to
    unstable regression estimates and distort the Type I error rate (Tabachnick
    and Fidell, 1983: 78). Ideally the set of variables should have a multi-
    variate normal distribution, but since this assumption is not readily
    testable the best approach is to examine the distribution of each variable.
    In a multivariate normal distribution each variable will have a univari-
    ate normal distribution. If variables do not display univariate normality
    then the set of variables will not achieve multivariate normality. Unfor-
    tunately, the opposite is not true. However, if the sample is large enough
    we need not worry too much since the central limit theorem (Problem 11)
    means that failures of normality will not have much effect.
7. The relationships between the variables will exhibit *homoscedasticity*.
    That is, the variance on one variable will be consistent across all values
    of the other variable. For example, homoscedasticity would exist
    between age and income where the variance in income was much the
    same regardless of how old people were. The opposite of homoscedas-
    ticity is *heteroscedasticity*. Heteroscedasticity degrades multiple regression
    analysis by underestimating the extent of the correlation between the
    variables. Heteroscedasticity would be present if incomes were more
    homogeneous among some age groups (e.g. young and old) than among
    others. Figure 46.1 provides two examples of heteroscedasticity.

How to Test to see if the Data Meet the Assumptions

Detecting Multicollinearity

There are a number of ways to detect multicollinearity problems.

EXAMINE BIVARIATE CORRELATIONS As part of the process of building a multiple regression model (see Problem 47) the bivariate correlations between the independent variables should be examined. Very high correlations (e.g. 0.95) will almost certainly produce collinearity problems.

MULTIPLE CORRELATION ANALYSIS Since multicollinearity can arise from very high correlations between a single variable and a *set* of independent variables it can be worth undertaking multiple correlation analysis. Suppose we have four independent variables, X_1, X_2, X_3 and X_4. Multiple correlation analysis can be conducted by treating one of these (e.g. X_4) as the Y variable and then examining the multiple correlation of the remaining three X variables with X_4. The multiple correlation coefficient (R) will indicate the correlation between the set of variables and X_4 in the same way that r indicates the correlation between a single X and a single Y variable. The same process can be repeated treating each of the other X variables (X_1, X_2 and X_3) as the Y variable. The simplest way of doing this is to use the tolerance statistic which is based on this logic (see below).

MULTICOLLINEARITY DIAGNOSTICS WITHIN MULTIPLE REGRESSION PROCEDURES Two such diagnostic statistics are the *variable inflation factor* (VIF) and *tolerance* measures. The latter are based on the multiple correlation approach described above. Variables that have a *low* tolerance indicate a likely problem with multicollinearity. As a general rule of thumb any variable that has a tolerance of 0.2 or less or a VIF of 5 or more could indicate problems with multicollinearity.

Failure of Normality

The main way of checking for violations of normality is to examine the distribution of single variables. Methods of checking *univariate normality* are discussed in detail in Problem 11. Briefly these methods involve:

- examining skewness and kurtosis statistics;
- inspecting histograms with a superimposed normal curve;
- using tests such as the Kolmogorov–Smirnov Z test;
- examining the distribution of dichotomous variables – If about 80 or 90 per cent of cases are in the one category of a dichotomous variable the variable can be considered to be skewed (Tabachnick and Fidell, 1983: 78).

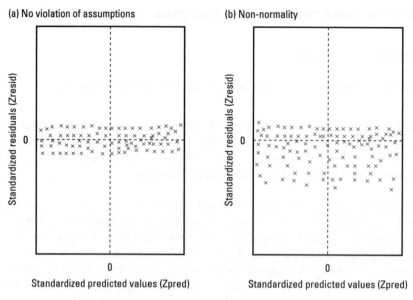

Figure 46.2 *Patterns of residuals in normal and non-normal distributions*

Multivariate violations of normality can be identified by examining the patterns of *residuals*. Statistical programs such as SPSS produce two types of residual plots that help identify such violations.

- *Standardized predicted values plotted against standardized residual values*. Where normality assumptions are met, the distribution of the residuals should show no pattern. Figure 46.2a provides an example of a good distribution of residuals. The cases are distributed evenly across the predicted values and evenly each side of the midpoint of the standardized residual values. In models where relatively little variance is explained the same general picture should be evident, except that the cases would be distributed more on the vertical axis. The distribution would nevertheless be even both sides of the midpoint on the vertical axis. Figure 46.2b illustrates the pattern of residuals if the variables display multivariate skewness. In such cases the residuals are more scattered on one side of the horizontal axis.
- *Histogram of standardized residuals*. These residuals should approximate a normal distribution. If they do not then one or more of the variables is most likely not normally distributed. In Figure 46.3 the distribution of the residuals appears somewhat skewed.

Testing for Linearity

Bivariate nonlinearity can be examined using a scatterplot of the two variables. This can be effective with smaller samples, but with large samples the

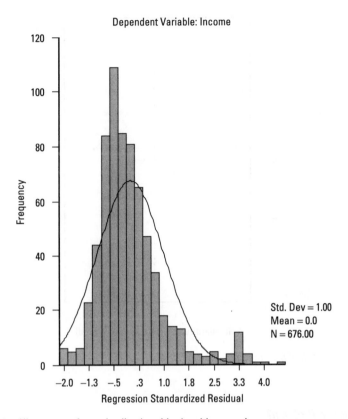

Figure 46.3 *Histogram of standardized residuals with normal curve*

scatterplots can be very difficult to read, especially when there are a large number of cases at the same coordinates.

In a *multivariate* analysis, an examination of the actual standardized residual values of Y against the predicted residual values of Y (predicted from the set of independent variables) can indicate a nonlinear relationship. Where the residuals have a nonlinear pattern (Figures 46.4 and 46.5c) then at least one of the independent variables or a combination of the independent variables has a nonlinear relationship with Y.

Is Heteroscedasticity Present?

The main way of checking for the presence of heteroscedasticity is to examine residual plots of the actual standardized residual values of Y against the predicted residual values of Y. The plots in Figure 46.5 illustrate hetero-scedasticity. This can be seen from the observation that the vertical spread of cases differs across the plot.

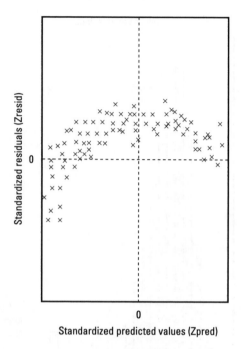

Figure 46.4   *Residual plot indicating nonlinear relationships*

Are Outliers a Problem?

An outlier may appear in univariate, bivariate and multivariate analysis. Any type of outlier can present problems in a multiple regression. There are a variety of methods for detecting outlier problems. These were discussed in detail in Problem 13. Briefly, these methods involve:

- examining the frequency distributions and standard deviations (univariate);
- inspecting scatterplots or standardized residual plots (bivariate and multivariate).

What to do if Assumptions are Violated

If any Variable is at the Wrong Level of Measurement

If an *independent* variable is not measured at the interval level or is not dichotomous, the solution is to create a set of dummy variables (Problem 48). If the *dependent* variable is not at the interval level or is dichotomous, a different type of regression is required (Problem 50).

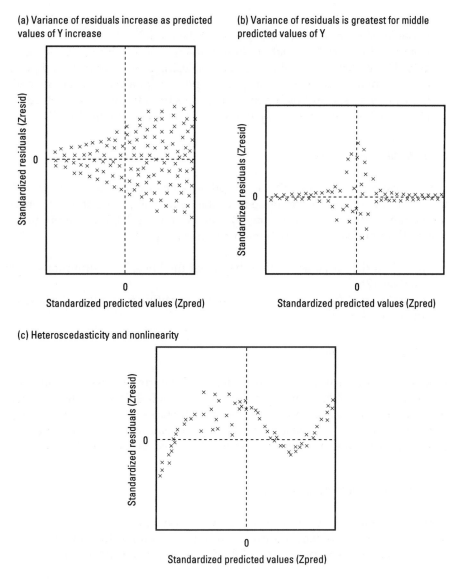

Figure 46.5 *Residual plots indicating various forms of heteroscedasticity*

Dealing with Multicollinearity

There are two main ways of dealing with multicollinearity.

*   Drop the most problematic variable from the analysis. This should cause no problems since multicollinearity is due to very high intercorrelations between variables. When variables are highly intercorrelated only one of

them helps explain variance in the Y variable, so dropping one of the variables should not affect the power of the model.

- Combine the variables that are highly intercorrelated into a single variable. These variables could be combined using a number of techniques, but one method is to use principal components analysis (closely related to factor analysis) and use component scores from this analysis instead of the variables that were highly intercorrelated (see Problem 19).

Fixing Nonlinearity Problems

Since violations of the linearity assumption can cause the regression model to miss all the nonlinear components of the relationships and thus underestimate the predictive and explanatory value of the model, it is important to deal with nonlinearity. The two main alternatives are to:

- transform the variables so that they meet the linearity assumptions (see Problem 12);
- use a different form of regression that is sensitive to nonlinear relationships (Problem 50).

Adjusting for Non Normality

Depending on the sample size, the failure of the normality assumption may not be a major problem. In larger samples the central limit theorem means that departure from normality will not normally have much effect. However, a distribution can be transformed to approximate a normal distribution using one of the transformation methods discussed in Problem 11.

What to do With Heteroscedasticity

Heteroscedasticity is often due to skewness on one variable or another. Should this be a problem, transforming the distribution to normality will often eliminate heteroscedasticity (Tabachnick and Fidell, 1983: 81).

How to Reduce Outlier Problems

A variety of methods are available for dealing with outliers (Problem 13). Briefly, the alternatives are:

- check data for coding or data entry error and correct any mistakes;
- transform the variable;
- change the score of the outlier case;
- delete the variable;
- remove cases with outlier values.

Using SPSS

The SPSS selections for many of the procedures mentioned in this chapter have been covered elsewhere in this book. I will only cover the procedures that have not.

Obtaining a Set of Bivariate Correlations

Since multiple regression usually requires interval variables, a set of Pearson correlations are required. These are best obtained as a set of correlations in the form of a correlation matrix.

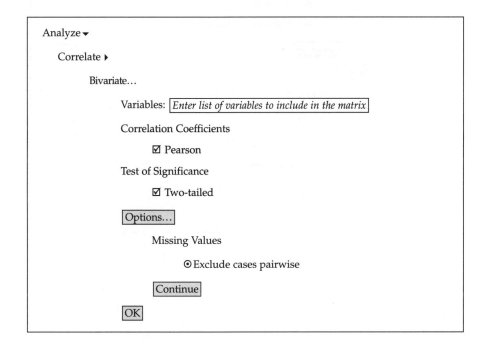

Analyze ▾

    Correlate ▶

        Bivariate...

            Variables: *Enter list of variables to include in the matrix*

            Correlation Coefficients

                ☑ Pearson

            Test of Significance

                ☑ Two-tailed

            Options...

                Missing Values

                    ⊙ Exclude cases pairwise

                Continue

        OK

Residual Plots and Histogram of Standardized Residuals, Tolerance and VIF Statistics

A variety of residual plots are available. I will only show how to obtain the plots of standardized residuals against the standardized predicted residuals as described in this chapter.

Analyze ▾

  Regression ▶

    Linear...

       Dependent: | *Insert Y variable* |

       Independent(s): | *Insert X variables* |

       Method: | *Select method* | ▾ [see Problem 47]

       | Statistics... |

         Regression Coefficients

           ☑ Estimates

           ☑ Collinearity diagnostics

         | Continue |

       | Plots... |

         Y: | *ZRESID |

         X: | *ZPRED |

         Standardized Residual Plots

           ☑ Histogram

         | Continue |

       | OK |

47

How to do a Multiple Regression

Building a regression model is not just a matter of selecting a dependent variable and 'throwing in' a few independent variables and seeing 'what happens'. Apart from meeting statistical assumptions (Problem 46), there are a number of decisions that must be made in the selection of variables for analysis and the way in which the analysis is executed.

The Basics of Multiple Regression

Multiple regression is a simple extension of bivariate regression. Like bivariate regression, there are three main aspects to multiple regression:

- Explaining variance in Y. In multiple regression the R^2 statistic indicates the amount of variance explained in Y (r^2 in bivariate regression).
- Estimating the impact of each X variable on the Y variable (regression coefficients). Multiple regression examines the impact of each variable with the impact of the other X variables controlled, and compares the *relative impact* of each X variable using standardized regression coefficients.
- Predicting Y values, from a set of regression coefficients, for individuals or for categories of cases (e.g. young males, unemployed young women).

Multiple regression is based on one interval Y variable and two or more interval X variables. At its most basic, a multiple regression model will include just two X variables without any propositions about causal relationships among the X variables (Figure 47.1a). However, regression models can include more than two X variables and propose causal relationships among the independent variables and different paths of causal influence of the independent variables (Figure 47.1b).

The regression model to be tested is represented by a multiple regression equation. The regression equation has the same form as the bivariate regression equation ($Y = a + bX$) except that it adds terms for the additional X variables, distinguishing the X variables and the associated regression

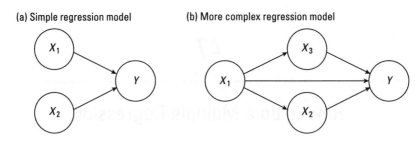

Figure 47.1   *Two regression models*

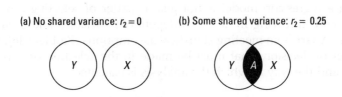

Figure 47.2   *Venn diagrams illustrating the concept of shared variance*

coefficients by subscripts. Thus the regression equation for the model in Figure 47.1a is

$$Y = a + b_1 X_1 + b_2 X_2.$$

Explaining Variance in Y

In bivariate regression the amount of variance that X explains in Y is indicated by Pearson's r^2 statistic. An r^2 of 0.25 means that 25 per cent of the variation in Y is 'explained' by variation in X. To be more precise, an r^2 of 0.25 means that there is 25 per cent overlapping variation between the two variables. The concept of overlapping variation can be illustrated with Venn diagrams. Figure 47.2a represents the variance of two variables as circles. The variance of the two circles does not overlap at all, so there is no shared variance. In this case $r^2 = 0$. In Figure 47.2b the variance of the two variables overlaps, so that 25 per cent of each circle is overlapping variance. This would be indicated by an r^2 of 0.25.

In multiple regression the power of a regression model (i.e. the extent to which a *set* of X variables explains variance in Y) is indicated by the R^2 statistic; this is the equivalent of r^2 except that two or more X variables are used to explain variance in Y. For example, rather than just using gender to explain income variations we will also use age. This enables us to see if these two variables together explain more variation in income than one variable can on its own.

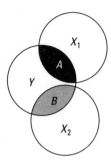

Figure 47.3 *R^2 with two uncorrelated X variables*

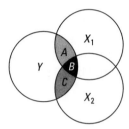

Figure 47.4 *Two independent variables with shared variance*

Correlated Independent Variables and R^2

When the two independent variables are uncorrelated with each other they will both explain separate amounts of the variance in Y (Figure 47.3) In such situations we could simply add the amount of variance explained by X_1 to that explained by X_2 to obtain R^2.

However, X variables are rarely completely uncorrelated so we cannot simply add the r^2 for X_1 to the r^2 of X_2. When independent variables are correlated with each other and they are each correlated with Y they will have some *overlapping* correlation with Y. In Figure 47.4 the shaded area marked as B is variance in Y that *either* X_1 or X_2 can explain.

However, when working out how much variance in Y we explain with the two variables, we cannot count the overlapping area twice. If the variance has already been explained by X_1 then it is not available for X_2 to explain. To count the overlapping variance (i.e. of Y with all of X_1 and of Y with all of X_2) twice would exaggerate how much variance in Y was explained and inflate the value of R^2. We must have a way of only counting the B area once.

Where X_1 and X_2 are moderately correlated they will share a fair amount of common variance with Y. In such cases the *extra* amount of variance that X_2

(a) X_1 and X_2 quite strongly correlated. Both X_1 and X_2 only have a small amount of unique (or independent) variance with Y.

(b) X_1 and X_2 are very highly correlated. X_2 adds no additional explained variance of Y (despite haveing as much bivariate variance in common with Y as does X_1)

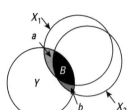
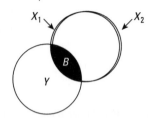

Figure 47.5 *Venn diagrams illustrating the unique variance explained by a second X variable*

explains in Y may be quite limited (Figure 47.5a). Where X_1 and X_2 are highly intercorrelated then X_2 will add virtually nothing beyond that contributed by X_1. In Figure 47.5b there would be no point in using both X_1 and X_2 in the model – only one is required.

How Many Variables to Use

Multiple regression programs permit the inclusion of a large number of X variables. In analyses where the goal is to maximize the explained variance in Y the temptation is to include as many variables as possible on the principle that the greater the number of variables included the more variance will be explained.

This approach should be avoided. A general principle of explanation is to seek the simplest powerful model (parsimony). However, simplicity and power are not always compatible so we must achieve a balance between the number of variables and the amount of variance explained (size of R^2). Variables that add virtually nothing to the predictive value of the model unnecessarily complicate the model for negligible return.

When testing theories the theoretical model should guide the selection of variables – not the goal of maximizing R^2. But care should be taken to control the number of variables included in the models.

Apart from parsimony, the number of variables should be limited since increasing the number of variables artificially inflates the R^2 – especially in small samples. The sample size is an important consideration when deciding how many variables to include in the model. The *variable to case ratio* helps identify the sample size required to accommodate the number of variables you wish to include. If your sample size is not large enough you will need to reduce the number of variables.

The following guidelines are widely used:

- When all variables are entered into the model in a single block (see below) the ratio of cases to variables should be at least $20 : 1$ (Tabachnick and Fidell, 1983).
- In stepwise or hierarchical regression models (see below) larger sample sizes and sample to variable ratios are required. Tabachnick and Fidell (1983) recommend that the ratio of cases to variables should be at least $40 : 1$. Thus for a model with six independent variables the minimum sample size when using stepwise procedures should be 240 cases.
- The minimum suggested sample to variable ratio is $5 : 1$ (Tabachnick and Fidell, 1983). When the ratio is this low it is particularly important that the residuals are normally distributed (see Problem 46).

Newton and Rudestam (1999) recommend the following rules of thumb:

- When computing R^2 the sample size should equal at least $50 + 8k$, where k is the number of independent variables. Thus if you wanted to use six independent variables you would require a sample size of $50 + (8 \times 6) = 98$.
- When computing regression estimates for individual variables, the sample size should be at least $104 + k$. With six independent variables this means the minimum sample size should be 110.

There is nothing absolute about these estimates of sample size. A number of considerations will mean that sample sizes may need to be increased above these sizes (Newton and Rudestam, 1999). Where only weak or moderate relationships exist (i.e. low R^2 and modest regression coefficients) the sample size should be increased. Similarly, if the Y variable is not normally distributed the sample size should be increased to dampen any effect of non-normality.

What is the Difference Between the Methods of Entering Variables?

What is Overlapping Variance?

Computing regression estimates can be single-stage or a multistage process. That is, a multiple regression analysis can proceed as a single step or as a series of steps. In this context a 'step' refers to a point in the analysis in which one or more X variables are 'entered' into the regression calculations. We can enter all the variables in a single step and examine the R^2. This will indicate how much variance in Y is explained by the *set* of variables. Alternatively, we can enter a single variable to see how much variance that variable explains, then add an additional variable to see how much *extra* variance that variable explains and so on.

The different methods of entering variables into the regression analysis can provide very different sorts of information. The *order* in which variables are entered will produce very different estimates about the relative importance of each of the individual variables. Since the method of entering variables can produce quite different results, it is important to understand both the consequences of the order of entry and the reasons for selecting one method over another.

To understand the importance of the different methods of entering X variables into the regression analysis it is useful to return to the diagrams used earlier to illustrate overlapping variance.

In Figure 47.3, X_1 and X_2 are uncorrelated with each other. They share no common variance with Y. In this case it makes no difference in which order these two variables are entered into the regression. In Figure 47.4, where X_1 and X_2 are correlated with each other and share some common variance with Y (area designated as B), it makes a great deal of difference how the variables are entered.

When calculating the R^2 for Y, we can only count the B area in Figure 47.4 once. If X_1 is entered into the model first it will account for the amount of variance in Y indicated by area $A + B$ (since the B area has not already been explained). When X_2 is entered the B area is already explained so X_2 cannot also explain this amount of variance in Y. X_2 can only explain the area marked C.

For example, let us assume that:

- the total variance in Y explained by X_1 is 15 per cent $(A + B)$;
- the total variance in Y explained by X_2 is 20 per cent $(C + B)$;
- the shared area (B) represents an area of 7 per cent of the variance of Y.

Therefore, if X_1 is entered into the regression model first it will explain 15 per cent of the variance in Y. Suppose X_2 is then entered. It will only explain 13 per cent (20 per cent less the 7 per cent already 'taken' by X_1). This makes it appear that X_1 explains more variance in Y than does X_2. In this case R^2 would be $0.15 + 0.13 = 0.28$.

However, if we entered X_2 first then X_2 would explain the full 20 per cent it shares with Y, and X_1 would only explain 8 per cent (since 7 per cent of its variance with Y has been taken). After both variables were included R^2 would be the same as if they were entered in the opposite order $(0.20 + 0.08 = 0.28)$ but the relative contribution of the two variables would be different.

If both variables are entered at the same time we cannot distinguish how much variance each X variable contributes. If X_1 and X_2 were entered at once the R^2 would still be 0.28 but we could not say anything about the relative contribution of each of the variables to R^2.

Figure 47.6 illustrates an extreme case of the above scenario. Here X_1 adds nothing to the explanation of variance in Y that is not already explained by X_2.

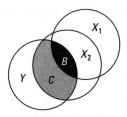

Figure 47.6 *Overlapping variance where the second variable adds nothing to the model*

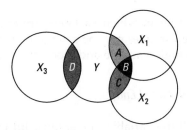

Figure 47.7 *Effect of order of entry of uncorrelated X variable*

If X_2 were entered into a model before X_1 then R^2 at that point would be approximately 0.50. If X_1 were then added R^2 would remain unchanged and it would appear that X_1 had nothing to do with Y. However, If X_1 were entered first the R^2 after it was entered would be approximately 0.15. Adding X_2 would increase the R^2 by an additional 0.35 and yield a total R^2 of 0.50. Clearly the order of entering variables matters to any assessment we make of their importance.

The order of entry does not always matter. If an X variable such as X_3 in Figure 47.7 is completely uncorrelated with the other X variables then it will have the same effect regardless of when it is entered.

Since the order in which variables are entered affects the apparent contribution of each X variable (but not the final R^2) it is important to know whether variables need to be entered step by step or whether they can all be entered in the one step. This decision will depend on the purpose of the analysis. If variables are to be entered in steps then the particular method of selecting the order of entry becomes important since this affects the results and the interpretation of the results.

There are three main methods of linear regression, differing in their method of entering variables into the analysis:

- *Standard*. All variables are entered at the one time.
- *Stepwise*. One variable is added at a time according to set criteria. Once the criteria are set the researcher has no control over what variables are entered or the order in which they are entered.

Table 47.1   *List of variable names and descriptions for a multiple regression analysis*

Name	Description	Name	Description
Y	Social withdrawal		
X_1	Anxiety	X_5	Academic achievement
X_2	Social skills	X_6	Development score
X_3	Symptoms of psychosis	X_7	Hyperactivity score
X_4	Depression	X_8	Delinquency

- *Hierarchical.* The order in which variables are entered is determined by the researcher. The variables may be entered one at a time, in blocks or by a combination of single-variable and block entry (p. 364).

What is the Standard Method of Entry

Using this method, all the variables are entered into the regression analysis in a single step. This method is most appropriate when we simply wish to describe:

- how much variance the model explains (R^2);
- how much impact each of the independent variables has on Y, net of the influence of the other independent variables (regression coefficients);
- the relative importance of each of the independent variables.

The single step method of entry does not allow us to explore theoretical models or test the causal relationships among the independent variables. It simply allows us to estimate the direct impact of each independent variable on the Y variable.

This method can be illustrated with a set of variables for a study of social withdrawal among a sample of adolescents (see Table 47.1). The purpose of the analysis is simply to see which of these variables are related to withdrawal and to see how well we have 'explained' variations in social withdrawal. I have no theory about any causal relationships among the X variables, which variables might be causally prior, and so on. The initial results of this analysis are reported in Table 47.2.

The analysis provides some clear results. Quite a bit of the variation in social withdrawal (59 per cent) is explained by this set of variables. We learn that anxiety, psychosis, depression and hyperactivity are all linked to social withdrawal (all are statistically significant) and that depression is the most important (highest beta – see Problem 48) followed by hyperactivity (negative beta: the higher the hyperactivity, the lower the social withdrawal), anxiety (the greater the anxiety, the greater the withdrawal) and psychosis.

Table 47.2 *Regression statistics and R^2 for variables listed in Table 47.1*

	b (unstandardized regression coefficients)	Beta (standardized regression coefficients)	Significance
X_1 Anxiety	0.25	0.28	0.01
X_2 Social skills	0.10	0.11	0.24
X_3 Symptoms of psychosis	0.14	0.21	0.04
X_4 Depression	0.61	0.72	0.00
X_5 Academic achievement	0.11	0.09	0.26
X_6 Social Development score	−0.04	−0.04	0.65
X_7 Hyperactivity Score	−0.23	−0.29	0.00
X_8 Delinquency	−0.02	−0.03	0.70

$R^2 = 0.59$, Sig. > 0.001
Dependent variable: Social withdrawal

Academic achievement, social development, delinquency and social skills were not linked to social withdrawal (none of these coefficients was statistically significant, so none is significantly different from 0). In other words, social withdrawal seemed to be more closely linked to psychological and psychiatric traits than to social characteristics.

How does Stepwise Regression differ from Standard Single-step Regression?

Using the same variables as above, a stepwise regression will compute up to eight regression models. Each model will add an additional predictor (X) variable. The stepwise procedure will only include variables that are significantly linked to Y. We already know that only four variables are significantly linked to Y so four regression models will be computed. Each one will add an additional variable. The order in which they are added will be set. In this case variables were entered in terms of amount of variance they explain. Table 47.3 presents the R^2 results from this stepwise analysis. Model 1 includes the X variables listed as footnote a; model 2 includes those variables listed in footnote b and so on. The footnotes to the table make it clear in which order the variables were added to the model. Depression was entered first because it explained the most variance.

Since variables are entered in steps R^2 can be calculated for each step. This allows us to see how much *extra* variance each extra variable adds to the explanation of variance in Y.

In this case depression explains 45 per cent of the variance in Y. Notice that in the fourth model R^2 is 56 per cent. The addition of the extra three variables

Table 47.3 *Model summary for stepwise regression*

Model	R	R Square	Adjusted R Square	Change Statistics R Square Change	Sig. F Change
1	0.68	0.46	0.45	0.46	0.00
2	0.71	0.50	0.49	0.04	0.00
3	0.74	0.55	0.54	0.05	0.00
4	0.76	0.58	0.56	0.03	0.00

a Predictors: (Constant), DEPRESS
b Predictors: (Constant), DEPRESS, HYPERACT
c Predictors: (Constant), DEPRESS, HYPERACT, ANXIETY
d Predictors: (Constant), DEPRESS, HYPERACT, ANXIETY, PSYCHOSIS

Table 47.4 *Statistics for excluded variables in stepwise regression*

Model		Beta In	t	Sig.
4	ACHIEVE	0.065	1.091	0.277
	DEVELOP	0.029	0.461	0.646
	DELINQ	−0.005	−0.070	0.945
	SOCSKILL	0.098	1.096	0.275

adds only another 11 per cent to the explained variance. However, the R^2 change and Sig. of change columns indicate that these three variables do add to the explanation and their contribution is not just due to sampling error.

In the final model, four variables were deemed unworthy of inclusion. Table 47.4 indicates that had these variables been included they would have had very low and statistically non-significant beta values.

Since the goal of stepwise regression is to produce a parsimonious model, it has identified the four variables that best predict Y and has eliminated those that contribute nothing significant. Of those it has identified as helping predict Y, it has identified which ones explain most variance in Y. If we wanted to use fewer variables in future research to predict Y we might settle for just the depression measure and do without the others that contribute relatively little. That choice is a matter of judgement and the constraints on data collection.

What is the Hierarchical Method of Entering Variables and when to use it?

This method of entering variables gives the data analyst most control over the regression model and enables the testing of hypotheses and theories. Hierarchical entry methods require the researcher to specify the order in which the variables are entered. This order depends on the purpose of the analysis. What factors might influence the order of entry of variables?

REMOVING THE INFLUENCE OF EXTRANEOUS VARIABLES   Controlling the order of entering variables enables the researcher to carry out 'statistical experiments' by controlling for sets of extraneous variables before undertaking the core part of the analysis. In experimental research the researcher removes contaminating factors that might confound the results by matching or random allocation to experimental and control groups. These matching or randomizing methods remove the effect of these extraneous variables so that the 'pure' effect of X on Y can be examined. While these methods of removing the effect of extraneous factors cannot be used in a great deal of social science research, we can remove some such factors using statistical techniques. Hierarchical methods in multiple regression are one such technique.

For example, if we were interested in gender differences in attitudes and behaviour we might first try to remove known differences between men and women (e.g. income, workforce participation, type of education). Once such 'background' factors are removed (controlled) we can get on with the business of examining gender differences without these factors confusing the analysis. If we find gender differences in attitudes and behaviour despite these controls at least we know that the gender differences are not due to *these* factors.

FOCUS ON EXTRA EXPLANATORY CONTRIBUTION OF A VARIABLE   A second factor that might influence the order of entry is that we specifically want to know how much *extra* explanatory power a particular variable or set of variables has. We may know that particular variables affect Y but our real interest may be in how much additional explanatory power another specified variable has. In this context we would first enter in the variables for which the impact is known and then add in the variable for which we want to test the additional impact.

TESTING PARTICULAR CAUSAL PROPOSITIONS   A third reason for controlling the order in which variables are entered is to test particular *causal propositions*. In Figure 47.8 four simple multivariate models are outlined. How would we test these and interpret the results by controlling the entry of variables?

To test the model in Figure 47.8a we would enter Z first and examine R^2. We would then enter X as a second step. If the model is correct then adding X after Z should not make any significant difference to R^2. Since this model asserts that all the influence of X is via Z then X should add nothing once Z has been taken into the model.

The same logic would apply to the model in Figure 47.8b. In this model Z is an *extraneous variable*. It will produce a correlation between X and Y simply because both are *outcomes* of Z. By entering Z first the influence of Z is removed. If any variables added subsequently have an effect on Y (i.e. increase R^2) then this effect it is *not* due in any way to any relationship that variable has with Z. If this model is correct then adding X after Z should not

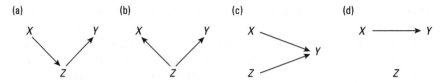

Figure 47.8 *Four simple multivariate models*

lead to any increase in R^2. This is the same pattern as would be expected for the model in Figure 47.8a. To work out which proposition makes most sense, see Problem 42.

If the model in Figure 47.8c is correct, the variables would be entered in the same order as for the previous models but we would expect a different pattern. In this case we would expect that R^2 would increase significantly with the addition of X. That is, X has an independent (or direct) impact additional to and separate from that of Z.

We would test the model in Figure 47.8d by first entering Z and then entering X. If this model is correct we would expect that R^2 will be non-significant after entering just Z. However, when X is added R^2 should change and become statistically significant.

In these four cases the order of entry of the variables is the same. In more complex models the order could vary. In these four cases the pattern of changes in R^2 is central to the interpretation of causal relationships. If a single-step regression model were used none of these causal propositions could be tested. If the stepwise model were used we would have no control over the order of their entry and thus could not test our particular propositions unless the automatic order in which they were entered using stepwise regression happened to be the same as we required.

BLOCK ENTRY Rather than entering variables one at a time, they can be entered in blocks. There are a number of reasons why we might enter variables as a block, including the following:

- We are unable to specify any causal order among the set of variables within the block.
- We are using the set of variables to measure an underlying construct. Rather than combine the variables into a single construct they are entered into the model as a block to represent the construct. For example, we may have a number of variables designed to tap social class. By entering these variables, on their own, in one step and examining the change in R^2 we can estimate the influence of social class on the Y variable.
- When a set of dummy variables need to be added (see Problem 48).

Overview of Methods of Entry

All three methods of managing the way in which variables are entered into a regression model have their place. In summary:

- The standard single-step entry method is appropriate when the purpose of the analysis is simple *description*.
- The stepwise procedure is appropriate when the purpose is maximizing *prediction* with as few variables as possible. It can also be useful as an exploratory, model-building approach to analysis.
- Hierarchical entry methods are necessary for *testing models and causal propositions* and conducting what I have called 'statistical experiments'.

Using SPSS

Standard Regression

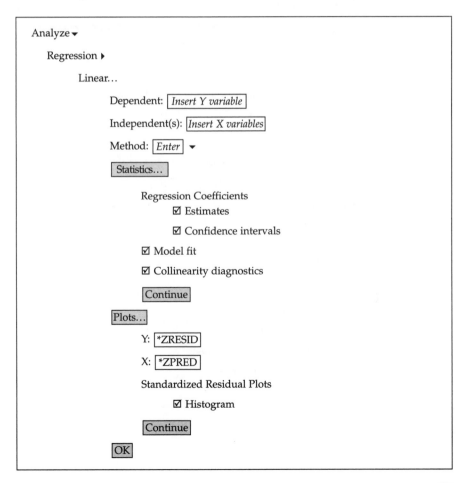

Analyze ▾

  Regression ▶

    Linear...

      Dependent: | Insert Y variable |

      Independent(s): | Insert X variables |

      Method: | Enter | ▾

      | Statistics... |

        Regression Coefficients

          ☑ Estimates

          ☑ Confidence intervals

        ☑ Model fit

        ☑ Collinearity diagnostics

        | Continue |

     | Plots... |

        Y: | *ZRESID |

        X: | *ZPRED |

        Standardized Residual Plots

          ☑ Histogram

        | Continue |

    | OK |

Stepwise

The same procedure is used as for standard regression except that Stepwise is selected as the method, rather than Enter. In addition, select the ☑ R squared change option on the Statistics menu to obtain R^2 change statistics.

Hierarchical

Analyze ▾

  Regression ▸

    Linear…

        Dependent: [Insert Y variable]

        Independent(s): [Insert X variables for step 1]

        Method: [Enter] ▾

        [Next] [above Independents panel] Click to go to enable entry of 2nd step

        Independent(s): [Insert X variables for step 2]

        Method: [Enter] ▾

        [Next] [above Independents panel] Click to go to enable entry of 3rd step

        Independent(s): [Insert X variables for step 3]

        Method: [Enter] ▾

        [Next] [above Independents panel] Click to go to enable entry of 4th step

        Independent(s): [Insert X variables for step 4]

        Method: [Enter] ▾

        [Statistics…]

            Regression Coefficients
                ☑ Estimates

                ☑ Confidence intervals

            ☑ Model fit

            ☑ R squared change

            ☑ Part and partial correlations

            ☑ Collinearity diagnostics

            [Continue]

        [Plots…]

Y: *ZRESID

X: *ZPRED

Standardized Residual Plots

☑ Histogram

Continue

OK

48

How to Use Non-interval Variables in Multiple Regression

What is the Problem?

Frequently in social science research we work with discrete variables measured at the nominal and ordinal levels. Normal regression requires that variables are measured at the interval level or are dichotomous. This requirement appears to preclude using variables such as marital status, race, country of birth, religion and a vast number of other important categorical variables. How can the power of regression analysis be used when some of the variables are nominal or discrete ordinal (i.e. categorical) variables?

When the Y variable is nominal, the type of regression described in this book cannot be used. Other methods, such as logistic regression and discriminant analysis, can be used in such cases (Problem 50).

However, where an *independent* variable (X) is nominal or discrete ordinal, ordinary regression methods can be applied. Since dichotomous variables can be used in multiple regression, the solution is to convert categorical variables into dichotomous variables. One way of doing this is to collapse the categorical X variable into two categories. However, this is unsatisfactory in many cases as we lose too much information by combining very different people into the same category. For example, collapsing marital status into two categories might result in the categories married and not married. But this would mean that the never married, separated, divorced and widowed would all be lumped into one category. This is unlikely to be a good way of analyzing data. A better solution is to use a set of *dummy variables* and enter these into the regression equation.

What is a Dummy Variable?

A categorical variable with three or more categories can be broken up into a set of separate dichotomous (dummy) variables coded 0 and 1. Doing this makes it possible to identify the impact of membership of any particular category of the variable on the Y variable. The process of creating and using dummy variables is best illustrated with an example.

Table 48.1   *Creating dummy variables for marital status*

Category	New variable name	Values
Married/cohabiting	MARR	1 = married/cohabiting 0 = everyone else
Separated/divorced	SEPDIV	1 = separated/divorced 0 = everyone else
Widowed	WID	1 = widowed 0 = everyone else
Never married	This category will not be 'dummied'. It will serve as the 'reference category'	

Table 48.2   *Codes of each category of marital status on the set of three dummy variables*

	MARR	SEPDIV	WID
Married/cohabiting	1	0	0
Separated/divorced	0	1	0
Widowed	0	0	1
Never married	0	0	0

Suppose we want to include marital status in a regression model. The variable has the following categories: never married; married/cohabiting; separated/divorced; widowed. This variable can be converted into a set of dummy variables. For reasons that will become clearer later, the number of dummy variables must be one less than the number of categories of the variable. In this case three dummy variables will be used to represent marital status (Table 48.1).

Setting up the variables in this way enables each different marital status to be identified by examining the codes on the *set* of variables. Each marital status (including the never married) will have a unique combination of codes on the set of dummy variables (see Table 48.2).

What do the Results from Dummy Variable Analysis Mean?

In the first instance I will illustrate the use and interpretation of a set of dummy variables without using other independent variables.

Single Set of Dummy Variables

When a set of dummy variables is created they must be entered as a *block* in one step (see Problem 47). Table 48.3 reports the results of entering our three dummy variables for marital status in a single step. Income is the *Y* variable.

Table 48.3   *Multiple regression output for a set of three dummy variables: income by marital status*

(a) Model Summary

Model	R	R Square	Adjusted R Square	Std. Error of the Estimate
1	0.27	0.08	0.08	28322

a Predictors: (Constant), WID, SEPDIV, MAR
Dependent variable: Income

(b) ANOVA

Model		Sum of Squares	df	Mean Square	F	Sig.
1	Regression	110962137391	3	36987379130	46.11	0.00
	Residual	1363689355419	1700	802170209		
	Total	1474651492811	1703			

a Predictors: (Constant), WID, SEPDIV, MAR

b Dependent Variable: Income

(c) Coefficients

Model		Unstandardized Coefficients		Standardized Coefficients	t	Sig.
		B	Std. Error	Beta		
1	(Constant)	$37 996	1733.3		21.9	0.00
	SEPDIV	−$10 304	2784.0	−0.11	−3.7	0.00
	MAR	$8628	1918.2	0.14	4.5	0.00
	WID	−$20 153	3609.9	−0.15	−5.6	0.00

a Dependent Variable: Income

Taken together, the dummy variables account for 8 per cent of variation in income (adjusted R^2 in Table 48.3a; see problem 49). How are the regression coefficients for these marital status dummy variables to be interpreted? To assist with the interpretation, remember that no dummy variable was created for the never married members of the sample. These people are called the *reference category*.

The general equation for the multiple regression is

$$Y = a + b_1X_1 + b_2X_2 + b_3X_3 + \dots$$

(see Problem 47). In the current example a dummy variable is substituted for each of the X variables. This gives the equation

$$Y = a + b_{MAR} X_{MAR} + b_{SEPDIV} X_{SEPDIV} + b_{WID} X_{WID}.$$

By substituting the b values obtained from Table 48.3c (unstandardized coefficients) for these variables we get:

$$Y = 37\ 996 + 8628\ X_{MAR} - 10\ 304\ X_{SEPDIV} - 20\ 153\ X_{WID}.$$

Those who *never married* (the reference category) have a value of 0 on each of the dummy variables (since they are not married, not separated or divorced and not widowed). To estimate the income of the never married respondents we simply substitute these zero values for the X value of each dummy variable. The equation becomes:

$$Y = 37\ 996 + 8628 \times 0 - 10\ 304 \times 0 - 20\ 153 \times 0 = \$37\ 996.$$

In other words, when only the dummy variables are in the regression equation the value for the variable relegated to the reference category is the same as the constant (the a value).

What do the regression coefficients for each of the dummy variables mean? These coefficients must be read in *relative* terms – that is, relative to the reference category. In this case the b coefficient for married people is 8628. This means that on average married people earn $8628 *more than* the reference category (the never marrieds). That is, the marrieds earn $37 996 + $8628. Those who are separated or divorced, on average, earn $10 304 *less* (notice the negative sign) than the never marrieds. Finally, widowed respondents earn, on average, $20 153 *less* than the never marrieds.

Including Additional Variables

When additional independent variables are included with the dummy variables the interpretation of the coefficients of each dummy variable will change, but the general interpretation remains the same. The regression coefficients are still interpreted in relative terms. For example, when gender is added (coded $0 =$ female, $1 =$ male) we obtain the regression figures reported in Table 48.4.

Here the coefficient for gender is 3401. Given the coding where males were coded as 1, this means that, given the same marital status, males, on average earn $3401 more than females. The other coefficients have changed a little but their *relative* interpretation remains the same. Thus the figure of 8720 for the variable MAR means that married people on average earn more than never married people.

What does the constant mean? The constant is the value for people who are coded 0 on *all* the independent variables. In this case this means that the constant is the predicted average income of *females* who have *never married*. *Males* who have never married score 0 on MAR, SEPDIV and WID but score 1 on the sex variable. Accordingly never married males are estimated to earn $36 098 plus an additional $3 401 by virtue of being male.

Table 48.4   *Regression coefficients for Income by marital status (dummy variables) and gender*

Model		Unstandardized Coefficients		Standardized Coefficients		
		B	Std. Error	Beta	t	Sig.
1	(Constant)	$36,098	$1,895		19.0	0.00
	SEPDIV	−$9,714	$2,790	−0.10	−3.5	0.00
	MAR	$8,720	$1,916	0.14	4.6	0.00
	WID	−$19,147	$3,628	−0.14	−5.3	0.00
	SEX	$3,401	$1,385	0.06	2.5	0.01

a Dependent Variable: Income; Sex is coded 0 = female; 1 = male

Using SPSS

Creating Dummy Variables

Regression using dummy variables is the same as with other variables except for the following points:

- The set of dummy variables representing a categorical variable must be entered as a single block. Stepwise regression will not do this, so you should use either standard regression or hierarchical regression with block entry.
- Before doing the regression analysis you will need to create the dummy variables. This is accomplished via variable transformations. The example below contains the instructions for creating the set of marital status dummy variables.

Transform ▾

    Recode ▸

        Into Different Variables...

            Input Variable → Output Variable: [*MARITAL*]

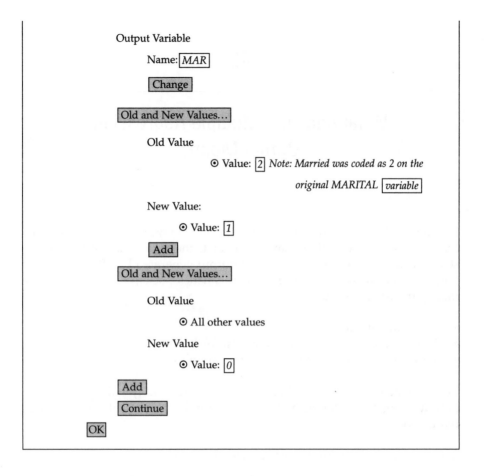

Repeat the same procedure for Separated and divorced, except that:

- the output variable name will be SEPDIV;
- the old value is 4.

Repeat the same procedure for Widowed, except that:

- the output variable name will be WID;
- the old value is 3.

49

What does the Multiple Regression Output Mean?

Having produced output from a well–developed regression model in which the regression assumptions have been met, the next problem is to make sense of the output. This section uses output generated by SPSS, but much the same output is produced by most statistics packages. There are three main parts to the output:

- the model fit – R^2;
- ANOVA output – the significance test for R^2;
- regression coefficients for individual variables.

Throughout this section a single example (Table 49.1) will be used, but output using the different methods of entering the variables will also be discussed.

Table 49.1   *Variable definitions for multiple regression example*

Variable	NAME	Description
Y	INC	Respondent's annual income in dollars
X_1	GENDER	Gender: 0 = female; 1 = male
X_2	HOURS	Weekly hours of work of respondent
X_3	AGE	Respondent's age in years
X_4	FED	Father's years of education
X_5	MED	Mother's years of education
X_6	FPRES	Father's occupational prestige, scored 18–70: high score = high prestige
X_7	RED	Respondent's years of education
X_8	RPRES	Respondent's occupational prestige, scored 18–70: high score = high prestige

How to Read the Model-fit Statistics

We begin by examining the model-fit output.

Table 49.2 *Model fit for single-step regression*

Model	R	R Square	Adjusted R Square	Std. Error of the Estimate
1[a]	0.62	0.38	0.38	17673.5

a Predictors: (Constant), GENDER, AGE, RED, HOURS, FPRES, MED, RPRES, FED
Dependent variable: Income

Model-Fit Output in Standard (Single-Step) Regression

There are two statistics of interest, R^2 and adjusted R^2.

The R^2 statistic indicates the amount of variance in Y that is explained by the set of X variables. In our example 38 per cent of the variance in Y is explained by the set of eight X variables (Table 49.2).

However, R^2 can be inflated by a large number of X variables. The adjusted R^2 statistic takes the number of X variables into account. For large samples the two statistics will be quite close, but in smaller samples where the case-to-variable ratio is low they can differ considerably. The adjusted R^2 should be reported in preference to R^2, especially for smaller samples.

Model Fit in Stepwise Regression

In the model-fit output for stepwise and hierarchical regression a separate row is provided for each step in building the full regression model. Each step is labelled as a model. If five steps are taken, five models will be specified in the model-fit table (Table 49.3). The variables included at each step are indicated in the footnotes to the model-fit table. In model 1 RPRES, the respondent's occupational prestige, was entered first since this variable had the strongest correlation with income. In model 2 GENDER was added since this had the next strongest correlation with income. In total the stepwise regression tried five models, with the final model including RPRES, GENDER, HOURS, RED and AGE. These variables helped explain variation in the respondent's income. Knowing anything about the parent's education or father's occupational prestige adds nothing that the other variables do not tell us.

The model-fit output indicates the R^2 for each model. By itself RPRES explains 14 per cent of the variance in income. Entering GENDER explains an *additional* 11 per cent of the variance (see R^2 change for model 2). This amount of extra change is unlikely to be due to sampling error (Sig. F change) since the significance level is well below 0.01. Entering HOURS explains another 6 per cent of income variance, and RED accounts for an additional 4 per cent, while AGE explains only an additional 2 per cent.

Table 49.3   *Model fit for stepwise method of entry*

Model	R	R Square	Adjusted R Square	Std. Error of the Estimate	R Square Change	Change Statistics			
						F Change	df1	df2	Sig. F Change
1[a]	0.38	0.14	0.14	20705.5	0.14	100.8	1	596	.001
2[b]	0.50	0.25	0.25	19366.3	0.11	86.3	1	595	.001
3[c]	0.56	0.32	0.31	18558.4	0.06	53.9	1	594	.001
4[d]	0.60	0.36	0.35	18003.3	0.04	38.2	1	593	.001
5[e]	0.62	0.38	0.37	17684.5	0.02	22.6	1	592	.001

a Predictors: (Constant), RPRES
b Predictors: (Constant), RPRES, GENDER
c Predictors: (Constant), RPRES, GENDER, HOURS
d Predictors: (Constant), RPRES, GENDER ,HOURS, RED
e Predictors: (Constant), RPRES, GENDER ,HOURS, RED, AGE

Model Fit for Hierarchical Regression

The output for hierarchical regression has a similar form to that for stepwise regression. The model-fit table displays a number of models. However, the number of models and the variables that are entered at each step are defined by the user.

While stepwise regression only includes variables that add significantly to the R^2 and only adds one variable at each step, hierarchical regression adds the variables as it is instructed and can add a block of variables at a single step.

In our current example we examine the importance for income of family class characteristics (parental education and occupational status) relative to the respondent's education and job prestige. Model 1 in Table 49.4 controls for some characteristics known to affect income ($R^2 = 0.22$) and removes their influence from subsequent steps. Model 2 adds parental characteristics. These add an additional 6 per cent to R^2. Finally, the respondent's education and occupational prestige are added. These explain an additional 11 per cent of variance in income. That is, the respondent's education and occupational prestige affect income above and beyond parental class.

The important point in this model is that parental characteristics were entered first. The respondent's education and job prestige are very likely to be correlated with parental education and job prestige. By entering parental characteristics first, all of the correlation between respondent's education and job prestige that is due to parental characteristics is already included in the explained variance by the time we get to model 3. Adding the respondent's education and occupational prestige after parental characteristics in model 3 indicates the amount of variance that respondent characteristics add *independently* of their relationship to parental characteristics.

Table 49.4 *Model fit with hierarchical method: parental characteristics entered before respondent characteristics*

Model	R	R Square	Adjusted R Square	Std. Error of the Estimate	Change Statistics				
					R Square Change	F Change	df1	df2	Sig. F Change
1[a]	0.47	0.22	0.22	19808.3	0.22	55.8	3	594	.001
2[b]	0.53	0.28	0.27	19117.9	0.06	15.6	3	591	.001
3[c]	0.62	0.38	0.38	17673.5	0.11	51.3	2	589	.001

a Predictors: (Constant), GENDER, AGE, HOURS
b Predictors: (Constant), GENDER, AGE, HOURS , FPRES, MED, FED
c Predictors: (Constant), GENDER, AGE, HOURS , FPRES, MED, FED, RPRES, RED

Table 49.5 *Model fit with hierarchical method: parental characteristics entered after respondent characteristics*

Model	R	R Square	Adjusted R Square	Std. Error of the Estimate	Change Statistics				
					R Square Change	F Change	df1	df2	Sig. F Change
1[a]	0.47	0.22	0.22	19808.3	0.22	55.8	3	594	.001
2[b]	0.62	0.38	0.37	17684.5	0.16	76.6	2	592	.001
3[c]	0.62	0.38	0.38	17673.5	0.004	1.2	3	589	.29

a Predictors: (Constant), GENDER, AGE, HOURS
b Predictors: (Constant), GENDER, AGE, HOURS , RPRES, RED
c Predictors: (Constant), GENDER, AGE, HOURS , RPRES, RED, FPRES, MED, FED

Had the respondent's characteristics been entered at step 2 and parental characteristics entered at step 3, the amount of variance explained by the former would have been much higher. Table 49.5 provides these figures for comparison purposes. When respondent characteristics are entered at step 2 the change in R^2 is 0.16, and adding parental characteristics after respondent characteristics adds nothing to the explained variance – the change in R^2 is small and statistically non-significant (see also Figure 47.6 and the related discussion of overlapping variance and the effect of the order of entry on the amount of variance explained by a particular variable).

Which Part of the ANOVA Output is Important?

The main value of the ANOVA table lies in the F test and its significance level. The significance level helps test the null hypothesis that $R^2 = 0$. If the significance of F is less than 0.05 or 0.01 the null hypothesis will be rejected, and we will assume that the R^2 reflects a real pattern in the population.

Table 49.6   *ANOVA output for single-step regression*

Model		Sum of Squares	df	Mean Square	F	Sig.
1	Regression	114739059437.5	8	14342382429	45.9	.001
	Residual	183976053438.7	589	312353231		
	Total	298715112876.3	597			

Table 49.7   *ANOVA output for three-step hierarchical model*

Model		Sum of Squares	df	Mean Square	F	Sig.
1	Regression	65647525756	3	21882508585	55.7	.001
	Residual	233067587120	594	392369675		
	Total	298715112876	597			
2	Regression	82708379089	6	13784729848	37.7	.001
	Residual	216006733786	591	365493627		
	Total	298715112876	597			
3	Regression	114739059437	8	14342382429	45.9	.001
	Residual	183976053438	589	312353231		
	Total	298715112876	597			

In single-step regression the output provides the significance level for the overall model (Table 49.6). For the stepwise and hierarchical methods a separate ANOVA table is provided for each step of the analysis so that the statistical significance of R^2 at any step of the analysis can be examined. Table 49.7 provides the ANOVA output for the hierarchical three-step model described above.

What do all the Regression Coefficients for Individual Variables Mean?

This part of the output reports information at the level of the individual variable. The variables for which information is provided will depend on the method of entering variables. In single-step and hierarchical regression details are provided on all variables. For stepwise regression details are provided only for variables that 'made it' into the model.

The information provided for each variable depends on the options selected when the regression was run. The outline below describes the most important information. Table 49.8 provides the output for each variable using the single-step regression model.

Table 49.8 *Regression estimates for individual variables in the single-step regression model*

Model	Unstandardized Coefficients (B)	Std. Error	Standardized Coefficients (Beta)	t	Sig.	95% Confidence Interval for B Lower Bound	Upper Bound	Correlations Zero-order	Partial	Part	Collinearity Statistics Tolerance	VIF
1 (Constant)	-$56961.6	5521.1		-10.3	.00	-67805.0	-46118.2					
HOURS	$393.9	53.7	.25	7.3	.00	288.4	499.4	.33	.29	.24	.92	1.1
RPRES	$294.6	63.5	.18	4.6	.00	170.0	419.3	.37	.19	.15	.70	1.4
FPRES	-$57.1	68.3	-.03	-.8	.40	-191.1	77.0	.12	-.03	-.03	.65	1.5
AGE	$409.2	68.0	.21	6.0	.00	275.7	542.8	.21	.24	.19	.86	1.2
RED	$2083.3	336.4	.26	6.2	.00	1422.7	2743.9	.38	.25	.20	.61	1.6
FED	$377.2	282.8	.07	1.3	.18	-178.3	932.7	.13	.05	.04	.42	2.4
MED	$173.1	292.3	.02	.6	.55	-401.0	747.3	.12	.02	.02	.59	1.7
GENDER	$12490.8	1477.0	.28	8.5	.00	9590.0	15391.6	.31	.33	.27	.96	1.0

a Dependent Variable: Income; Gender is coded 0 = female; 1 = male

Interpreting the Unstandardized Coefficient (B)

- This is the unstandardized regression coefficient that is symbolized as b in the regression equations.
- This figure is expressed in the units of measurement of the Y variable. Since Y is measured in dollars the regression coefficient is expressed in dollars in Table 49.8.
- The b coefficients represent the impact of each X variable on Y *independently* of the impact of the other independent variables in the model. The estimate of the impact of any particular X variable has removed from it any impact due to the joint effect of other X variables. This means that if everything else was the same regarding the other X variables, then an extra hour of work per week yields an average of an extra $393.90 per year (row 2 in Table 49.8). Other things being equal, being male yields an extra $12 490.80 (row 9 in Table 49.8).
- The value of b can be positive or negative. A positive coefficient means that, for an additional unit of X, Y will increase by b. A negative coefficient means that, for an additional unit of X, Y will decrease by b.
- In multiple regression the various X variables will usually be measured in different units. Where this is so the b coefficients cannot be compared with one another. Thus the impact of age on income and gender on income cannot be compared. A 'unit of gender' which is measured on a 0–1 scale is not equivalent to a unit of age which is measured on a scale of years. The size of each 'unit' is not equivalent.
- In the multistep regression models the regression estimates differ between each step. As each variable is entered the estimates change. In hierarchical regression the b coefficients at the final step are the same as for single-step regression. In stepwise regression the final b coefficients can be a little different from those calculated using single-step or hierarchical regression. This is because stepwise regression excludes some variables from the final solution.

Standard Error of B

These standard error figures are used in the calculation of the confidence intervals for b (see below).

How to Compare the Importance of Each Variable – Using Standardized Coefficients (Beta)

Since b coefficients are measured in different units, the effects of the various X variables cannot be compared. The standardized regression coefficient (also called beta) adjusts for these differences so that the impact of each

X variable can be compared. Beta coefficients are b coefficients re-expressed in standard deviation units of the Y variable. They range from 0 to 1 and can be either positive or negative. The larger the beta value (ignoring the sign) the greater the impact of that variable relative to the other X variables in the model. In Table 49.8 GENDER has the strongest impact (beta = 0.28) followed by RED (0.26) and HOURS (0.25).

What are T and Sig.?

Of these two columns the 'Sig.' figures matter most. These test the null hypothesis that the regression coefficients (both unstandardized and standardized) are zero. When the significance level is below 0.05 or 0.01 the null hypothesis of no impact is rejected. In Table 49.8 the significance figures for FED, MED and FPRES are higher than 0.05 so we cannot be confident that their impact is greater than 0. The other variables have low significance levels, which means that in the population their impact is greater than zero.

What does the Confidence Interval for B Mean?

The confidence interval for B provides a way of estimating the likely impact of the variable in the population. It is the confidence interval for the unstandardized regression coefficient at the 95 per cent confidence level. The predicted impact of each X variable in the population is likely to be within the range specified by the lower and upper bounds. Where this range is wide the predictions based on this variable will have a wide margin of error; this tends to occur when R^2 is low.

What are the Zero-order, Partial and Part Correlations?

The zero-order correlations are Pearson r correlations that indicate the bivariate correlation between each X variable and Y without controlling for any other X variables (see Problem 35). The value of the zero-order correlation is unaffected by the method of entering variables into the model.

Partial correlations refer to the correlation of X with Y with the influence of other variables removed (see Problem 45). The partial correlation is always larger than the part correlation, but can vary depending on the method of entering variables into the model.

Part correlations represent the amount by which the R^2 would be reduced if the X variable were removed from the regression equation (Newton and Rudestam, 1999).

How to Read the Collinearity Statistics

These two statistics indicate whether a variable could be producing multi-collinearity problems. Tolerance values can range between 0 to 1. If the tolerance is less than 0.2 the variable may produce multicollinearity problems. VIF refers to the variable inflation factor: a VIF greater than 5 indicates a problem with multicollinearity.

Using SPSS

Previous chapters have indicated how to run a multiple regression in SPSS. The instructions below specify how to obtain the output that has been discussed in this chapter.

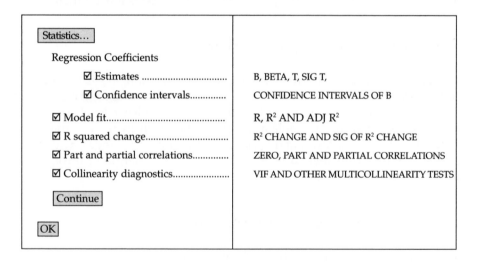

50

What Other Multivariate Methods are Available?

The purpose of this chapter is to provide pointers to an appropriate method of analysis for multivariate research questions. Many considerations will determine the choice of method, and I simply provide some of the questions to ask as you narrow down the choice. Following the list of questions is a summary indicating some features of some common multivariate techniques.

Questions to ask When Selecting a Multivariate Method

Purpose of the Analysis

1. What is the purpose of the analysis. Is it:

    - data reduction?
    - description of relationships?
    - explanation and theory testing?

2. If the purpose is explanation, do you plan to:

    - examine causal relationships?
    - examine direct and indirect causal paths?
    - focus on explaining a bivariate relationship?

Questions about the Design

3. What type of research design do you have?

    - Is it a repeated measures design?
    - Are there covariates that need to be controlled statistically?
    - Is it cross-sectional?

Questions about the Sample

4. Is the sample a probability sample?
5. How large is the sample?

Questions about the Independent Variable

6. How many independent variables will be examined?

   - One?
   - Two or more?

7. What is the level of measurement of the variables?

   - Are they all interval?
   - Is there a mixture of interval and dichotomous variables?
   - Is there a mixture of interval and discrete categorical variables?

8. Are the independent variables likely to be normally distributed in the population?
9. Are the relationships between the independent variables likely to be linear or nonlinear?
10. Are the relationships between the independent variable(s) and the dependent variable likely to be linear or nonlinear?

Questions about the Dependent Variable

11. How many dependent variables will be used in a single analysis?
12. What is the level of measurement of the dependent variable(s)?
13. Is the dependent variable dichotomous?
14. What is the likely distribution of the dependent variable in the population?

Aspects of Some Common Multivariate Methods of Analysis

Factor Analysis (Exploratory)

Main uses
- to reduce the number of variables for later analysis;
- to explore the underlying structure of a set of variables;
- to eliminate multicollinearity in other multivariate methods by reducing collinear variables into one construct.

Design
- data are normally collected at one point in time;
- should avoid factor-analyzing data from different samples or from repeated measures.

Sample
- the larger the sample, the more reliable and stable the factor analysis. Comrey and

		Lee (1992) recommend at least 300; Tabachnick and Fidell (1983) recommend at least 150.
Independent variables	•	the distinction between independent and dependent variables is not relevant;
	•	all variables are assumed to be caused by an underlying unmeasured variable;
	•	variables should not be causally related to one another.
Number	•	at least two, but it is highly desirable that far more variables are included.
Level of measurement	•	based on Pearson's correlation, therefore interval variables are assumed;
	•	however, ordinal variables are frequently used in factor analysis if the variable can be assumed to have an underlying continuous character;
	•	correlations are robust so can accommodate ordinal variables without too much distortion.
Dichotomies OK?	•	not generally desirable.
Assumes normality?	•	yes, but factor analysis can still be used with a non-normal distribution if it is simply being used to describe a sample.
Assumes linearity	•	based on Pearson's correlation and therefore it is only sensitive to linear relationships between the variables;
	•	can be used on variables that do not have a linearrelationship, but the analysis will be degraded.
Other	•	the set of variables to be factor-analysed should have a fair number of bivariate correlations if the solution is to be meaningful.
Dependent variable	•	not relevant.

Discriminant Analysis

Main uses	•	description and prediction;
	•	to identify variables that best predict group membership.
Design	•	assumes observations are uncorrelated;
	•	therefore discriminant analysis is inappropriate in paired or repeated measures designs.
Sample	•	easier to detect violations of assumptions in larger sample;
	•	sample size of smallest group should exceed the number of predictor variables.

Independent variables

Number	• two or more.
Level of measurement	• interval.
Dichotomies OK?	• yes.
Assumes normality?	• assumed to be from a multivariate normal distribution.
Assumes linearity?	• yes.

Dependent variable

Type	• discrete;
	• the categories of the Y variable are the groups whose membership discriminant analysis predicts.
No. of categories	• two or more.
Number	• one.

Logistic Regression

Main uses	• description, prediction and causal analysis for dichotomous dependent variables.
Design	• assumes that outcomes (i.e. membership of categories of the Y variable) are independent;
	• logistic regression is inappropriate in paired or repeated measures designs.
Sample	• requires larger samples than linear regression if testing hypotheses;
	• a minimum of 50 cases per predictor variable is recommended (Aldrich and Nelson, 1984).

Independent variables

Number	• two or more.
Level of measurement	• interval.
Dichotomies OK?	• yes;
	• can dummy-code categorical variables in same way as in normal regression.
Assumes normality?	• assumed to be from a multivariate normal distribution.
Assumes linearity?	• yes.

Dependent variable

Level of measurement	• does not matter.
No. of categories	• two;

- can be extended to dependent variables with three or more categories by using multinomial logistic regression.

Number	• one.
Assumes normal distribution?	• no.
Relationship between X and Y	• assumed to be nonlinear.

Loglinear Analysis

Main uses	• to describe relationships among categorical (nominal or discrete ordinal) variables;
	• to test predictive models consisting of categorical variables.
Design	• assumes that outcomes (i.e. membership of categories of the Y variable) are independent;
	• therefore loglinear analysis is inappropriate in paired or repeated measures designs;

Independent variables

Number	• two or more.
Level of measurement	• nominal or ordinal but discrete.
No. of categories	• best with relatively small number of categories;
	• where ordinal variables have large number of categories they are frequently treated as interval and normal regression is used.
Dichotomies OK?	• yes.
Assumes normality?	• no.
Assumes linearity?	• no.

Dependent variable

Type	• discrete but can be ordered.
No. of categories	• two or more;
	• can handle more than two categories more readily than logistic regression.
Number	• one.
Relationship between X and Y	• assumed to be nonlinear.

Multiple Regression and Multiple Correlation

Main uses	• description: analysis of joint impact and explained variance of a set of independent variables;

- prediction: identifies which variables from a set of variables best predict the values of Y;
- explanation: tests causal models and propositions;
- examines independent impact of individual variables and identification of the relative importance of each independent variable.

Design
- normally used in cross-sectional design;
- can be used in panel designs but can encounter problems with correlated error, measurement error.

Sample
- variable to sample size ratio is important in reliability of estimates.

Independent variables

Number
- two or more.

Level of measurement
- interval.
- categorical variables can be used if converted to dummy variables.

No. of categories
- continuous.

Dichotomies OK?
- yes.

Assumes normality?
- yes, but less important with larger samples.

Assumes linearity?
- yes.

Dependent variable

Type
- interval.

No. of categories
- continuous.

Number
- one.

Relationship between X and Y
- linear.

Path Analysis

Main Uses
- describe relationships among interval-level independent variables and interval-level dependent variables;
- test causal models;
- evaluate the importance of direct and indirect causal paths.

Design
- normally used with cross-sectional data.

Sample
- same as for multiple regression.

Independent variables

Number	•	two or more.
Level of measurement	•	interval.
Dichotomies OK?	•	yes.
Assumes normality?	•	yes, but less important as sample gets larger.
Assumes linearity?	•	yes.
Other	•	path analysis is based on a series of multiple regression equations. It therefore has the same data requirements as multiple regression.

Dependent variable

Type	•	interval level.
No. of categories	•	dichotomous variables are not appropriate.
Number	•	one.
Relationship between X and Y	•	assumed to be linear.

Anova

Main uses	•	to test the statistical significance of differences between means;
	•	to examine the separate effects of each independent variable on the means of the dependent variable;
	•	to examine the joint influence of the independent variables on the means of the dependent variable.
Design	•	repeated measures ANOVA and independent samples ANOVA are available.

Independent variables

Number	•	two or more.
Level of measurement	•	nominal or ordinal but discrete.
No. of categories	•	best with relatively small number of categories;
	•	where ordinal variables have large number of categories, they are frequently treated as interval and normal regression is used.
Dichotomies OK?	•	yes.
Assumes normality?	•	Assumes multivariate normal.

Dependent variable

Type	•	interval.
No. of categories	•	two or more;

- can handle more than two categories more readily than logistic regression.

Number • one.

Relationship between
X and Y • can be nonlinear.

Multivariate Analysis of Variance

Main uses • an extension of ANOVA to situations in which there are several dependent variables;
- may reveal differences not identified with ANOVA;
- helps identify which dependent variables are most affected by an independent variable.

Design • can be applied to repeated measures designs.

Independent variables

Number • one or more.
Level of measurement • nominal or ordinal but discrete.
No. of categories • best with relatively small number of categories.
Dichotomies OK? • yes.
Assumes normality? • no.
Assumes linearity? • no.

Dependent variable

Type • all interval level.
No. of categories • assumed to be continuous.
Number • two or more.
Relationship between • assumed to be linear;
Y variables • assumed to be correlated.

References

Aldrich, J.H. and Nelson, F.D. (1984) *Linear Probability, Logit and Probit Models*. Beverly Hills, CA: Sage.

Bean, C., Gow, D. and McAllister, L. (1998) *Australian Election Survey, 1998* [computer file]. Canberra: Social Science Data Archives, Australian National University.

Campbell, D.T. and Fiske, D.W. (1959) 'Convergent and discriminant validity by the multitrait–multimethod matrix', *Psychological Bulletin*, 56: 85–105.

Carmines, E.G. and Zeller, R.A. (1979) *Reliability and Validity Assessment*. Beverly Hills, CA: Sage.

Carver, R.P. (1978) 'The case against statistical significance testing', *Harvard Educational Review*, 48: 387–99.

Carver, R.P. (1993) 'The case against statistical significance testing, revisited', *Journal of Experimental Education*, 61: 287–92.

Cohen, J. (1988) *Statistical Power Analysis for the Behavioral Sciences*. Hillsdale, NJ: Lawrence Erlbaum Associates.

Cohen, J. (1990) 'Things I have learned (so far)', *American Psychologist*, 45: 1304–12.

Cohen, J. (1994) 'The world is round ($p < .05$)', *American Psychologist*, 49: 997–1003.

Comrey, A.L. and Lee, H.B. (1992) *A First Course in Factor Analysis*. Hillsdale, NJ: Lawrence Erlbaum Associates.

Cook, T.D. and Campbell, D.T. (1979) *Quasi-experimentation: Design and Analysis Issues for Field Settings*. Boston: Houghton Mifflin Co.

Davis, J.A. (1971) *Elementary Survey Analysis*. Englewood Cliffs, NJ: Prentice Hall.

de Vaus, D.A. (2001a) *Surveys in Social Research*. London: Routledge.

de Vaus, D.A. (2001b) *Research Design in Social Research*. London: Sage.

Foddy, W.H. (1993) *Constructing Questions for Interviews and Questionnaires: Theory and Practice in Social Research*. New York: Cambridge University Press.

Fox, J. (1997) *Applied Regression Analysis, Linear Models and Related Methods*. Thousand Oaks, CA: Sage.

Hayes, W.L. (1973) *Statistics for the Social Sciences*. New York: Holt, Rinehart, and Winston.

Kaiser, H.F. (1974) 'An index of factorial simplicity', *Psychometrica*, 39: 31–6.

Kalton, G., Roberts, J. and Holt, D. (1980) 'The effect of offering the middle response option with opinion questions', *The Statistician*, 29: 65–78.

Kendall, M.G. (1970) *Rank Correlation Methods*. London: Griffin.

Kendall, P.L. and Lazarsfeld, P.F. (1950) 'Problems of survey analysis' in R.K. Merton and P.F. Lazarsfeld (eds), *Continuities in Social Research*, Glencoe: Free Press.

Kim, J.O. and Mueller, C.W. (1978) *Introduction to Factor Analysis: What It Is and How to Do It*. Beverly Hills, CA: Sage.

Kirk, R.E. (1996) 'Practical significance: A concept whose time has come', *Educational and Psychological Measurement*, 56: 746–59.

Labovitz, S. (1970) 'The nonutility of significance tests: The significance of significance tests reconsidered', *Pacific Sociological Review*, 13: 141–8.

Labovitz, S. (1971) 'The zone of rejection: Negative thoughts on statistical inference'. *Pacific Sociological Review*, 14: 373–81.

Marsh, C. (1988) *Exploring Data: An Introduction to Data Analysis for Social Scientists*. Cambridge, U.K: Polity Press.

McIver, J.P. and Carmines, E.G. (1981) *Unidimensional Scaling*. Beverly Hills, CA: Sage.

McNemar, Q. (1969) *Psychological Statistics*. New York: Wiley.

Morrison, D.E. and Henkel, R.E. (eds) (1970) *The Significance Test Controversy*. Chicago: Aldine.

Newton, R.R. and Rudestam, K.E. (1999) *Your Statistical Consultant: Answers to Your Data Analysis Questions*. Thousand Oaks, CA: Sage.

Peatman, J.G. (1947) *Descriptive and Sampling Statistics*. New York: Harper and Brothers.

Reynolds, H.T. (1977) *The Analysis of Cross-classifications*. New York: Free Press.

Rozeboom, W.W. (1960) 'The fallacy of the null-hypothesis significance test', *Psychological Bulletin*, 57: 416–28.

Rummel, R.J. (1970) *Applied Factor Analysis*. Evanston, IL: Northwestern University Press.

Schuman, H. and Presser, S. (1980) 'Public opinion and public ignorance: The fine line between attitudes and nonattitudes', *American Journal of Sociology*, 85: 1214–25.

Schuman, H. and Presser, S. (1981) *Questions and Answers in Attitude Surveys: Experiments on Question Form, Wording and Context*. New York: Academic Press.

Selvin, H. (1957) 'A critique of tests of significance in survey research', *American Sociological Review*, 22: 519–27.

Sheskin, D. (1984) *Statistical Tests and Experimental Design: A Guidebook*. New York: Gardner.

Siegel, S. (1956) *Nonparametric Statistics for the Behavioral Sciences*. New York: McGraw-Hill.

Smith, T.W. (1984) 'Nonattitudes: A review and evaluation', in C.F. Turner and E. Martin (eds), *Surveying Subjective Phenomena, Volume 2*. New York: Russell Sage Foundation, pp. 215–55.

Sudman, S. (1983) 'Applied sampling', in P.H. Rossi, J.D. Wright and A.B. Anderson (eds), *Handbook of Survey Research*. New York: Academic Press, pp. 145–94.

Sudman, S. and Bradburn, N.M. (1982) *Asking Questions: A Practical Guide to Questionnaire Design*. San Francisco: Jossey-Bass.

Tabachnick, B.G. and Fidell, L.S. (1983) *Using Multivariate Statistics*. New York: Harper & Row.

Trochim (2000a) *http://trochim.human.cornell.edu/kb/rel&val.htm* Accessed 16/12/2001.

Trochim (2000b) *http://trochim.human.cornell.edu/kb/cmconval.htm* Accessed 16/12/2001.

Wilkinson, L. and Task Force on Statistical Inference (1999) 'Statistical methods in psychology journals: Guidelines and explanations'. *American Psychologist*, 54: 594–604.

Yin, R.K. (1989) *Case Study Research. Design and Methods*. London: Sage.

Index